T0211275

Reusable Firmware Development

A Practical Approach to APIs, HALs and Drivers

Jacob Beningo

Apress®

Reusable Firmware Development: A Practical Approach to APIs, HALs and Drivers

Jacob Beningo
Linden, Michigan, USA

ISBN-13 (pbk): 978-1-4842-3296-5   ISBN-13 (electronic): 978-1-4842-3297-2
https://doi.org/10.1007/978-1-4842-3297-2

Library of Congress Control Number: 2017961731

Cover image by Freepik (www.freepik.com)

    Managing Director: Welmoed Spahr
    Editorial Director: Todd Green
    Acquisitions Editor: Steve Anglin
    Development Editor: Matthew Moodie
    Technical Reviewers: Ahmed Hag-ElSafi and Rami Zewail
    Coordinating Editor: Mark Powers
    Copy Editor: April Rondeau

Distributed to the book trade worldwide by Springer Science+Business Media New York, 233 Spring Street, 6th Floor, New York, NY 10013. Phone 1-800-SPRINGER, fax (201) 348-4505, email orders-ny@springer-sbm. com, or visit www.springeronline.com. Apress Media, LLC is a California LLC and the sole member (owner) is Springer Science + Business Media Finance Inc (SSBM Finance Inc). SSBM Finance Inc is a **Delaware** corporation.

For information on translations, please email rights@apress.com, or visit http://www.apress.com/ rights-permissions.

Apress titles may be purchased in bulk for academic, corporate, or promotional use. eBook versions and licenses are also available for most titles. For more information, reference our Print and eBook Bulk Sales web page at http://www.apress.com/bulk-sales.

Any source code or other supplementary material referenced by the author in this book is available to readers on GitHub via the book's product page, located at www.apress.com/9781484232965. For more detailed information, please visit http://www.apress.com/source-code.

Printed on acid-free paper

To my lovely wife, children, parents, and siblings.

Table of Contents

About the Author

Jacob Beningo is an embedded software consultant with over 15 years of experience in microcontroller-based real-time embedded systems. After spending over ten years designing embedded systems for the automotive, defense, and space industries, Jacob founded Beningo Embedded Group in 2009. Jacob has worked with clients in more than a dozen countries to dramatically transform their businesses by improving product quality, cost, and time to market. He has published more than 200 articles on embedded software development techniques and is a sought-after speaker and technical advisor. Jacob is an avid writer, trainer, consultant, and entrepreneur who transforms the complex into simple and understandable concepts that accelerate technological innovation.

Jacob has demonstrated his leadership in the embedded-systems industry by consulting and working as a trusted advisor at companies such as General Motors, Intel, Infineon, and Renesas. Jacob also speaks at and is involved in the embedded track-selection committees at ARM Techcon, Embedded System Conferences, and Sensor Expo. Jacob holds bachelor's degrees in electrical engineering, physics, and mathematics from Central Michigan University and a master's degree in space systems engineering from the University of Michigan.

In his spare time, Jacob enjoys spending time with his family, reading, writing, and playing hockey and golf. When there are clear skies, he can often be found outside with his telescope, sipping a fine scotch while imaging the sky.

About the Technical Reviewers

Ahmed S. Hag-ElSafi (Khartoum, 1978) holds Bachelor of Science and Master of Science degrees in electronics and communications engineering from the Arab Academy for Science and Technology, earned in 2002 and 2004 respectively.

He has 15 years of experience of research and industrial development in the areas of embedded systems and machine learning. He has published more than fifteen papers in the areas of IOT security, biometrics, machine learning, and medical image processing. He is currently the co-founder and principal researcher at Smart Empower Innovation Labs Inc. in Alberta, Canada.

Mr. Hag-ElSafi is a member the Smart City Alliance in Alberta, Canada, and the Association of Professional Engineers and Geoscientists of Alberta (APEGA).

Rami Zewail received Bachelor of Science and Master of Science degrees in electronics and communications engineering from the Arab Academy for Science and Technology, Egypt, earned in 2002 and 2004 respectively. He earned his PhD in electrical and computer engineering from the University of Alberta, Canada, in 2010.

He has over 15 years of academic and industrial R&D experience in the areas of embedded systems and machine learning. He has contributed to the scientific community with a patent and over 19 publications in the areas of embedded computing, machine learning, and statistical modeling. Currently, he is co-founder and staff researcher at Smart Empower Innovations Labs Inc., a Canada-based R&D and consulting corporation specialized in the fields of embedded systems and machine learning.

Dr. Zewail is a member of the Institute of Electrical and Electronics Engineers (IEEE), the Association of Professional Engineers & Geoscientists (APEGA), and the Canadian Association for Artificial Intelligence. He also served as a reviewer for the *Journal of Electronics Imaging* and the *Journal of Optical Engineering* for the SPIE society in the United States.

Acknowledgments

I would like to thank my parents, teachers, and family for inspiring me and encouraging me to pursue my passions. Without their help, this book and the very direction my career has taken would never have happened.

I would also like to thank the countless and often nameless software engineers who came before us and laid the foundation upon which this book sits. Without their contributions to this industry and their inspiration, I would never have embarked on such an undertaking.

I would also like to thank Salvador Almanza and Benjamin Sweet for acting as sounding boards and reviewing portions of the manuscript.

Finally, I would like to thank Max "The Magnificient" Maxfield for encouraging me to write this book and sharing his publishing experiences with me.

Preface

In 2001, when I was a bright-eyed college sophomore, I would spend my evenings doing something a bit unusual—writing embedded software. Writing embedded software is not necessarily unusual, except that any observer would think that I wasn't writing the software for any particular purpose. I was not designing any specific product or experimenting to understand how things work. Instead, I was focused on understanding how to write portable and reusable software for microcontroller-based systems.

My idea and hope was that I could develop libraries and code modules that would allow me to quickly meet any project requirements that might be thrown my way. In theory, these libraries would allow me to get a microcontroller up and running and interface with external communication devices at a fraction of the time and cost that it would take if I started from scratch every time.

Looking back on this endeavor, I realize that this was a pivotal period that would permeate my professional career, even now. Unfortunately, as a college student in 2001, the libraries and components that I created were written in assembly and closely tied to a single target device. Assembly language compilers were freely offered in those days, and the preferred C compilers cost several thousand dollars, with no code-size limitation trials. (The microcontrollers I was using did not have a GCC variant available at that time).

The fortunes of time have thankfully made C compilers more readily available, and assembly language code has gone nearly the way of the dinosaurs. What is perhaps far more interesting about this tale is that this early interest in developing modular and reusable components in assembly language found its way into my professional career developing embedded software in C/C++. The result has been a steadily improving set of techniques, APIs, HALs, components, and design patterns that can be applied to resource-constrained embedded systems.

As a consultant and technical educator, each year I work with companies by the dozens and engineers by the thousands who struggle to develop portable and reusable embedded software. Many efforts are repeated from one project to the next, resulting in wasted time, effort, money, and potential to innovate.

One of my hopes with this book and the associated API and HAL Standard is to share my experiences and provide a framework that other developers may leverage and use in their own development efforts. My goal is that readers won't just become better developers but will also be able to keep pace with the demanding modern development cycle and still have time to innovate and push the envelope.

Implementing the processes and techniques contained in this book should help any developer decrease their development costs and time to market while improving the portability and reliability of their software. At a minimum, developers will find that they no longer need to keep reinventing the wheel every time a new project starts.

Happy coding,
Jacob Beningo
September 2017

Introduction

Since the turn of the twenty-first century, microcontroller-based systems have become extremely complex. Microcontrollers started out as simple 8-bit devices running at bus speeds in the 8 MHz to 48 MHz range. Since then, microcontrollers have become complex and powerful 32-bit devices running at clock speeds faster than 200 MHz with every imaginable peripheral, including USB, TCP/IP, and Wi-Fi, and some microcontrollers now even have an internal cache. This dramatic explosion of capability and complexity has left the embedded software developer scrambling to understand how to do the following:

- Shorten time to market

- Keep budgets under control

- Get to market on time

- Manage their system's complexity

- Meet the client's feature and innovation needs

Traditionally, many embedded systems were written in such a way that the code was used once, on a single platform, and then tossed out. Software, for the most part, could be referred to as spaghetti code and did not follow any object-oriented or software-reuse model. In today's development environment, developers need to write their software with reusability and portability in mind. The teams that are the most successful can leverage existing intellectual property and quickly innovate on it.

The purpose of this book is to help the embedded software engineer learn and understand how they can develop reusable firmware that can be used across multiple microcontroller platforms and software products. The fundamental pieces to firmware reuse that we will be focusing on are HALs, APIs, and drivers. These are the core pieces that will allow us to develop a layered software architecture and define how those different layers interact with each other.

Chapters 1 through 5 lay the foundation on which a developer can start writing reusable firmware. In these chapters, we examine the C constructs that best lend themselves to portability and define what a hardware abstraction layer (HAL) is and how it differs from application programming interfaces (APIs). We will discuss different design methodologies developers can use to write low-level drivers and examine the design patterns, along with their pros and cons. Along the way, we'll look at real-world examples and even take a chapter to discuss how reusable firmware should be documented.

With the foundation laid, Chapters 6 through 10 examine the processes that can be followed to create HALs and APIs. We examine common elements, such as GPIO, SPI, and external memory devices, before moving on to looking at high-level application frameworks that can aid reuse and accelerate software design.

Chapter 11 discusses how developers should develop tests to ensure that their reusable software remains usable with a minimal bug count. Finally, Chapter 12 walks developers through how they can start developing reusable software no matter the environment or challenges that they may be facing and how they can succeed in those environments.

The chapters don't necessarily need to be read in order, but they are put together in an order that builds upon what came before. A developer with reasonable experience developing reusable software could easily skip around whereas developers new to writing reusable software should read the chapters in order.

CHAPTER 1

Concepts for Developing Portable Firmware

"A good scientist is a person with original ideas. A good engineer is a person who makes a design that works with as few original ideas as possible."

—Freeman Dyson

Why Code Reuse Matters

Over the past several decades, embedded systems have steadily increased in complexity. The internet's birth has only accelerated the process as our society has been in a race to connect nearly every device imaginable. Systems that were once simple and stand-alone must now connect through the internet in a secure and fail-safe manner in order to stream critical information up into the cloud. Complexity and features are increasing at an exponential rate, with each device generation forcing engineers to reevaluate how to successfully develop embedded software within the allotted time frame and budget.

The increased demand for product features, along with the need to connect systems to the internet, has dramatically increased the amount of software that needs to be developed to launch a product. While software complexity and features have been increasing, the time available to develop a product has for the most part remained constant, with a negligible increase in development time (two weeks in five years), as can be seen in Figure 1-1. In order to meet project timelines, developers are forced to either purchase commercial off-the-shelf (COTS) software that can decrease their development time or reuse as much code as possible from previous projects.

1

© Jacob Beningo 2017
J. Beningo, *Reusable Firmware Development*, https://doi.org/10.1007/978-1-4842-3297-2_1

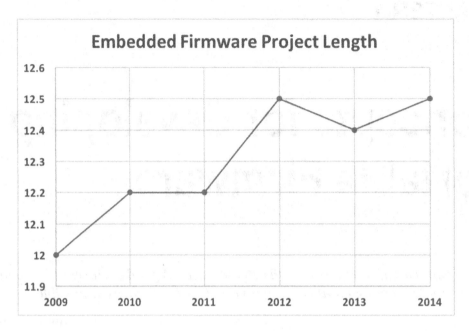

Figure 1-1. *Average firmware project development time (in months)[1]*

Firmware for microcontrollers has conventionally been developed for a specific application using functional design methodologies (if any methodology has been used at all) that typically tie the low-level hardware directly into the application code, making the software difficult if not impossible to reuse and port on the same hardware architectures let alone reuse on a different architecture. The primary driving factor behind developing throw-away firmware has been the resource-constrained nature many embedded products exhibit. Microcontrollers with RAM greater than a few kilobytes and flash sizes greater than 16 kB were once expensive and could not be designed into a product without destroying any hope of making a profit. Embedded-software developers did not have large memories or powerful processors to work with, which prevented modern software-design techniques from being used in application development.

Modern microcontrollers are beginning to change the game. A typical low-end ARM Cortex-M microcontroller now costs just a few U.S. dollars and offers at a minimum 16 kB of RAM and 64 kB of flash. The dramatic cost decreases in memory, larger memory availability, and more efficient CPU architectures are removing the resource-constrained nature that firmware developers have been stuck with. The result is that developers

---

[1]Embedded Marketing Study, 2009 – 2015, UBM

can now start utilizing design methods that decouple the application code from the hardware and allow a radical increase in code reuse.

Portable Firmware

Firmware developed today is written in a rather archaic manner. Each product-development cycle results in limited to no code reuse, with reinvention being a major theme among development teams. A simple example is when development teams refuse to use an available real-time operating system (RTOS) and instead develop their own in-house scheduler. Beyond wanting to build their own custom scheduler, there are two primary examples that demonstrate the issue with reinvention.

SOFTWARE TERMINOLOGY

Portable firmware is embedded software that is designed to run on more than one microcontroller or processor architecture with little or no modification.

First, nearly every development team writes their own drivers because microcontroller vendors provide only example code and not production-ready drivers. Examples provide a great jump-start to understanding the microcontroller peripherals, but it still requires a significant time investment to get a production-intent system. There could be a hundred companies using the exact same microcontroller, and each and every one will waste as much as 30 percent or more of their total development time getting their microcontroller drivers written and integrated with their middleware! I have seen this happen repeatedly among my client base and have heard numerous corroborating stories from the hundreds of engineers I interact with on a yearly basis.

Second, there are so many features that need to be packed into a product, and with a typical design cycle being twelve months,[1] developers don't take the time to properly architect their systems for reuse. High-level application code becomes tightly coupled to low-level microcontroller code, which makes separating, reusing, or porting the application code costly, time consuming, and buggy. The end result—developers just start from scratch every time.

In order to keep up with the rapid development pace in today's design cycles, developers need to be highly skilled in developing portable firmware. Portable firmware is embedded software that is designed to run on more than one microcontroller or processor architecture with little to no modification. Writing firmware that can be ported from one microcontroller architecture to the next has many direct advantages, such as:

- Decreasing time to market by not having to reinvent the wheel (which can be time consuming)

- Decreasing project costs by leveraging existing components and libraries

- Improving product quality through use of proven and continuously tested software

Portable firmware also has several indirect advantages that many teams overlook but that can far outweigh the direct benefits, such as:

- More time in the development cycle to focus on product innovation and differentiation

- Decreased team stress levels due to limiting how much total code needs to be developed (happy, relaxed engineers are more innovative and efficient)

- Organized and well-documented code that can make porting and maintenance easier and more cost effective

Using portable and reusable code can result in some very fast and amazing results, as seen in the case study "Firmware Development for a Smart Solar Panel," but there are also a few disadvantages. The disadvantages are related to upfront time and effort, such as:

- The software architecture's needing to be well thought through

- Understanding potential architectural differences between microcontrollers

- Developing regression tests to ensure porting is successful

- Selecting real-time languages and understanding their interoperability or lack thereof

- Having experienced and high-skilled engineers available to develop a portable and scalable architecture

For development teams to successfully enjoy the benefits of portable code use, extra time and money needs to be spent up-front. However, after the initial investment, development cycles have a jump-start to potentially decrease development time by months versus the traditional embedded-software design cycle. The long-term benefits and cost savings usually overshadow the up-front design costs, along with the potential to speed up the development schedule.

Developing firmware with the intent to reuse also means that developers may be stuck with a single programming language. How does one choose a language for software that may stick around for a decade or longer? Using a single programming language is not a major concern in embedded-software development, despite what one might initially think. The most popular embedded language, ANSI-C, was developed in 1972 and has proven to be nearly impossible to usurp. Figure 1-2 shows the popularity of programming languages used in embedded systems. Despite advances in computer science and the development of object-oriented programming languages, C has remained very popular as a general language and is heavily entrenched in embedded software.

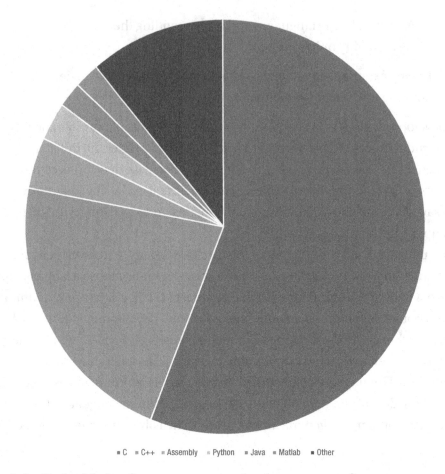

■ C   ■ C++   ■ Assembly   ■ Python   ■ Java   ■ Matlab   ■ Other

Figure 1-2. *Embedded-software programming language use[2]*

The C programming language's popularity and steady use doesn't appear to be changing anytime soon. When and if the Internet of Things (IoT) begins to gain momentum, C may even begin to grow in its use and popularity as millions of devices are developed and deployed using it. Developing portable and reusable software becomes a viable option when one considers the steady and near-constant use that the C language has enjoyed in the industry for developing embedded systems. When a development team considers the timelines, feature needs, and limited budgets for the product-development cycle, developing portable code should be considered a mandatory requirement.

---

[2]Aspencore Embedded Systems Survey, 2017, www.embedded.com

CASE STUDY—FIRMWARE FOR A SMART SOLAR PANEL

When it comes to product development, the single constant in the universe is that the development either needs to be done yesterday or by some not-so-distant future date. A few years ago, on December 1, I received a call from a prospective client I had been talking with for the better part of the year. The client, a start-up in the small satellite industry, had just received news that they had an opportunity to fly their new flagship spacecraft on an upcoming launch. The problem was that they had just six weeks to finish building, testing, and delivering their satellite!

One of the many hurdles they faced was that their smart solar panels (smart because they contained a plethora of sensors critical to stabilizing the spacecraft) didn't have a single line of firmware written. The solar panels' firmware had to be completed by January 1, leaving just four weeks over a holiday month to design, implement, test, and deploy the firmware. To give some quantification to the project scope, the following are some of the software components that needed to be included:

- GPIO, SPI, I2C, PWM, UART, Flash, ADC

- Timer and system tick

- H-bridge control

- Task scheduler

- Accelerometer

- Magnetometer

- Calibration algorithms

- Fault recovery

- Health and wellness monitoring

- Flight computer communication protocol

An experienced developer knows the preceding list would be impossible to successfully complete in four weeks from scratch. I2C alone could take two weeks to develop, and the realistic delivery date for the project would be three to four months, not weeks.

I accepted the project and leveraged the very same HAL and driver techniques presented in this book to complete the project. A day was spent pulling in existing drivers and making minor modifications for the microcontroller derivative. The second week was spent pulling together the application code and remaining drivers. Finally, week three was test, debug, and deliver— just in time for Christmas and to the client's delight.

The decision to develop portable firmware should not be taken lightly. In order to develop truly portable and reusable firmware, there are a few characteristics that a developer should review and make sure that the firmware will exhibit. First, the software needs to be modular. Writing an application that exists in a single source file is not an option (yes, I still see this done even in 2016). The software needs to be broken up into manageable pieces with minimal dependencies between modules and similar functions being grouped together.

10 QUALITIES OF PORTABLE FIRMWARE

Portable Firmware …

1. is modular

2. is loosely coupled

3. has high cohesion

4. is ANSI-C compliant

5. has a clean interface

6. has a hardware abstraction layer (HAL)

7. is readable and maintainable

8. is simple

9. uses encapsulation and abstract data types

10. is well documented

Portable software should follow the ANSI-C programming language standard. Developers should avoid using compiler intrinsics and C extensions, because they are compiler specific and will not easily port between tool chains. In addition to avoiding these add-ons, developers should select a safe and fully specified subset for the C programming language. Industry-accepted standards such as MISRA-C or Secure C might be good options to help ensure that the firmware will use safe constructs.

Developers will want to make sure that the reusable code is also well documented and contains detailed examples. The firmware needs to have a clean interface that is simple and easy to understand. Most important, developers will want to make sure that a simple, scalable hardware-abstraction layer is included in the software architecture. The hardware-abstraction layer will define how application code interacts with the lower underlying hardware. Let's examine in greater detail a few key characteristics that portable firmware should exhibit before diving into hardware-abstraction layers.

Modularity

On more than one occasion over the last several years, I have worked with a client whose entire application, 50,000-plus lines of code, was contained within a single main.c module. Attempts to maintain the software or reuse pieces of code quickly turned into a nightmare. These applications were still using software techniques from back in the 1970s and 1980s, which was not working out so well for my client.

Modularity emphasizes that a program's functionality should be separated into independent modules that may be interchangeable. Each module contains a header and source file with the ability to execute specialized system functions that are exposed through the module's interface. The primary benefit of employing modularity in an embedded system is that the program is broken up into smaller pieces that are organized based on purpose and function.

Ignoring the preceding facts and lumping large amounts of code into a single module, even if it is well organized or makes sense in the beginning, usually results in a decay into a chaos and a software architecture that resembles spaghetti. Breaking a program up into separate modules is so important when developing portable and reusable firmware because the independence each module exhibits allows it to be easily moved from one application to the next, or in some cases even from one platform to the next. There are a few advantages associated with breaking a program up into modular pieces, such as:

- Being able to find functions or code of interest very quickly and easily

- Improved software understanding through the modules' organization

- The ability to copy modules and use them in new applications

- The ability to remove modules from a program and replace them with new functionality

- Easing requirements' traceability

- Developing automated regression testing for individual modules and features

- Overall decreased time to market and development costs

Each module added to a program does come with the disadvantage that the compiler will need to open, process, compile, and close the module. The result in the "old days" would have been slower compilation times. Development machines today are so fast and efficient that increased compile time is no longer an excuse for writing bulking, clunky code.

Module Coupling and Cohesion

Breaking a program up into smaller, more manageable pieces is a good step forward toward developing portable firmware, but it is only the first step. For a module to be truly portable, it must exhibit low coupling to other modules within the code base and a high level of cohesion. Coupling refers to how closely related different modules or classes are to each other and the degree to which they are interdependent. The higher the coupling, the less independent the module is.

Portable software should minimize the coupling between modules to make it easier to use in more than one development environment. Take, for example, the file-dependency chart in Figure 1-3. Attempting to bring the top-level module into the code base will be a small nightmare, like peeling an onion. The top module will be brought in, only for the developer to realize that it is dependent upon another, which is dependent upon another and another and so on. In short order, the developer might as well have just brought in the entire application or simply started from scratch. Attempting to use modules that are tightly coupled is very frustrating and can cause the code size to balloon out of control if care is not taken.

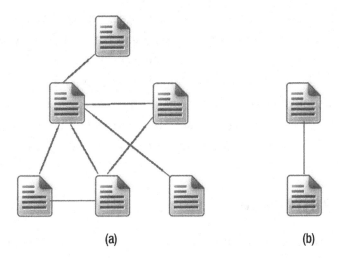

(a)   (b)

Figure 1-3. *Module coupling*

The software base in Figure 1-3a shows a completely different story. The modules in Figure 1-3b are loosely coupled. A developer attempting to bring in a top-level module won't be fraught with continuous compiler errors of missing files or spend hours on end trying to track down all the dependencies. Instead, the developer quickly moves the loosely coupled module into the new code base and is on to the next task with little to no frustration. Low coupling is the result of a well-thought-out and well-structured software design.

SOFTWARE TERMINOLOGY

Coupling refers to how closely related different modules or classes are to each other and the degree to which they are interdependent.

Cohesion refers to the degree to which module elements belong together.

Module coupling is only the story's first part. Having low module coupling doesn't guarantee that the software will exhibit easily portable traits. The goal is to have a module that has low coupling and high cohesion. Cohesion refers to the degree to which the module elements belong together. In a microcontroller environment, a low-cohesion example would be lumping every microcontroller peripheral function into a single module. The module would be large and unwieldy. The microcontroller peripheral functions could instead be broken up into separate modules, each with functions specific to one peripheral. The results would be the benefits listed in the previous section on modularity.

11

Portable and reusable software attempts to create modules that are loosely coupled and have high cohesion. Modules with these characteristics are usually easy to reuse and maintain. Consider what would happen in a tightly coupled system if a single module were changed. A single change would result in changes being forced in at least one other module, if not more, and it could be time consuming to hunt down all the necessary changes. Failure to make the change or a simple oversight could result in a bug, which in the worst case could cause project delays and increased costs.

Following a Standard

Creating firmware that is portable and reusable can be challenging. For example, the C language has gone through several different standard revisions: C90, C99, and C11. In addition to the different C versions, there also exist non-standard language extensions, compiler additions, and even language offshoots. To develop firmware that is reusable to the greatest extent possible, a development team needs to select a widely accepted standard version, such as C90 or C99. The C99 version has some great additions that make it a good choice for developers. At the time of this writing, there is limited support for C11 in firmware development, and C11 is five years old! Adopting C99 is the best bet for following a standard.

The long-term support for C and its general-purpose use has resulted in language extensions and non-standard versions that need to be avoided. Using any construct that is not in the standard will result in specialized modifications to the code base that can obfuscate the code. Sometimes using extensions or an intrinsic is unavoidable due to optimization needs, but we will discuss later how we can still write portable code in these circumstances.

In addition to using the C standard, developers should also restrict their use to well-defined constructs that are easy to understand and maintain and are fully specified. For example, standards such as MISRA-C and Secure-C exist to provide recommendations on a C subset and they should be used to develop firmware. MISRA-C was developed for the automotive industry, but the recommendations have proven to be so successful at producing quality software that other industries are adopting the recommendations.

Developers should not view a standard as a restriction but instead as a method for improving the quality and portability of the firmware that they develop. Identifying and following standard C dialects will take developers a long way in developing reusable firmware. Recognizing the need to follow the ANSI-C standard and having the discipline to follow it will guide a development team toward creating embedded software that can be reused for years to come.

Portability Issues in C—Data Types

The most infamous and well-known portability issues in the C programming language are related to defining the most commonly used data type, the integer. One needs only to ask a simple question to demonstrate a potential portability issue: What will be the value LoopCount contains when i rolls over to 0? The demonstration code that contains LoopCount can be found in in Figure 1-4.

```
static int i = 0;
static uint32_t LoopCount = 0;

for (i = 1; i != 0; i++)
{
   LoopCount++;
}
```

Figure 1-4. *Integer rollover test*

The answer could be 65,535 or 4,294,967,295. Both answers could be correct. The reason is that the storage size for an integer is not defined within the ANSI-C standard. The compiler vendors have the choice to define the storage size for the variable based on what they deem will be the most efficient and/or appropriate.

The storage size for an integer normally wouldn't seem like a big deal. For a code base an int will be an int, so who cares? The problem surfaces when that same code is compiled using a different compiler. Will the other compiler store the variable as the same size or different? What happens if it was stored as four bytes and now is only two? Perfectly working software is now buggy!

The portability issues arising from integers, the most commonly used data type, are solved in a relatively simplistic way. The library header file stdint.h defines fixed-width integers. A fixed-width integer is a data type that is based on the number of bits required to store the data. For example, a variable that needs to store unsigned data that is 32 bits wide doesn't need to gamble on int being 32 bits, but instead a developer can simply use the data type uint32_t. Fixed-width integers exist for 8, 16, 32, and in some cases even 64 bits. Table 1-1 shows a list of the different fixed-width integer definitions that can be found in stdint.h.

Table 1-1. *Fixed-Width Integers*[3]

Data Type	Minimum Value	Maximum Value
int8_t	-128	127
uint8_t	0	255
int16_t	-32,768	32,767
uint16_t	0	65535
int32_t	-2,147,483,648	2,147,483,647
uint32_t	0	4,294,967,295

The library file stdint.h doesn't contain just the data types found in Table 1-1 but also a few interesting and less-known gems. Take, for example, uint_fastN_t, which defines a variable that is the fastest to process at least *N* bits wide. A developer can tell the compiler that the data must be at least 16 bits but could be 32 bits if it can be processed faster using a larger data type. Another great example is uintmax_t, which defines the largest fixed-width integer possible on the system. A personal favorite is uintptr_t, which defines a type that is wide enough to store the value of a pointer.

Using stdint.h is an easy way to help ensure that embedded-software integer types preserve their storage size no matter which compiler the code may be compiled on. It is a simple and safe way to ensure that integer data types are properly preserved.

Portability Issues in C—Structures and Unions

The C standards have some unfortunate ambiguities in the definition of certain language constructs; take, for example, structures and unions. A developer can declare a structure containing three members, x, y, and z, as shown in Figure 1-5. As one might expect,

---

[3]ISO/IEC 9899:1999, C Language Specification

when a variable is declared of type Axis_t, the data members will be created in the order x, y, and z in memory. However, the C standard does not specify how the data members will be byte aligned. The compiler has the option to align the data members in any way that it chooses. The result could be that x, y, and z occupy contiguous memory, or there could be padding bytes added between the data members that space the members by two, four, or some other byte value that would be completely unexpected by a programmer.

```
typedef struct
{
    uint8_t x;
    uint8_t y;
    uint8_t z;
}Axis_t;
```

Figure 1-5. *Structure definition*

The unspecified structure and union behavior makes it the developer's job when porting the firmware to understand how the structure is being defined in memory and whether the structure is being used in such a way that adding padding bytes could affect the application's behavior or performance. The structure could include padding bytes or even holes depending on the data type being defined and how the compiler vendor decided to handle the byte alignment.

Portability Issues in C—Bit Fields

The situation with structures gets even worse when it comes to the definition of bit fields. Bit fields are declared within a structure and are meant to allow a developer to save memory space by tightly packing data members that don't occupy an entire data space. An example of using bit fields is to declare a flag within a structure that has a true or false value, as shown in Figure 1-6.

```c
typedef struct
{
   uint8_t x;
   uint8_t y;
   uint8_t z;
   uint8_t x_flag:1;
   uint8_t y_flag:1;
   uint8_t z_flag:1;
}Axis_t;
```

Figure 1-6. *Bit field definition*

The problem with bit fields is that the implementation is completely undefined by the standard. The compiler implementers get to decide how the bit field will be stored in memory, including byte alignment and whether the bit field can cross a memory boundary. Another problem with bit fields is that while they may appear to save memory, the resulting code required to access the bit field may be large and slow, which can affect the real-time performance of accessing it. The general recommendation when it comes to bit fields is that they are non-portable and compiler dependent and should be avoided for use in firmware that is meant to be reusable and portable.

Portability Issues in C—Preprocessor Directives

All preprocessor directives are not created equal. A developer will have different preprocessor directives available depending on whether GNU C, IAR Embedded Workbench, Keil uVision, or any other compiler is used. ANSI-C has a limited number of preprocessor directives that are included in the standard and can be considered portable.

Compiler vendors have the ability to add preprocessor directives that are not part of the standard. For example, #warning is a commonly used preprocessor directive that is not supported by C90 or C99! The #error preprocessor directive is part of the standard, and #warning was added by compiler vendors to allow a developer to raise a compilation warning. Developers who rely heavily on #warning may port code to a compiler that doesn't recognize #warning as a valid preprocessor directive or may recognize it as having a different purpose!

A developer interested in writing portable code needs to be careful about which preprocessor directives are used within the embedded software. The most obvious non-portable preprocessor directive is #pragma, which can generally be considered to declare implementation-defined behaviors within an application. The use of #pragma should be avoided as much as possible within an application that is expected to be ported to other tool chains.

Using #pragma or other specialized preprocessor directives and attributes cannot always be avoided without dramatically increasing code complexity and structure. One example where #pragma may be necessary is to specify an optimization that should be performed on an area of code. A developer in a similar situation can use compiler-predefined macros and conditional compilation to ensure that the code is optimized and that if it is ever ported to another compiler an error is raised at compile time. Each compiler has its own set of predefined macros, including a macro that can be used to identify the compiler that is in use. Figure 1-7 shows an example of a compiler-defined macro that may be of interest to a developer.

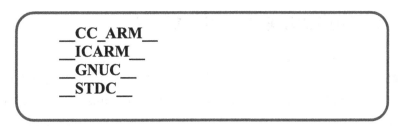

Figure 1-7. *Compiler-defined macros*

The predefined macros from Figure 1-7 that identify the compiler can be used as part of a preprocessor directive to conditionally compile code. Each compiler that may be used can then be added to the conditional statement with the non-portable preprocessor directive that is needed for the task at hand. Figure 1-8 shows how a developer might take advantage of the predefined compiler macros to conditionally compile a fictitious #pragma statement into a code base.

```
#if defined (__ICARM__)
    #pragma loop unroll 3
#elif defined (__GNUC__)
    #pragma unroll 3
#else
    #error Loop unroll optimization not defined!
#endif
```

Figure 1-8. Using conditional compilation for non-portable constructs

Developers interested in writing portable ANSI-C code should consult the ANSI-C standard, such as C90, C99, or C11, and check the appendices for implementation-defined behaviors. A developer may also want to consult their compiler manuals to determine the extensions and attributes that are available to developers.

Embedded-Software Architecture

Firmware development in the early days used truly resource-constrained microcontrollers. Every single bit had to be squeezed from both code and data memory spaces. Software reusability was a minor concern, and programs were monolithically developed. The programs would be one giant 50,000-line program, all contained within a single module, with little to no thought given to architectural design or reuse. The only goal was to make the software work. Thankfully, times have changed, and while many microcontroller applications remain "resource constrained," compiler capabilities and decreasing memory costs now allow for a software architecture that encourages reuse.

Developing software that is complex, scalable, portable, and reusable requires a software architecture. A software architecture is the fundamental organization a system embodies in its components, their relationship to each other and to the environment, and the principles guiding its design and evolution.[4] In other words, a software architecture is the blueprint from which a developer implements software. A software architecture is literally analogous to the blueprint an architect would use to design a building or a bridge.

---

[4]ISO/IEC/IEEE 42010:2011, Systems and software engineering — Architecture

The software architecture provides a developer with each component and major software structure, supplies constraints on their performance, and identifies their dependencies and interactions (the inputs and outputs). For our purposes, we will only be looking at software architecture from the perspective of organizing firmware into separate software layers that have contractually specified interfaces to improve portability and code reuse. Each software has a specific function, such as directly controlling the microcontroller hardware, running middleware, or containing the system's application code. Properly architected software can provide developers with many advantages.

First, a layered architecture can provide a functional boundary between different components within the software. Take, for example, low-level driver code that makes the microcontroller work. Including driver code directly within the application code tightly couples the microcontroller to the application code. Since application code normally contains algorithms that may be used across multiple products, mixing in low-level microcontroller code will make it difficult and time consuming to reuse the code. Instead, a developer who architects layered software can separate the application and low-level code, allowing both layers to be reused in other applications or on different hardware.

Second, a layered architecture hints at the locations where interfaces within the software need to be created. For a development team to create firmware that can be reused, there needs to be an identifiable boundary where an interface can be created that remains consistent and unchanging as time passes. The interface contains declarations and function prototypes for controlling software in lower layers.

Third, a layered architecture allows information within the application to be hidden from other areas that may not need access to it. Consider the example with the low-level driver. Does the application code really need to know the implementation details for how the driver works? Surely, someone working at the application level would rather have a simple function to call, with the desired result happening behind the scenes. This is the idea behind abstractions, which hide the implementation behavior from the programmer and simply provide them with a black box. Developing a simple software architecture can help developers take advantage of these benefits.

Developers looking to create portable firmware that follows a layered software-architecture model have many different possible models that can be chosen from and many custom hybrid models that they could undoubtedly develop. The simplest layered architecture can be seen in Figure 1-9 and contains a driver and application layer operating on the hardware. The driver layer includes all the code necessary to get the microcontroller and any other associated board hardware, such as sensors, buttons, and so forth, running. The application code contains no driver code but has access to the low-level hardware through a driver-layer interface that hides the hardware details from the application developer but still allows them to perform useful functions.

Figure 1-9. *Two-layer embedded-software architecture*

The next model that a developer could choose to implement breaks the software up into three layers, similar to Figure 1-10. In a three-layer model, the driver and application layers still exist, but a third "middle" layer has been added. The middle layer may contain software such as a real-time operating system (RTOS), USB and/or Ethernet stacks, along with file systems. The middle layer contains software that isn't directly the end application code but also does not drive the low-level hardware. For this reason, components in this layer are often referred to as middleware.

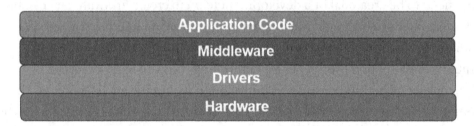

Figure 1-10. *Three-layer embedded-software architecture*

Beyond the three-layer model, developers may find it worthwhile to start breaking the software up into more refined layers of operation and maybe even provide pathways for high-level layers to circumvent layers and get direct access into lower software layers. The architectures can become quite complex and are well beyond the scope of this book. For now, a four-layer model will be as complex an example as we will examine. For example, a developer may decide that the board-support package—the integrated circuits outside of the microcontroller—should be separated from the microcontroller driver layer. The board-support drivers are usually dependent on the microcontroller drivers anyway, and in order to improve portability probably should be separated. Doing this results in one possible four-layer model like the one shown in Figure 1-11.

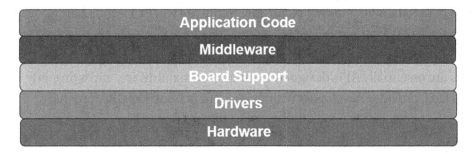

Figure 1-11. *Four-layer embedded-software architecture*

Many formal models exist for developing layered software architectures, including the well-known OSI model, which contains over seven layers. A developer should examine their requirements and their portability and reuse needs and pick the simplest architecture that can meet their requirements. Don't be tempted to build a 30-layer software architecture if three layers will meet the requirements! The goal is to avoid complex spaghetti code that is intertwined and entangled and instead develop layered lasagna code! (Just the thought makes my stomach growl!)

Hardware Abstraction Layers (HAL)[5]

Each software layer has at least one interface to an adjoining software layer. The software type that is contained within the next layer determines the name given to the interface. Each layer, if developed properly, can appear as a black box to the developer, and only the interface specification provides insight into how to get the needed behavior and result. The interface has many benefits, such as the following:

- Providing a consistent method for accessing features

- Abstracting out the details for how the underlying code works

- Specifying wrapper interfaces for how to merge inconsistent code to the software layer

The most interesting firmware layer that developers now have the ability to utilize is the hardware abstraction layer (HAL). A HAL is an interface that provides the application developer with a standard function set that can be used to access hardware functions

---

[5]http://whatis.techtarget.com/definition/layering

without a detailed understanding of how the hardware works. Despite being commonly referred to as a HAL, it is not the infamous artificial intelligence from *2001: A Space Odyssey*, although sometimes they can be just as devious.

HALs are essentially APIs designed to interact with hardware, and a properly designed HAL provides developers with many benefits, such as software that

- is portable

- is reusable

- has a lower cost (result of reuse)

- is abstracted (I don't need to know how the microcontroller does what it does)

- has fewer bugs due to repeated use

- is scalable (moving to other MCUs within a part family)

SOFTWARE TERMINOLOGY

Driver Layer refers to the software layer that contains low-level, microcontroller-specific software. The driver layer forms the basis from which higher-level software interacts with and controls the microcontroller.

Board-Support Package refers to driver code that is dependent upon lower-level microcontroller driver code. These drivers usually support external integrated circuits such as EEPROM or flash chips.

Middleware refers to the software layer that contains software dependent upon the lower-lying hardware drivers but does not directly contain application code. Application code is usually dependent upon the software contained within this middle layer of software.

Application Layer refers to a software layer used for system- and application-specific purposes that is decoupled from the underlying hardware. The application code meets product-specific features and requirements.

Configuration Layer refers to a software layer used to configure components within the layer.

A poorly designed HAL can result in increased costs and buggy software and can leave the developer wishing that they were dealing with the previously mentioned infamous HAL. An example software architecture that utilizes a HAL might look something like Figure 1-12. We will be discussing HAL design throughout the book.

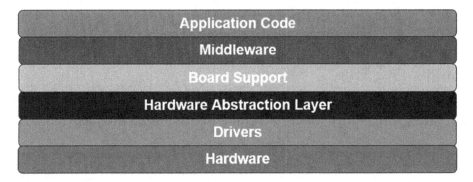

Figure 1-12. *Software architecture with a HAL*

SOFTWARE TERMINOLOGY

Hardware abstraction layer (HAL) refers to a firmware layer that replaces hardware-level accesses with higher-level function calls.

Application programming interface (API) refers to functions, routines, and libraries that are used to accelerate application software development.

Application Programming Interfaces (APIs)[6]

Application programming interfaces, often referred to as APIs, are a set of functions, routines, and libraries that are used to accelerate application software development. APIs are usually developed at the highest software layers. There are many cases where developers will use the term API to include the HAL, since the HAL is really a specialized API designed to interact with hardware. An example where the API might exist in a software stack can be seen in Figure 1-13.

---

[6]http://whatis.techtarget.com/definition/interface

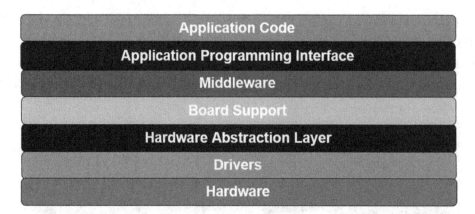

Figure 1-13. *Architecture with application programming interfaces (APIs)*

A specific application may have multiple middleware components, such as an RTOS, TCP/IP stack, file system, and so forth. Each component may have their very own API associated with their software package. There could even be application-level components that have their own APIs in order to facilitate speedy development. The rule of thumb is that wherever you see two software layers touch, there is an interface there that defines an API or HAL.

Project Organization

Organizing a project can help improve both portability and maintainability. There are many ways that developers can organize their software, but the easiest is to attempt to follow the software layer stack-up. Creating a file system and project folder structure that matches the layers makes it easy to simply replace a folder (a layer) with new software, which would also include the components within that layer.

The project should also be organized in such a way within each layer that modules, tasks, and other relevant code are easily locatable. Some developers like to create folders for modules or components and keep all configuration, header, and source modules within the folders. Organizing the software in this way makes it very easy to add and remove software modules. Other developers prefer to break up and keep header and source files separate. The method used is not important so much as being consistent and following a methodology is.

The following is an example organization that a developer may decide to implement to organize their project:

- Drivers

- Application

- Task Schedulers

- Protocol Stacks

- Configuration

- Supporting Files and Docs

Getting Started Writing Portable Firmware

Developers who want to reuse software have several challenges to overcome in order to be successful. These include:

- Endianness

- Processor architecture

- Bus width

- Ambiguous standards

- Development time and budget

- Modularity

- Code coupling

This is just to name a few. Getting started can be overwhelming and can lead to more stress and confusion than simply writing very functional code that is discarded later. The key to successfully developing portable code is to determine how well your firmware currently meets the portable software characteristics. Once we understand where we are, we can decide where we want to go and set in motion the steps necessary to get there.

To determine where we are today with developing portable firmware, start by drawing a diagram like that shown in Figure 1-14. In the diagram, label each spoke with a portable firmware characteristic and select the eight characteristics most important to you.

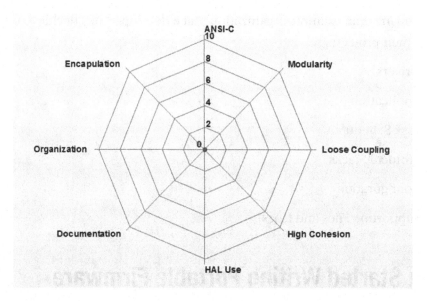

Figure 1-14. *Portable code evaluation*

In each identified category, a developer can evaluate how well their code exhibits these properties. For example, a developer who has been trying to transition into writing more portable code may evaluate themselves with a diagram result like Figure 1-15.

A quick look at Figure 1-15 can tell a developer a lot of information. First, we have strengths in documentation and modularity. That's a great step toward developing portable firmware, and we are just getting started. The figure also shows us where our weaknesses are, such as code coupling and cohesion.

From this glance, we can now determine where we should focus our attention. Which characteristic, if improved by just a couple points, will most drastically improve our code? Let's choose code coupling as an example. If a developer is going to improve code coupling, they need to determine how they are going to go about making that improvement. They might decide that the best way to do this is to do one or more of the following:

- Schedule code reviews

- Find a tool that can provide a module-dependency graph

- Use the dependency-graph tool (just because we have a tool doesn't mean we have the discipline to use it)

- Develop a high-level architecture that considers module coupling

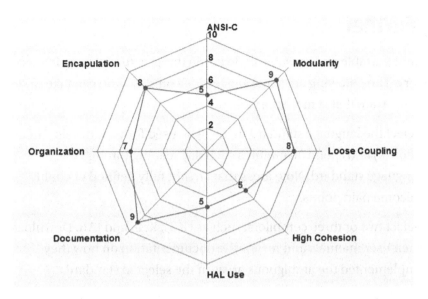

Figure 1-15. *Evaluated firmware characteristics*

A developer may decide that improving in one area is good enough to start or that all need to be done. The point is that we aren't going to start writing perfect, reusable code overnight. The process is iterative and may take a few years before all the rough edges are smoothed, but that is okay.

The following is a simple process that developers can use to improve their firmware portability:

1. Analyze their code characteristics.

2. Identify strengths and weaknesses.

3. Determine which characteristic to improve in the next three months.

4. Identify what can be done to make the incremental improvement.

5. Implement the improvement.

6. After the specified period, repeat.

Going Further

Reading about portable and reusable code is one thing; actually doing it is a completely different story. The following are some suggestions on steps you can take to start developing firmware that is more portable:

- Select the language standard that will be used for your development effort(s) and spend 30 minutes each day reading through the language standard. Note areas that are not fully defined or could become pain points.

- Select two or three compilers, such as GCC, Keil, and IAR. Download their user manuals and review the documentation on how they implemented the ambiguous areas in the selected standard.

- Purchase a copy of MISRA C/C++ and become familiar with the recommended best practices.

- Develop your own coding standard on the constructs that are allowed within an application and how compiler intrinsics and extensions should be handled.

- Review your typical software architecture. Does it have well-defined layers? Does each layer have a well-defined interface? If not, now is the perfect time to spend a few minutes architecting your firmware stack-up. (Don't be concerned with defining the interface just yet. We'll be covering how to do this in the coming chapters.)

- Review the last section on "Getting Started Writing Portable Firmware." On a sheet of paper, draw your own spider diagram and rank how well your code exhibits the portable-firmware characteristics. Select one or two characteristics that you feel will have the biggest impact on your code and focus on improving those. Periodically review and reevaluate.

CHAPTER 2

API and HAL Fundamentals

"Software is a great combination between artistry and engineering."

—Bill Gates

The Wonderful World of HALs

There are many tools that embedded-software developers can use to develop software consistently, but the greatest tools available to improve code reuse and portability are APIs and HALs. Designing a HAL is a great first step toward developing firmware that is reusable and hardware independent. The HAL, or hardware abstraction layer, provides the application developer with a standard function set that can be used to access hardware functions without a detailed understanding of how the underlying hardware works. A HAL is not the infamous artificial intelligence from *2001: A Space Odyssey*. HALs are essentially APIs designed to interact with hardware rather than to provide high-level program blocks that ease application development. A properly designed HAL provides developers with many benefits, such as code that is portable, reusable, lower cost, abstracted, and potentially with fewer bugs. A poorly designed HAL can result in increased costs and buggy software and can leave the developer wishing that they were dealing with the previously mentioned infamous HAL.

© Jacob Beningo 2017
J. Beningo, *Reusable Firmware Development*, https://doi.org/10.1007/978-1-4842-3297-2_2

APIs Versus HALs

Traditionally, embedded-software developers have done a poor job developing software that can be easily reused and ported. The reason is not necessarily the developers' fault but rather has its roots in the fact that the available hardware has been very resource constrained, compiled code wasn't the most efficient, and project pressures result in software being developed in a hurry. For these reasons, most embedded-software projects start out with a clean slate with little code being reused.

A major barrier to creating reusable software has been the very technologies that developers are using, along with the microcontroller itself being a big culprit. Two major factors for skipping APIs and HALs have been the fact that they can add a little overhead because of function calls and that code space can creep up slightly. When flash memory was expensive, a little code bloat could easily cause a significant increase in hardware costs. Developers also considered using HALs to be a waste because the variability in capabilities and low-level register and memory-map layouts make reuse appear very difficult.

Embedded-software development needs in the twenty-first century are driving major changes to the way software is developed. Hardware capabilities have dramatically increased while costs have fallen significantly. The major project costs are no longer with the hardware design and manufacturing but instead in the software development. These factors are driving the need to reuse embedded software.

Embedded software can be easily developed that is reused from one application to the next and even from an 8-bit microcontroller to a 32-bit microcontroller. Computer scientists solved porting or reusing software many decades ago. Desktop programmers have taken advantage of frameworks and components since the dawn of the personal computer (if not earlier). One of the most important tools that embedded-system developers have tended to neglect is the use of an API or a HAL.

An API is an application programming interface that defines a set of routines, protocols, and tools for creating an application.[1] An API defines the high-level interface of the behavior and capabilities of the component and its inputs and outputs. An API should be created so that it is generic and implementation independent. This allows the API to be used in multiple applications with changes being made only to the API implementation and not to the general interface or behavior.

---

[1]http://www.webopedia.com/TERM/A/API.html

A HAL is a hardware abstraction layer that defines a set of routines, protocols, and tools for interacting with the hardware. A HAL is focused on creating abstract, high-level functions that can be used to make the hardware do something without requiring detailed knowledge of how the hardware is doing it. A HAL can come in extremely handy for developers who work with multiple microcontroller hardware types and need to port applications from one platform to the next.

APIs and HALs are related. It could be argued that they do nearly the same thing. The difference is that an API is designed to make application software easier while a HAL is designed to make interacting with low-level hardware easier. An embedded system that is well designed would have both a HAL to interact with the low-level hardware and an API that interacts with the HAL to produce a set of APIs that simplify application development.

The API and HAL Landscape

As microprocessor capabilities have increased in recent years, the technical expertise required and the time necessary to get a microcontroller up and running have also been increasing dramatically. Setting up a simple UART can require days as one digs through thousands of pages of technical documents to figure out exactly which registers and bits need to be manipulated to establish basic serial communication with an embedded system. Given the pressure on many development teams to deliver faster and at lower costs, providing a HAL and an API can be a huge advantage.

Nearly every microcontroller manufacturer now has an API set that goes with their microcontroller. Beyond just the microcontroller manufacturers' APIs (and in many cases the terms API and HAL are used synonymously), there exist several APIs that embedded-systems developers can leverage that are attempting to be industry standards but differ drastically in their capabilities and the engineer type that they are targeting. In many cases, the APIs, HALs, components, and frameworks are referred to as a *platform*.

SOFTWARE TERMINOLOGY

Platform is a collection of APIs, HALs, modules, components, libraries, and frameworks designed to work together to speed up embedded-software development and decrease project costs.

The first, and probably the most famously known, are the Arduino APIs.[2] Every Arduino board can use common software components and function calls from the Arduino software library on any Arduino-based board. Arduino provides huge flexibility in hardware use, and most developers using Arduino know little to nothing about microcontrollers and sometimes even programming. These libraries provide an excellent way for non-computer-programming folks to create functional applications. The problem is that the API is targeted toward rapid prototyping and the maker community and lacks a professional touch that would be easy to use in a professional development environment.

Another well-known API example is ARM's mbed platform. Mbed is like Arduino in that it provides a common set of software features and functions that can be used to develop software quickly with little knowledge of the underlying hardware. Professional developers, though, will once again struggle with the fact that this platform is not designed to be production intent and lacks important underlying error handling and software analysis features that would be associated with a production-intent product. Lacking these important tools and capabilities once again make mbed a great prototyping platform but not a production-intent system. (There have been massive efforts under way to fill in these gaps and make mbed a fully production-intent platform that includes an RTOS).[3]

Beyond Arduino and mbed, there are professional production-intent standards that developers can leverage to develop their embedded software and improve its reusability and portability. A great example is AUTOSAR, which is used in the automotive industry. AUTOSAR provides a great HAL for interacting with the low-level hardware. The problem is that AUTOSAR is a bit convoluted and expensive to use as far as processing power goes and doesn't play well on resource-constrained microcontroller systems running under 200 MHz.

Unfortunately, a generic, industry-wide accepted standard does not exist for microcontroller-based systems. ARM has attempted to create standards through their CMSIS and mbed offerings, but in most cases these can only cover a standard way for interacting with the microcontroller core and not with the entire microcontroller. Every microcontroller manufacturer still has their own peripherals and other intellectual property that are designed to be key differentiators and differ from competitor offerings.

---

[2]https://www.arduino.cc/
[3]https://www.mbed.com/en/

For this reason, in many cases these "industry standards" fail, and each vendor is now producing their own unique and custom standard.

The Good, Bad, and Ugly

The ability to leverage an API or HAL that a microcontroller vendor has created can offer many advantages. The microcontroller manufacturer is the expert in how their part works, so it only makes sense that they have the necessary knowledge to create software that fully utilizes and is compatible with the microcontroller at a minimal cost. Nearly every microcontroller manufacturer has their own API. A few choice examples to explore include the Renesas Synergy™ Platform, Microchip Harmony, and ST Microelectronics STM32CubeMX toolchain.

There are many benefits that developers can experience by using an off-the-shelf HAL produced by a microcontroller vendor. First, if the vendor leveraged their internal hardware understanding, then developers would expect the interfaces to be fast and to utilize all the tricks that can be used within the microcontroller itself. Second, a development team doesn't need to spend months developing an API and HAL to interface with the microcontroller. They can get the microcontroller doing what it should be doing right out of the box. The ability to just use an existing API and HAL is a major benefit to developers, which is why microcontroller vendors have started to supply them. Teams can immediately start developing their application code rather than having to spend months diving into highly technical datasheets trying to understand how the microcontroller works.

Another benefit to developers is that in many instances the APIs and HALs have been integrated into easy-to-use development tools that include configurators to help ease the development burden. Engineers can select what components to include in an application and specify how those components should be configured from a simple Graphical User Interfaces (GUI). These tools vary drastically, however, in the software quality that is generated from the toolchain.

Potential Issues and the Boogeyman

All APIs and HALs are not created equal. Whether a development team is using an open source standard or a microcontroller vendor–provided standard, or have decided to roll their own standard, there are a few concerns that developers need to be aware of that can result in major software issues. The issues, if not considered up front, can come back to haunt a team, causing many sleepless nights as a result of an ill-considered boogeyman. These issues can include but are not limited to the following:

- Tied to a single toolchain

- Copyright infringement

- Execution efficiency

- Functionality limitations resulting from abstraction

- Integration issues

- Code bloat

- Readability

Microcontroller vendors have started to tie their APIs and HALs into automated toolchains that allow a developer to select which components they need in a project and easily configure them. For a developer using these toolchains, life is simplified and huge time and cost savings can be realized throughout the project. For some, though, it won't be all blue skies. A potential issue arises when a team wants to change microcontroller vendors. Suddenly, all their application code is tied to the vendor's APIs and functionality, which are tightly integrated together. Attempting to port that application code to a new API and HAL can be time consuming and costly.

This brings us to the second issue. A development team may decide that while they are tightly tied to the toolchain, they can easily just modify the low-level register accesses to use a different microcontroller and maintain the same API. The problem is that if you read the fine print for any vendor-supplied software, it is quite clear that the software, APIs, HALs, and so on are only to be used with their microcontrollers! Using them with a competitor's processor is a copyright violation. The result is having to rework or rewrite a fair amount of software or violate the copyright and nervously wait for potential legal ramifications (which of course is never the right solution).

Beyond the potential business and legal ramifications of using the software that is provided by microcontroller vendors, there is also the question of efficiency. Code that is written for a very specifically defined application can be very efficient. Abstracting the hardware and attempting to provide hooks for every possible use and application will add layers to the software. The more layers there are, the more function calls that execute before work is performed. This means that the system latency will begin to creep up. On a modern-day 32-bit microcontroller, this is not a problem; however, on an old 8-bit or 16-bit microcontroller, this could potentially be a big deal. Developers therefore need to look at how the provided software is architected and take some measurements to ensure that the execution efficiency is acceptable.

Abstracting a peripheral is a great technique to allow application developers to focus on the application and not worry about the underlying hardware. The problem is that through abstraction, sometimes little details and functionality get lost that could improve execution efficiency or simplify a task. Vendors will often write their automation tools to cover every device even though there are slight variations. Sometimes the details are abstracted out with no method to access that functionality through the API and HAL. In a later chapter, we will discuss how developers can deal with this issue.

There are also the inevitable integration issues. Most development teams use a mixture of commercial and open source software. In many cases, these software components were not designed to work with each other or ever tested together. The result is time wasted debugging and integrating software that from the surface appeared to be compatible but proved otherwise. Sometimes developers must add additional wrappers or create horrible constructs to make a square peg fit into a round hole.

The inevitable result of creating additional layers and abstractions within software is that the code gets slightly larger and larger until it is, well, bloated. Flash has become relatively inexpensive, and many developers don't worry as much today about code size as they did fifteen or twenty years ago. Still, it is something that needs to be considered by developers.

Finally, we have the potential for readability issues. When pulling in software vendor–supplied APIs, HALs, components, and so forth, the likelihood that they all used the same coding standard is rather slim. Functions and variables will use different naming conventions, which can be confusing and detract from the software function. Teams need to decide how best to deal with this, whether it's minor modifications, just dealing with it, or coming up with a unique and innovative solution. One potential solution is to compile the third-party components into libraries and include them in binary form so that the source code is not available in the project. However, this can potentially cause issues for developers during debugging.

Additional potential issues exist, but these are the ones that developers will find have the greatest impact on their development efforts. Each issue needs to be carefully considered and weighed before diving into a development effort and selecting or building the API.

Characteristics Every HAL Should Exhibit

Just because a platform or framework provides a HAL does not mean that it is going to be easy to use or will improve the software. I've encountered many instances where the HAL designers went overboard in their design and abstracted the HAL so much that it would take weeks to make heads or tails of how the HAL was working. Those designers seemed to believe in obfuscation, not abstraction. So, how can developers distinguish between the good HALs and the bad ones? There are probably more than two dozen different characteristics we could examine, but there are ten key characteristics that bear the most weight. Before going into detail on each characteristic, the following is a summary to provide the reader with the roadmap for where the discussion is going:

- Contains a well-defined coding standard

- Reasonable documentation and comments

- Written in C99

- Can be complied with any modern compiler

- Abstracts useful hardware features

- Easily extensible

SOFTWARE TERMINOLOGY

Coding standards contain a set of programming rules, naming conventions, and layout specifications that provide a consistent software.[4]

- Modular and adaptable

- Deterministic and well-understood behavior

- Error handling and diagnostic capabilities

- Integrated regression testing

With this preview in mind, let's now examine the characteristics in greater detail.

---

[4]http://www.decision-making-confidence.com/kepner-tregoe-decision-making.html

Characteristic #1: Contains a Well-Defined Coding Standard

In my experience, I have found that most HALs do not have a well-defined coding standard associated with them. Now, don't get me wrong—some microcontroller vendor–supplied HALs followed a coding standard, but after reviewing and searching their documentation, I discovered that it wasn't published or explicitly stated anywhere for the developers. Perhaps this is just a minor gripe, but the HAL is taking very specific microcontroller hardware and features and creating tidy and easy-to-use black boxes. A few pages stating the coding standard and mechanisms used to create the HAL doesn't seem like too much to ask, especially given the fact that developers could then incorporate that standard into their own documentation and practices to help provide a clean and consistent look to the entire code base.

Characteristic #2: Reasonable Documentation and Comments

I love open source software, but I also hate it. Open source software is usually sparsely populated with comments, which forces a developer to infer or guess at what the code is doing. Just because I can see the code doesn't mean that I will know what on Earth it is doing or, most important, why the developer is doing it that way. Running into even the smallest hiccup or problem results in a herculean effort to understand and resolve the issue. The documentation doesn't have to be a book, but a few clear and concise comments sprinkled throughout the source code that explain to an engineer how to configure and use the HAL is critical. A few examples certainly wouldn't hurt by any means either, or references to documents that can shed light on the code.

WHEN ARE THERE ENOUGH COMMENTS?

Ask just about any developer this question and you will get a spectrum of answers ranging from "Commenting is a time waste" through "There are never enough comments." The answer is that there should be enough comments for a developer who is new to maintaining the software to clearly understand what the code is doing and why. Sometimes a developer can get away with no comments if the code is self-explanatory, while at other times a developer may need to write a giant comment block.

Chapter 5 will dig into documenting firmware in greater detail.

Characteristic #3: Written in C99

There are so many choices for languages and language versions available to developers that one's head can begin spinning quite quickly trying to decide which to select. Typically, as low-level hardware programmers, the language of choice is going to be either C or C++, but given tradition the C programming language is the best bet. That leaves a simple choice between using C90, C99, or C11. C90 is a bit antiquated and is missing some very useful constructs that are included in C99. C11 is too new and very few compilers targeting microcontrollers support the updated and new features, although more support is being added with each passing year. The safest bet for any development team is to make sure any HAL that is being used conforms to the C99 standard. C99 provides the most flexibility and by now is supported by every compiler. If the compiler you are using does not support C99, then it is time to change compilers.

Characteristic #4: Can Be Compiled in Any Modern Compiler

The HAL should be designed to be capable of being compiled on any compiler. Whether a development team selects GCC, IAR, Keil, or some other compiler (there are probably only 100 different ones on the market), the HAL that is used should be able to be easily moved from one compiler to the next without any changes. Standard ANSI-C should be used, with compiler-specific additions such as attributes and #pragmas being kept to a minimum. Where there are compiler-specific features needed, the HAL should make that very clear using pre-processor directives for the desired compiler and flagging an error if the compiler has not yet been specified. Chapter 1 showed an example of how this could be done.

It is easy to start developing with one compiler only to discover compiler deficiencies, develop a new partnership with a vendor, get a great deal on a new license, or have team member preferences change. Keeping to ANSI-C and even occasionally checking compilation against multiple compilers can help ensure that the HAL will be easily portable to multiple compilers. Numerous teams that I've worked with have used more than one compiler for different product lines or even had their own compiler that they would periodically compare to GCC. (Maintaining your own custom compiler is also not recommended even if the company you work for is a silicon behemoth).

Characteristic #5: Abstract Useful Hardware Features

Microcontroller peripherals have become extremely complex and are designed to cover every possible design need conceivable. A development team could easily create a HAL with dozens of interfaces to handle all those possible nuances and features. A developer who does that would be wasting their time. In most applications, only a few common features are used from any single peripheral. The neat custom features like GPIO clock validation aren't commonly used, so there is no need to put them in the HAL unless you are a silicon vendor designing the APIs and HALs for your end users. Special features can be added to the HAL by extension, which will be discussed in a later chapter. Minimizing the features in the HAL can make the HAL more manageable and easier to use.

RECOGNIZING BAD APIS

APIs are the basic building blocks that applications are built upon. A good API should be small, efficient, and easily extensible. Throughout my career, I have had the opportunity to use both good and bad APIs. Developers can try to quantify what a good API is and what a bad API is, but the fact of the matter is that developers will know it when they see it. A bad API will often have the following characteristics:

- Has more than 12 interfaces

- Can be refactored to decrease the interface complexity

- Doesn't follow an obvious coding standard

- Is not easily memorable and requires constant looks at the reference manual

- Requires intense study, integration, and testing to get it to work properly

A good API will seem natural to developers.

Characteristic #6: Easily Extensible

Keeping the HAL common and to general peripheral features to make it more manageable is a great idea. The problem, however, is what if I selected a microcontroller specifically for that specialized peripheral feature and now don't have access to it through my HAL. A HAL should contain a pre-defined and standard function set, and then from those interfaces the HAL should be extensible to include the custom features that are included in many microcontrollers. For example, the HAL can expose an interface for directly accessing peripheral registers in a specific memory region that a higher level Board Support Package (BSP) or application module can use to configure the special behavior. The HAL then stays simple and common from one application and microcontroller to the next while at the same time allowing additional custom features.

Characteristic #7: Modular and Adaptable

A HAL should not be a single massive file that contains every possible feature for the microcontroller. The HAL needs to be modular, with the different microcontroller peripherals each existing in its own module. Separating the peripherals makes the code more modular and reusable and allows developers to adapt to different application needs. If a project doesn't need the SPI peripheral, they can simply exclude that module from the code base and save precious flash space. Using a modular HAL also makes it much easier to parallel the work that needs to be done so that multiple engineers can all be working at the same time.

CASE STUDY—ONE MODULE TO RULE THEM ALL!

The *Lord of the Rings* is a great movie. I'm a huge fan, but having a single code module to rule the entire application does not sound like fun. It's 2017 when I'm writing this, and I still encounter customers who write their embedded software in a single source module named `main`. In most instances, these single-module applications contain at least 100,000 lines of code!

During one particular encounter, we had multiple engineers working on a new product that was an improvement over an earlier prototype. The goal was to reuse as much code as possible from the original product in order to save time and costs and bring it up to the latest and greatest in organization and software architecture. The product had separate hardware components, so we assigned one engineer to port the code for each device.

Trying to pull code from the 100 KLOC-plus code base was a nightmare since everything was tightly coupled and hardware dependent. In frustration, I finally said the heck with it and started from scratch. When I was finally done with my code, the other two engineers were still frantically trying to make sense of the code they had before them. Countless time was spent on their part searching and sifting through the code looking for things. Poor code organization and a single module made their lives a nightmare and cost the company countless weeks if not months in additional engineering costs.

The only time that One Module should be used to rule them ALL is if that one module is a configuration module that is used to enable and disable features and configure the project.

Characteristic #8: Deterministic and Well-Understood Behavior

As teams develop and use a HAL implementation, data should be collected and analyzed that provide information related to the HAL performance. A good HAL will be deterministic and have well-defined and -understood behavior. A developer should know that calling `Gpio_PinWrite` will require a minimum of 15 microseconds and a maximum of 25 microseconds to execute but that it will always be within that range on specific target processors running at a specified frequency. In most cases, HALs are provided for microcontrollers but contain no intimate details as to how the HAL behaves in a real-time environment. Sure, one could argue that different microcontroller architectures and clock rates will change these characteristics, but even the data provided for one or two architectures with the test details can help an engineer infer the behavior they can expect. Once implemented in their own design, an engineer can then verify that assumption themselves, record the new values, and push those back to the HAL producer to provide yet more data for engineers to make ever better decisions.

Characteristic #9: Error-Handling and Diagnostic Capabilities

I would guess that 99 percent of the HALs I have seen give little to no thought to error handling or diagnostic capabilities. I suspect the reason is that using HALs in microcontroller-based applications is so new that the whole focus is on just getting the first cut done. I suppose the alternative could be that the HAL developers just assumed that there would never be an error or problem and that the system would just run flawlessly. I've met quite a few teams in my career that had that mentality.

Error handling doesn't have to be perfect. Returning a value indicating if the intended interfaced call was successful or not could be enough. Alternatively, perhaps requiring a full check on the peripheral to ensure that it is configured properly is necessary. Developers should look for at least some minimal amount of error handling in the HAL. Otherwise, something will go wrong and it will be up to the developer to dig in and try to discover what.

CASE STUDY—ASSUMING EVERYTHING WILL BE OKAY

Software engineers are very optimistic creatures. If the software runs correctly one time, it is often assumed that it will always run correctly no matter what the circumstances may be. Unfortunately, this is not the case!

On numerous occasions, I have encountered application code that just did not seem to work the way that was expected. After being called in to help identify the issue, I discovered that the developers not only didn't include any error handling or checks in their software, they also did not check return values for functions.

After sprinkling error checking throughout the code, I discovered that one function was returning a value that stated there was insufficient memory available. After making a slight adjustment, the code ran fine.

Debugging software can be time consuming and expensive, both financially and emotionally. Don't assume that everything will be okay; in fact, assume that nothing is going to go right! Make sure that all return values are checked for errors. Adding in extra checks may use some extra time and extra code space and cause a negligible performance hit, but these minor costs will save far more time, budget, and emotional wear and tear than they cause harm.

Characteristic #10: Integrated Regression Testing

The major benefit of using a HAL is to abstract out the lower-level hardware and to create a clean interface that is easily ported. If code is going to be reused, there should also be regression tests associated with that code. At a minimum, developers should create a test-case list that can be walked through to verify the HAL behavior. Manual checking can be error prone and extremely labor intensive. In many cases, a team will pick only a few boundary conditions and just assume the rest are correct. Automated regression tests, on the other hand, can walk through all the possible combinations and completely verify all the test cases. As the HAL matures and grows, new test cases can be added or removed to fit the team needs. Just remember: If the software hasn't been tested then it doesn't work! Figure 2-1 provides an example of what an integration server might look like.

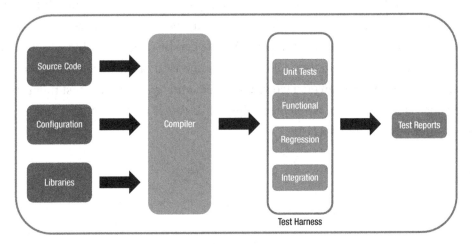

Figure 2-1. *Integration server performing automated testing*

An integration server will pull the latest source code, configuration, and libraries and verify that there are no problems compiling the code. Some setups will even perform static code analysis and generate reports based on the compilation and code analysis. Additional analytics can be performed, such as measuring the software function complexity.

Once the compiler has successfully compiled the code, the executable can be passed to the test harness. The test harness can use either mock hardware—that is, hardware that is simulated in memory—or it can use real hardware and integrate into GDB or other debugging tools. The test harness should have tests that are traceable to the system requirements. Example tests that would be performed are unit tests on functions, functional tests to verify that hardware performs as expected, regression tests that cover all previous test cases and ensure that they still pass, and then perhaps even integration testing.

Evaluating HAL Characteristics

There are many ways that a developer can evaluate whether a HAL is going to meet the system requirements, but one method that I have found provides a very unbiased opinion is the KT Matrix. The KT Matrix[4] allows a developer to identify all the characteristics that they are interested in evaluating concerning a decision that they need to make. Each characteristic can be provided a weight to show how important it is to the decision-making process. The KT Matrix can be used to decide which HAL to use. The potential HALs can then all be evaluated based on how well they meet the characteristics. Each HAL is given a weighted value, and the HAL that best meets the characteristics is the HAL that is selected. Figure 2-2 shows an example KT Matrix that a developer might use to select a HAL.

		Criteria	Weight	HAL #1 Rating 1	2	3	4	5	Weighted Rating	HAL #2 Rating 1	2	3	4	5	Weighted Rating	HAL #3 Rating 1	2	3	4	5	Weighted Rating
	Performance	Smallest RAM footprint	4	3	5	3	5	3	60	2	2	2	2	2	40	1	1	1	1	1	20
		Smallest ROM footprint	4	2	2	2	2	2	40	1	1	1	1	1	20	3	3	3	3	3	60
		Highest degree of determinism	5	2	1	1	1	2	35	1	2	2	2	1	40	3	3	3	3	3	75
		Best meets reliability requirements	5	1	2	2	1	1	35	3	1	1	3	2	50	2	3	3	2	3	65
	Features	Written in C99	3	2	1	2	3	1	27	1	2	1	1	2	27	3	3	1	2	3	36
		Multiple Compiler Support	4	2	3	1	2	3	44	3	1	2	3	1	40	1	2	3	1	2	36
		Easiest to scale	5	3	2	3	2	2	65	1	3	1	1	1	45	2	1	2	1	2	40
		Easiest to configure features	5	2	2	3	1	1	45	1	1	2	2	2	40	3	1	1	3	3	65
		Processor derivative fully supported	5	2	2	2	2	2	50	1	1	1	1	3	25	3	3	3	3	3	75
		Conforms to required interface standards (i.e. POSIX, DO-178B)	3	1	1	1	1	1	15	3	3	3	3	3	45	2	2	2	2	2	30
		Extensible	5	3	3	3	3	3	75	3	3	3	3	3	75	3	3	3	3	3	75
		Modular	5	3	3	3	3	3	75	3	3	3	3	3	75	3	3	3	3	3	75
		Integrated Regression Testing	4	2	1	3	1	1	32	2	1	3	1	1	32	2	1	3	1	1	32
		Easiest to port to other MCU's and architectures	3	1	2	3	1	2	27	3	3	1	2	3	33	3	1	2	3	1	30
		Most relevant safety certifications	4	3	2	3	2	3	52	2	3	1	3	1	40	1	1	2	1	2	28
	Cost	Lowest upfront licensing costs	5	3	3	3	3	3	75	1	1	1	1	1	25	2	2	2	2	2	50
		Lowest royalty cost per unit	3	3	3	3	3	3	45	2	2	2	2	2	30	1	1	1	1	1	15
		Lowest time to get up to speed with RTOS specifics	3	1	2	3	3	2	33	3	3	1	1	3	30	3	1	2	1	3	27
		Lowest training investment	3	2	1	3	2	1	45	1	3	2	1	3	50	3	3	1	2	2	50
		Least open source (minimize new IP release)	3	1	1	1	1	1	15	2	3	3	2	2	36	3	2	1	3	3	39
	Ecosystem	Highest adoption rate in target industry	3	3	2	3	2	2	39	3	1	3	1	2	30	2	1	2	1	1	21
		Most architectures supported	3	2	2	2	2	2	30	3	3	3	3	3	45	1	1	1	1	1	15
		Largest and most vibrant forum community (fast to respond)	4	2	5	2	3	1	44	1	2	1	1	3	32	3	1	3	3	2	48
		Fastest technical support available	5	1	2	1	2	1	35	2	3	2	3	2	60	3	1	3	1	3	55
		Highest quality professional training available	2	2	1	2	1	2	16	1	1	3	1	1	18	3	2	3	2	3	26
		Example projects and source available	4	2	5	2	3	2	48	3	1	3	1	3	44	1	2	1	2	1	28
	Vendor	Best historical track record	3	2	2	1	3	1	27	3	3	2	1	2	33	1	1	3	2	3	30
		Most relevant certified development process	3	1	1	2	1	1	18	2	2	3	2	2	33	3	3	1	3	2	39
		Shortest support request times	5	1	1	1	2	2	35	2	2	2	3	3	60	3	3	3	1	1	55
		Best strategic fit	4	2	2	1	2	2	36	2	3	1	2	3	40	3	3	3	1	1	44
		Best code quality	4	1	1	2	2	1	28	2	2	3	3	2	48	3	5	1	1	2	40
		Best code documentation	4	2	2	1	2	2	36	3	2	3	3	2	56	1	1	3	1	1	28
	Engineer	Minimal professional growth potential	2	2	2	1	3	1	18	1	1	3	2	3	20	3	3	1	1	2	20
		Least amount of stress to implement	2	2	3	1	1	3	20	1	1	2	3	3	22	2	2	2	1	2	18
		Most fun / interesting	1	2	3	3	1	2	11	3	1	1	2	3	10	1	2	2	1	1	9
		Minimized labor intensity	3	1	2	3	1	3	30	2	3	1	2	1	27	3	1	2	3	2	33
		Least deadline constrained to get up to speed	2	2	1	1	2	1	18	1	1	3	1	1	22	1	3	1	3	2	20
		Most internal resources available	3	1	2	3	3	3	36	2	3	1	1	1	24	3	1	2	2	2	30
		Total	140	73	75	81	75	76	1428	73	82	75	81	78	1421	88	74	80	76	75	1402
						HAL #1						HAL #2						HAL #3				

Figure 2-2. *KT Matrix to select a HAL*

There are a few different ways that the KT matrix can be evaluated. In general, each characteristic in a group is given a rating from 1, being the worst rank in the category, to X, being the highest rank in that category. Every engineer involved in the decision provides a ranking for the HAL, and then the ranking is weighted and added to the other rankings. The rankings for all the criteria are then summed and the HAL with the highest score is the HAL that best meets the HAL criteria.

To Build or Not to Build

Chances are, there is no HAL on the planet for microcontrollers that currently meets all the characteristics that we just discussed or that meets every development team's needs. Certainly, some good HALs exist, but no single microcontroller HAL brings the best of all worlds. Some may be complete overkill for the application space or company needs while others may not go far enough. In these circumstances, a development team may need to build their own HAL. For those of you up to that challenge, we will be discussing how to do this in detail in this book, but for now let's talk about how to decide whether to build one ourselves, the potential cost, and how to make the process manageable.

There are several factors that a development team needs to consider before deciding to build their own HAL. These factors include:

- Availability of existing HALs

- Target microcontroller(s) and application

- Cost

- Development time

Before deciding to start designing your own HAL, it's critical to determine whether you need to design one yourself or if one exists that already meets your needs and requirements. A good starting place is to do some basic research and identify any HALs and standards that currently exist and get familiar with them. What are their strengths? What are their weaknesses? Having this information empowers a team to properly evaluate whether existing HALs will fit their company's needs.

The target microcontrollers and application can influence whether a development team will create their own HAL or use an existing HAL. For example, if a development team has decided that they will always use a microcontroller from a single microcontroller supplier, the team may be able to just use the HAL provided by the microcontroller vendor. This would save the time and cost of developing a HAL from scratch. However, it also ties the development team into that vendor's ecosystem and may make it extremely costly to change microcontrollers later on down the road. Consider the fact that in most cases those HALs have licenses or copyrights associated with them and using them with any other manufacturer would violate those licenses.

Developing a HAL from scratch can take some additional development time to be properly designed as well as some additional up-front costs. The costs are usually offset and easily recouped after one or two development cycles depending on the experience of the designing engineers. However, it is not uncommon for a HAL to require multiple iterations and multiple projects before it is finally fleshed out and covers all the possible permutations. The hope, however, is that developers can use the knowledge and experiences in this book to quickly and cost effectively implement their own HALs that will not tie them to any microcontroller toolchain.

A First Look at a HAL

To many readers, what a HAL looks like is completely obvious. A HAL is round, with a red optical center surrounded by a lens and gray trim. This is, of course, the description for how the HAL 9000 looked in *2001: A Space Odyssey*. The HAL that we are interested in as developers is a software interface that allows us to easily control a microcontroller. To a developer, these HALs are nothing more than a header and source module with a pre-defined function set. We will be going into a great deal of detail on this later, but to give a sneak peak, Figure 2-3 shows an example HAL for a GPIO peripheral.

```
void Dio_Init(const DioConfig_t * const Config);
DioPinState_t Dio_ChannelRead(DioChannel_t Channel);
void Dio_ChannelWrite(DioChannel_t Channel,
                        DioPinState_t State);
void Dio_ChannelToggle(DioChannel_t Channel);
void Dio_ChannelModeSet(DioChannel_t Channel,
                        DioMode_t Mode);
void Dio_ChannelDirectionSet(DioChannel_t Channel,
                        PinModeEnum_t Mode);
void Dio_RegisterWrite(uint32_t Address, TYPE Value);
TYPE Dio_RegisterRead(uint32_t Address);
Void Dio_CallbackRegister(DioCallback_t Function,
                        TYPE (*CallbackFunction)(type));
```

Figure 2-3. *Example GPIO HAL*

Figure 2-3 has a clear majority of the characteristics we previously discussed that all HALs should have. The characteristics that are lacking can be easily added by the reader. Throughout this book, we will go into the details of the HAL listed and discuss the design decisions and steps to put it together, not just for GPIO but for any microcontroller peripheral. Consider Figure 2-3 your sneak peek!

The API Scope

The API is a tool available to developers that can be used to dramatically speed up software development. Developers who want to write code that is reusable will break their software up into logical components that exhibit certain functions and features that are useful building blocks for the application. A developer doesn't necessarily want to understand every detail included in the component but simply what inputs are necessary to get the desired outputs. An API is provided for the component to abstract the underlying details and allow application developers to very rapidly develop software.

It is important to note that a HAL is really a specialized case for an API. Both APIs and HALs are used to abstract out the underlying component details and speed up software development. They both are used with components. The real difference between them is that a HAL is used to abstract hardware functionality while an API is used to abstract software components.

For most software developers, the HAL doesn't even exist in their minds because they are always writing code at the highest software levels available. Take, for example, web developers or mobile phone application developers. Sure, there is hardware that drives the entire system, but it is abstracted through so many software layers that, to the developer, there is only software.

APIs act as a standard—or, to some degree, as a contract—between the component that is being used and the necessary inputs and outputs necessary to make the component function. They provide the definition for how to use software libraries, real-time operating systems (RTOSes), and many other possible software components one might find in a system.

Embedded-software developers might wonder if there are any API standards that can be used to reuse code and speed up development. At first thought, the answer is that there aren't any. The truth is, though, that there are API standards that we use that we aren't even aware exist! Take, for example, any RTOS that is on the market today. Each RTOS has its own API standard that it adheres to that allows developers to consistently use and reuse the RTOS. Now, of course, each RTOS has a different API standard, and sure it would be great if they all had a single standard that they followed (something like POSIX), but unfortunately, that is not the case (for now).

There are many examples available to embedded-software developers of APIs. The following is a small list, but it should give you an idea about the APIs that are available:

- EEPROM JEDEC Standard (all EEPROMs have a standard hardware interface that can be used to create a standard API interface)

- FatFS (open source Fat File System library)

- AUTOSAR

- GUIX (graphical user interface APIs from Express Logix)

- Arduino (high-level components do have a standard interface)

API Characteristics to Look For

Many API characteristics that developers should look for will include the list that was previously discussed for the HAL. However, that list can be expanded to include generic characteristics that are considered good programming practices. For example, a few additional characteristics that we should consider include the following:

- Uses const on read-only parameters liberally

- Uses easily understood naming conventions

- Has consistent look and feel that is intuitive

- Well documented with examples

- Flexible and configurable

Let's take a quick look at why these five characteristics are so important.

Characteristic #1: Using const Frequently

The const keyword tells the compiler that the data being referred to by the const variable is read-only. The actual memory location may be writable, but through the variable the data should be treated as read-only. There are many times when a developer may have data that can change, but when passing it into an API call, doesn't want the data manipulated or modified. To protect that data, one can type the variable as const and pass it into the API. If the API doesn't need to modify the variable, it should treat it as read-only so that a maintaining engineer or just a simple coding mistake can't accidentally corrupt or change the data.

49

A good API will declare many parameters as const because it is just using the data to perform useful work and wants to protect the data that it is using. APIs that are light on using const aren't necessarily bad, but they do open themselves up to the opportunity for something to go wrong and behave unexpectedly.

Characteristic #2: Easily Understood Naming Conventions

A good API is easy to read and understand. As a developer becomes familiar with the API, they should be able to naturally remember the different API calls based on the function that is needed. This seems obvious, but in many circumstances the APIs that we use are quite bad and require us to constantly go back to the documentation to remember the exact name.

A great example is if a developer were to right now go and compare the API calls associated with FreeRTOS with those provided by Micrium's uOS II or III. FreeRTOS uses weird and non-intuitive APIs. Some calls have v's or x's in front, which can easily confuse developers. For one, they must figure out what the heck those v's and x's stand for. Once they do, they must try to remember what they mean! Was v for a macro or a direct function call? Was it the other way around? On the other hand, the uOS calls are obvious and straightforward and much easier to remember. Figure 2-4 shows a few examples from FreeRTOS and Figure 2-5 shows the corresponding calls in uOS III.

```
BaseType_t xTaskCreate(    TaskFunction_t pvTaskCode,
                           const char * const pcName,
                           unsigned short usStackDepth,
                           void *pvParameters,
                           UBaseType_t uxPriority,
                           TaskHandle_t *pxCreatedTask
                      )

void vTaskDelete( TaskHandle_t xTask )

SemaphoreHandle_t xSemaphoreCreateBinary( void )

void vSemaphoreDelete( SemaphoreHandle_t xSemaphore )

xSemaphoreTake( SemaphoreHandle_t xSemaphore,
                TickType_t xTicksToWait )

xSemaphoreGive( SemaphoreHandle_t xSemaphore )
```

Figure 2-4.   *Example FreeRTOS APIs[5]*

---

[5]http://www.freertos.org/a00106.html

```
        void OSTaskCreate (OS_TCB *p_tcb,
                           CPU_CHAR *p_name,
                           OS_TASK_PTR p_task,
                           void *p_arg,
                           OS_PRIO prio,
                           CPU_STK *p_stk_base,
                           CPU_STK_SIZE stk_limit,
                           CPU_STK_SIZE stk_size,
                           OS_MSG_QTY q_size,
                           OS_TICK time_quanta,
                           void *p_ext,
                           OS_OPT opt,
                           OS_ERR *p_err)

        void OSSemCreate ( OS_SEM *p_sem,
                           CPU_CHAR *p_name,
                           OS_SEM_CTR cnt,
                           OS_ERR *p_err)

        OS_OBJ_QTY OSSemDel (OS_SEM *p_sem,
                             OS_OPT opt,
                             OS_ERR *p_err)

        OS_SEM_CTR OSSemPend (OS_SEM *p_sem,
                              OS_TICK timeout,
                              OS_OPT opt,
                              CPU_TS *p_ts,
                              OS_ERR *p_err)

        OS_SEM_CTR OSSemPost (OS_SEM *p_sem,
                              OS_OPT opt,
                              OS_ERR *p_err)
```

Figure 2-5. *Example uOS III APIs*[6]

---

[6]https://doc.micrium.com/pages/viewpage.action?pageId=10753180

Characteristics #3: Consistent Look and Feel

The APIs for any component should have a consistent look and feel. They should follow a similar standard and be intuitive to the developer. APIs that are not consistent are error prone, and developers often find themselves digging through the documentation trying to figure out what is going on. The naming conventions should also follow a standard that gives the overall API a clean and professional look. Examining Figure 2-4 and Figure 2-5 again will demonstrate what a developer would expect from a professional API.

Characteristic #4: Well Documented

Good APIs will have great documentation associated with them, detailed documentation that shows the inputs, outputs, and expected results. Some APIs will even provide initial and post conditions, which is awesome! There should be examples that show how to use the APIs and maybe even a few that show a developer what not to do and identify the primary pain points developers will encounter when using the component.

Characteristic #5: Flexible and Configurable

APIs are at a high enough level that sometimes one size does not fit all. A good API should be flexible enough to work on multiple hardware platforms and provide a HAL to deal with differences in the hardware. The ability to configure the component to account for differences in hardware or even application is very critical. There are a lot of popular APIs available that just are not well developed, and the users end up struggling through them. That time and effort could have been spent innovating and coming up with improvements rather than just getting the component to function the way it is supposed to.

Designing Your Own APIs

In many instances, developers will be integrating components into their applications that already have a defined API that they have very little control over. However, there will be times when developers are creating their own components that they will be using for years as their own products evolve. In these instances, developers will want to create their own APIs that adhere to the characteristics that we just discussed.

A First Look at an API

APIs really don't look any different then HALs do. They are simply function calls within an application that have a public scope and can be accessed by any module. The only difference is that the APIs are designed to make application development easier versus working with hardware easier. A great API example to consider is for an RTOS. Figures 2-6 through 2-8 show the example API calls to create a task in Micrium's uC/OS-III, FreeRTOS, and Expresslogics's ThreadX real-time operating systems. Take a moment to look through them.

```
BaseType_t xTaskCreate(TaskFunction_t pvTaskCode,
                const char * const pcName,
                unsigned short usStackDepth,
                void *pvParameters,
                UBaseType_t uxPriority,
                TaskHandle_t *pxCreatedTask
                )
```

Figure 2-6. *FreeRTOS TaskCreate[7]*

```
void OSTaskCreate (OS_TCB *p_tcb,
                CPU_CHAR *p_name,
                OS_TASK_PTR p_task,
                void *p_arg,
                OS_PRIO prio,
                CPU_STK *p_stk_base,
                CPU_STK_SIZE stk_limit,
                CPU_STK_SIZE stk_size,
                OS_MSG_QTY q_size,
                OS_TICK time_quanta,
                void *p_ext,
                OS_OPT opt,
                OS_ERR *p_err)
```

Figure 2-7. *Micrium uc/OS-III OSTaskCreate[8]*

---

[7]http://www.freertos.org/a00125.html

[8]https://doc.micrium.com/display/osiiidoc/OSTaskCreate

```
UINT tx_thread_create(TX_THREAD *thread_ptr,
                CHAR *name_ptr,
                VOID (*entry_function)(ULONG),
                ULONG entry_input,
                VOID *stack_start,
                ULONG stack_size,
                UINT priority,
                UINT preempt_threshold,
                ULONG time_slice,
                UINT auto_start)
```

Figure 2-8. *Express Logic ThreadX tx_thread_create*[9]

Now, I am not knocking any RTOS, but from a quick look it is obvious that there
is no standard that is being followed either in naming convention or for features and
functionality. Each RTOS will fill a need and a niche, and some will meet the API
characteristics more than others. I'm not advocating one RTOS over another, but rather
simply sharing the API for three very popular and successful RTOSes. Starting with one
RTOS and then trying to switch to another obviously will require rework since the APIs
are not standardized.

Wrapping APIs

As I mentioned earlier, there may be certain components in an embedded system that
meet a common design challenge, such as real-time scheduling, but the components
available on the market do not have a standard interface. When this occurs, developers
can take the matter into their own hands and add an API wrapper to the components to
make them fit a standard interface.

---

[9]http://rtos.com/images/uploads/programmersguide_threadx.pdf

For example, I might have three different RTOSes I want to use in a design, and the product or process will determine which one I use. As a developer, I can look at the commonalities between the operating systems and create my own API functions that will call the desired function in the target RTOS. I could create an API for creating a task, using mutexes, semaphores, or even message queues. The API would then be a generic and standard call, which is replaced by my call into the specific RTOS function. Figure 2-9 shows an example of what the wrapper would look like. The application code would use this function, and then within that function call would be the RTOS-specific task-create function call.

```
int16_t OS_TaskCreate(tcb_t * TaskConfig);
```

Figure 2-9. *Using an API wrapper*

Using a general wrapper in this way has many advantages, and there are quite a few places where a developer may want to use a wrapper API, such as:

- RTOS calls

- Memory accesses

- File systems

- High-level components that require third-party software

- Circular buffers

- External devices

Using a wrapper is not all blue skies though. Every function call does incur a little bit of overhead on the processor, and passing parameters into the function does use some stack space. In most applications, the overhead performance hit and extra code will be negligible. Developers should still be careful and aware that the wrapper does affect performance and code size.

Why Design Your Own APIs and HALs?

Silicon vendors provide their own HALs to help speed development, or even tools like Processor Expert and STM32CubeMx that can automatically generate the HALs needed based on the project configuration. Microchip has MPLAB Harmony, Renesas, the Renesas Synergy™ Platform, so why not just use those? After all, a lot of time and effort has gone into developing these capabilities for developers, and they are offered free of charge. There are a few times when a development team may decide to overlook the silicon vendors' APIs and HALs and instead use their own. These include when the development team is concerned with the following:

- Not wanting to be stuck using the vendor's toolchain, which can be costly and time consuming to change

- API is under copyright so it cannot be ported without being completely rewritten

- API quality

- Coding standards

- Robustness

- Code size

- Quality

- Testability

Microcontroller manufacturers are making it easier and easier for developers to abstract the low-level hardware and focus their efforts on their application. For example, the Renesas Synergy Platform has tried to meet all these concerns by developing a strict software development life-cycle process and focusing heavily on quality. For some developers, this is great news since they no longer need to worry about that low-level driver design. For other developers, this is the end of embedded software as we know it, or they may have other concerns that will cause them to shy away from using these vendor-specific solutions. The truth is, microcontrollers have become extremely complex, and in order to deliver products within realistic time frames and budgets, developers need help to abstract out these complexities and work at a higher abstraction level.

Comparing APIs and HALs

Before we conclude this chapter, it is a useful exercise to examine the similarities and differences between APIs and HALs. As we have seen, APIs and HALs have a lot in common. In fact, in many circumstances developers may use the term API to include both the low-level software and the high-level application software. Remember, HALs interact with hardware at the lowest levels while an API interacts with other software at a high level. Beyond these differences, developers are looking for the exact same characteristics in both APIs and HALs. Take a few moments to examine Figure 2-10, which demonstrates the commonalities and differences between APIs and HALs. Developers will easily notice that APIs and HALs have far more in common than they do differences.

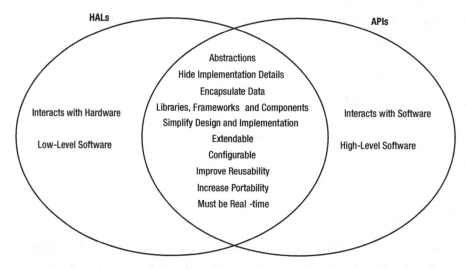

Figure 2-10. APIs versus HALs

Going Further

Understanding HALs and APIs requires more than just reading about them in this book. Practical experience and knowledge is crucial, especially for developers interested in developing their own portable HALs and APIs. The following are a few thoughts on what the reader can do to strengthen their understanding and start applying the concepts we've just discussed immediately in their own development efforts:

- Identify at least three different HALs that exist currently in the embedded-software industry. Schedule time to review these standards. While reviewing them, develop a simple chart that answers the following questions:

  - What strengths does this HAL exhibit?

  - What weaknesses does this HAL exhibit?

  - How well does it meet the characteristics every good HAL should have?

- Identify at least three different APIs that exist currently in the embedded-software industry. Schedule time to review these standards. While reviewing them, develop a simple chart that answers the following questions:

  - What strengths does this API exhibit?

  - What weaknesses does this API exhibit?

  - How well does it meet the characteristics every good API should have?

- Earlier in the chapter, three different microcontroller platforms were mentioned that utilize a HAL and API framework. Investigate each framework listed here and examine the similarities and differences:

  - Renesas Synergy Platform

  - Microchip Harmony

  - ST Microelectronics STM32CubeMx

- From the preceding platforms, how easy would it be to switch from one silicon vendor to the next? Are their APIs similar or completely different? List several advantages and disadvantages to using these platforms.

- Review the characteristics of HALs and APIs. Make a simple spreadsheet with each characteristic listed. Now, go online to a few RTOS vendors. Review their API interfaces for task management, semaphores, mutexes, and message queues. How well do these APIs meet the characteristics of good APIs?

- Create a KT Matrix that can be used to evaluate APIs and HALs from third-party sources. Pick a few external APIs, such as ones for an RTOS or HAL, and with a close group of engineers walk through the process for selecting the API.

- Review Figures 2-4 to Figure 2-8. Do real-time operating systems have a standard API interface that developers can follow? What does this mean for developers when it comes to porting to a new OS, development time, learning curve, and costs?

- Design a wrapper that could be used to interact with any RTOS function calls.

CHAPTER 3

Device Driver Fundamentals in C

"Software is like entropy. It is difficult to grasp, weighs nothing, and obeys the second law of thermodynamics; i.e., it always increases."

—Norman Ralph Augustine

Understanding the Memory Map

The memory in every microcontroller is broken up into different regions that relate to specific microcontroller functions. Despite similar behaviors and capabilities among microcontrollers, memory regions and organization vary from one microcontroller to the next, and sometimes even within the same microcontroller family. Even though each microcontroller is organized differently, a developer can still develop drivers that are reusable and easily portable from one microcontroller to the next.

To create a driver, a developer must understand the different memory regions, their purpose, and the techniques available in the C programming language to map to those memory regions. Memory is organized into different regions, such as CPU, ROM, RAM, FLASH, Peripheral, and EEPROM. These regions are connected to the CPU through various buses, but the specifics will vary from one architecture to the next. Figure 3-1 shows an example of what a developer would expect to find located within the memory map.

© Jacob Beningo 2017

J. Beningo, *Reusable Firmware Development*, https://doi.org/10.1007/978-1-4842-3297-2_3

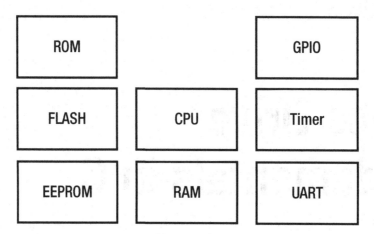

Figure 3-1. *Microcontroller memory regions*

ROM memory regions are programmed by the microcontroller manufacturer and can contain anything the manufacturer thought would be useful to their clients. For example, it is not uncommon to find bootloader, motor control, or flash algorithms permanently stored in these ROM regions. A ROM memory region cannot be modified by a developer, and the algorithms located there are permanent. A ROM region does not count toward the total code space that is available to a developer. Developers can access the algorithms stored in the ROM by mapping a function pointer to the code located there and de-referencing it.

RAM memory regions are volatile memory locations that can be programmed during the program's execution but will lose their data upon reset, power cycle, or power down. RAM contains the program stack, heap, and statically allocated variables. A developer must tell the compiler which memory areas will contain the program stack (for a bare-metal application) and the heap (which contains dynamically allocated variables such as the stack in an Real-time operating system (RTOS) and other on-the-fly application needs). Once these memory regions have been specified, the remaining memory can be used for general-purpose application variables and data storage.

Flash memory regions contain the executable application instructions, data tables (such as calibration data), and initialized variable values. In general, the flash memory regions are programmed when a device is a manufactured. However, the flash contents can be modified in the field through a bootloader application. The flash contents are carefully monitored during program development to ensure that the region is appropriately sized to hold the entire application. A good rule of thumb is to also size the flash region to allow new features to be added over the product's lifetime.

The CPU region contains control registers for the CPU itself, sometimes related to interrupts, faults, exceptions, and clock control. CPU registers are typically initialized by the start-up code, with vendors providing their own interfaces into the memory region. CPU regions are typically abstracted to hide the inner workings of the microcontroller from the developer.

CASE STUDY—ASSUMING RAM VALUES ARE PRESERVED

On numerous occasions, I have seen clients who get the ingenious idea to save memory and application time by using RAM to store data between power cycles. The assumption is that by writing data to RAM, performing a reset, and then powering up, the memory location can then be read with the previous application's values and state. I have seen developers most tempted to do this when creating a bootloader. The data stored is meant to tell the application whether the application or the bootloader should be loaded.

The problem with using RAM to store data between resets is that the data stored in memory is NOT guaranteed to persist between the power cycle or reset. The data may be preserved in most circumstances but undoubtedly is occasionally cleared out or corrupted, resulting in unexpected behavior. Assuming that the RAM data persists between power cycles will result in a software bug that is elusive and difficult to consistently repeat.

EEPROM regions are the rarest and typically will not be found on most microcontrollers. EEPROM provides a developer with a working region for calibration data that is separate from flash and provides a safe means for updating the data without the risk of accidentally erasing application code. Microcontrollers that don't include EEPROM will typically provide flash libraries that can be used to simulate EEPROM behavior but risk application code corruption.

The peripheral memory region is the most interesting to driver developers. The peripheral memory region contains the registers that control the microcontroller's peripherals, such as general-purpose input and output, analog-to-digital converters, serial peripheral interface, and many others. In order to create a driver, a developer must map the driver code to the memory region that the peripheral registers exist in. Once again, these regions will vary from one microcontroller to the next. In this chapter, we will discuss general techniques and strategies for driver development, and then in the next chapter we will dive into the nitty-gritty details.

The memory regions for a microcontroller are not required to be contiguous in any shape or form. A memory map may start with memory locations for application code, switch to RAM, then peripherals, and then back to application code. There can even be large spaces between usable memory locations that are commonly referred to as memory-map holes. An example of a memory map with holes can be seen in Figure 3-2.

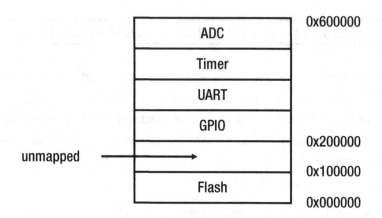

Figure 3-2. *Generic microcontroller memory map*

Planning the Driver Interfaces

Resource-constrained embedded-software development has a tendency toward chaos. Back when the C programming language was originally introduced, best practices and layered software architectures did not exist. Embedded software was littered with goto statements, driver code was tightly coupled to the application code, and there was no distinction as to where the middleware started or ended. The result was a giant code mess that rightly deserved the name spaghetti code.

Now, for those readers who have not yet drawn the connection, Beningo is an Italian name, and like any good Italian, a love of pasta is a given. In this instance, an analogy between pasta and the way that software is architected is completely appropriate. Take a moment to consider this: spaghetti is chaotic; noodles intertwine going this way and that way, resulting in a complete lack of structure. Writing unstructured code is exactly like spaghetti; with each bite you have no clue what you are going to get! (At least with spaghetti it will be tasty!)

On the other hand, there is lasagna! The noodles are layered, giving the meal structure and order. Code developed using layers is not only easier to understand, but it also has the potential to have one layer removed and a new layer added, basically allowing for reuse and ease in maintainability. (At times, I have been tempted to swap out lasagna layers, but I've always found it's just better to eat it!) Remember—we want to write lasagna code, not spaghetti code! Figure 3-3 is an example software architecture a developer might choose that decouples the different software layers. We discussed software architectures back in Chapter 1.

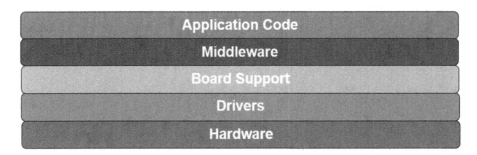

Figure 3-3. *The lasagna software architecture*

Writing software in a layered, lasagna-like manner allows the developer to easily define where one software type (layer) ends and another begins. At that point, we have what is known as a software interface. In Figure 3-3, we have four possible interfaces that need to be clearly defined. The interface allows the software layer directly above to interact with the software or possibly the hardware that exists beneath it. Defining a clean and extensible interface allows developers to not only organize their code but also provide a common interface that can be reused from one application to the next.

Starting in Chapter 6, we will be discussing in detail how to walk through and properly design and plan the interfaces. We will even walk through how to develop the interfaces for the hardware abstraction layer. At this point, in order to properly plan a software interface, a developer should look at the memory map that we discussed in the previous section and identify the low-level components that may be required in the driver layer. A similar list can be developed for each component that will exist in the middleware and application layers. The result may be a component diagram that looks like Figure 3-4.

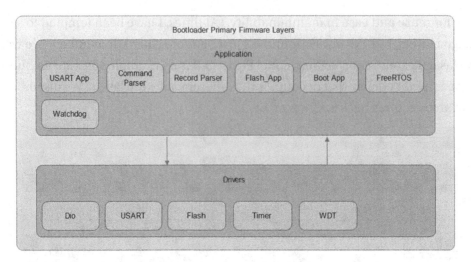

Figure 3-4. *Component identification*

The component interfaces occur where one layer touches another. The interface will consist of functions that result in some action being taken by the component, such as toggling a pin state, setting a register, or simply reading data. In order for those functions—the interface—to behave as expected, it can be extremely useful for developers to create a contract relationship between the interface and the developers who use it.

Design by Contract

Software interfaces can get complicated very quickly. A modern API and HAL may have over a hundred interfaces that are used to get the system to behave in the desired way. One method that can be used to ensure that developers have a clear understanding of how to use the interface is to use design-by-contract.[1] Design-by-contract is a methodology developers can use to specify pre-conditions, post-conditions, side effects, and invariants that are associated with the interface. Every component then has a contract that must be adhered to in order for the component to integrate into the application successfully. Figure 3-5 demonstrates how design by contract works.

---

[1]https://en.wikipedia.org/wiki/Design_by_contract

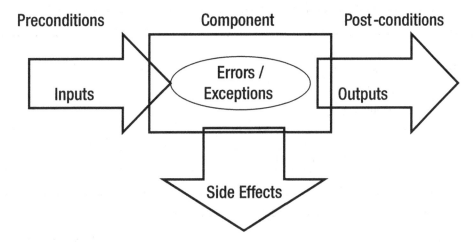

Figure 3-5. *Design by contract*

As developers, we must examine a component's inputs, outputs, and the work (the side effects) that will be performed. The pre-conditions describe what conditions must already exist within the system prior to performing an operation with the component. For example, a GPIO pin state cannot be toggled unless it first has the GPIO clock enabled. Enabling the clock would be a pre-condition or a pre-requisite for the GPIO component. Failing to meet this condition would result in nothing happening when a call to perform a GPIO operation occurs.

Once the pre-conditions for a function have been met, there may be inputs that are provided to the component so that it can carry out its function. An example would be toggling the state for a GPIO pin. The interface may have a function designed to elicit this behavior that requires the pin number to be passed in to properly identify the pin that will be toggled. Some interfaces may require no additional inputs other than making a call to the interface, while others may require a dozen or more inputs to get the desired behavior.

If the pre-conditions are met and the input data are valid, a developer would expect there to be a resulting side effect. A side effect is basically just that something in the system changes. Maybe a memory region is written or read, an i/o state is altered, or data is simply returned. Something useful happens by interacting with the component's interface. The resulting side effect then produces post-conditions that a developer can expect. The system state has changed into a desired state.

Finally, the outputs for the component are extracted. Perhaps the interface returns a success or a failure flag—maybe even an error code. Something is returned to let the caller know that everything proceeded as expected and the resulting side effect should now be observable.

```
                             DEFINITIONS
```

Pre-conditions are conditions required to be met prior to the function being called. Pre-conditions are specified in the component contract, which frees the function from having to check the conditions internally.

Post-conditions are conditions guaranteed to be met when the component has completed execution provided that all the pre-conditions have been met.

Side effects are the effects that the called function has on the system when it is executed. The side effect is the useful work that is performed by the function.

Invariants are conditions that are specified across the application that must be met to use the component. For example, when the restrict keyword is being used with a pointer, which tells the compiler the input will not be used anywhere else within the program.

Assertion Fundamentals

Before moving on to discuss driver models and the different methods embedded-software developers use to create drivers, it is important that we take a brief moment to review an important construct within the C programming language that is usually neglected or abused. The construct is the assert macro, which allows a developer to test assertions about the software.

The best definition for an assertion that I have ever encountered is as follows: "An assertion is a Boolean expression at a specific point in a program that will be true unless there is a bug in the program."[2] Assertions can be used to make sure that the program state is exactly what we expect it to be. If the state is something else, an assertion will stop execution and provide debug information, such as the file and line number where the assertion went wrong. A developer can then dive in and understand what happened before the application has the chance to change states.

The assert macro is defined in the assert.h header file. The assert macro generally takes the form shown in Figure 3-6. If the assertion is false, a developer-defined function is called to notify the user about the failed condition. In this case, when the assertion is false, a message will be printed over the UART that lists the file and line number of the failed assertion.

---

[2]http://wiki.c2.com/?WhatAreAssertions

```
288   void __aeabi_assert(const char *expr, const char *file, int line)
289 ⊟{
290      Uart_printf(UART1, "Assertion failed in %s at line %d\n", file, line);
291
292      for(;;);
293 }
```

Figure 3-6. *Example assert macro implementation*

The reason that I bring up assertions at this point, even though they are really beyond the scope of this book, is to point out that assertions are a great way to check inputs, outputs, pre-conditions, and post-conditions for interfaces and functions that are using design-by-contract interface definitions. A developer can use assert to verify that the conditions and inputs are met, and if not then there is a bug in the application code and the developer can be instantly notified that they did something wrong.

Using assertions is straightforward. A developer determines what the precondition is to the function and then develops an expression to test that condition. For example, if function x requires that the input be less than 150, a developer would check the pre-condition in the function using code like that found here:

```
void Function_X(uint8_t input)
{
   assert(input < 150);
   // Function main body
}
```

Every input and pre-condition should be checked at the start of a function. This is the developers' way to verify that the contract has been fulfilled by the component user. The same technique can also be used to verify that the post-conditions, output, and even the side effect are correct.

Now, some readers may be thinking to themselves that given enough assertions in the code, the overhead and the code space could quite quickly become too much. Assertions are meant to catch bugs in the program, and in many cases they are only enabled during development. Disabling assertions will reclaim code space and a few instruction cycles. Defining the macro NDEBUG will change the assert macro to an empty macro, essentially disabling the assertions.

Pay attention! This is critical! If assertions are going to be disabled for production, the final testing and validation needs to be performed with the assertions disabled. The reason for disabling them is that evaluating the expressions does affect the real-time performance, even if it is only a few clock cycles. Changing the execution time after testing could have completely unexpected consequences.

Device Driver Models

There are many ways that a low-level driver can be developed for a microcontroller. The two generic models that we are going to review are blocking and non-blocking drivers. Figure 3-7 compares each model using a sequence diagram, with lines representing the application's life line. The life line shows the application code's access to the CPU and the device driver's access to the CPU.

A blocking driver has exclusive access to the CPU and will not yield the CPU until the driver operation is completed. A typical example is the way that printf is set up in an embedded system. Calling printf first formats the desired string and puts the first character into the UART transmit buffer. The program then waits until the character is completely transmitted before entering the next character into the buffer. The process repeats until all characters are transmitted. Only then will printf return and allow the next line of code to execute. A blocking driver has the potential to destroy the real-time performance of an embedded system, and care must be taken to understand the minimum, maximum, and average execution times for drivers written in this manner.

The alternative strategy is to use a non-blocking driver. A non-blocking version for printf, which is a non-standard implementation, would prepare the string and place the first character into the transmit buffer. Once the character is in the buffer, printf would then return to the main application and allow it to continue executing while the character was being transmitted. The application would then use an interrupt to detect when the character transmission was complete so that the next character could be placed in the buffer.

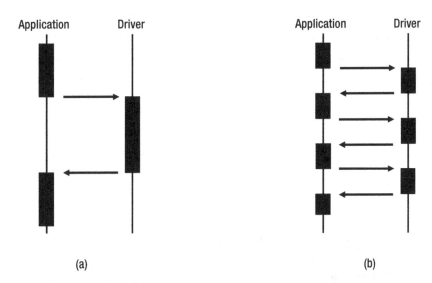

Figure 3-7. *(a) blocking driver model (b) non-blocking driver model*

On the one hand, blocking drivers can be very simple since they don't need to return to the main application and perform monitoring functions. The problem is that the real-time performance can be severely affected. Alternatively, non-blocking implementations can be used, which will preserve the real-time performance but will potentially increase the complexity for the application. The application must now in some way monitor for when the next character is ready to be placed into the buffer. The two primary ways that the buffer can be monitored are polling- or interrupt-driven behavior.

Polling Versus Interrupt-Driven Drivers

The easiest way to monitor that an event occurs in the system is to just periodically check if the complete flag has been set. Periodically checking a flag or register bit is known as *polling*. We basically ask, what's the flag state now . . . now . . . now . . . now . . . how about now . . . over and over until the flag is set. Once the flag is set, the application performs its next operation. Polled methods are simple but very inefficient. Clock cycles are wasted simply checking whether something should be done now or later.

A perfect example showing how the real-time performance can be dramatically affected by a blocking driver or function can be seen in Figure 3-8. The figure shows the timing required to print "Hello World" using a standard baud rate of 9600 bits per second. Using "Hello World" is a relatively simple string, yet, upon examining the figure, the reader will discover that it is taking approximately 12 milliseconds to execute!

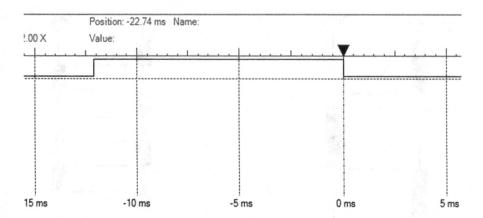

Figure 3-8. *Blocking printf timing to print "Hello World"*

The standard implementation for `printf` can get even worse! Printing a fixed string doesn't help when debugging a system. The data that is transmitted often includes variables and data that will change from one iteration to the next and require substitution. Figure 3-9 shows the same blocking implementation that is now printing out the system state using `printf("The system state is %d", State)`. The result is that, on average, the transmission takes 21 milliseconds!

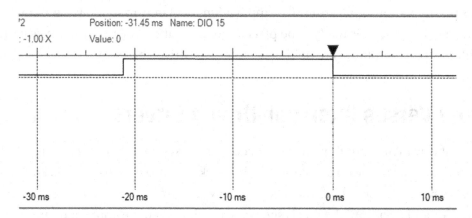

Figure 3-9. *Blocking printf timing to print "The system state is %d", State*

Obviously, blocking an application for tens of milliseconds is going to be unacceptable in a real-time application. The alternative to using polling is to use interrupts. Every microcontroller has interrupts for nearly any event-driven situation that a developer may be interested in. They can be much more efficient and by their very nature are non-blocking. Setting up and configuring an interrupt can be a complex and error-prone endeavor. A developer needs to carefully weigh their options and select the method that is most appropriate for the situation.

If a developer were to go back to their printf implementation and decide to implement a non-blocking solution that uses the UART transmission complete interrupt to load a new character into the transmit buffer, they would see a drastic change in their application's performance. First, the new implementation would process the string and prepare it to be transmitted, which, depending on the string's complexity, could take anywhere from 0.5 to 2.0 milliseconds for the strings used in the blocking example. Once the first character was transmitted, the remaining characters would be transmitted in an interrupt that executed approximately every 1.2 milliseconds, as shown in Figure 3-10.

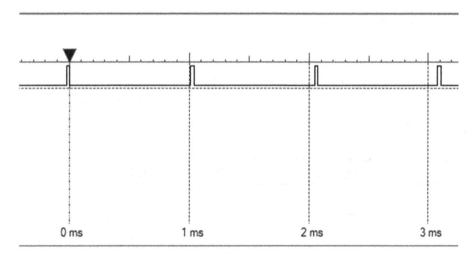

Figure 3-10. *Transmit interrupt frequency for 9600 bauds*

The major concern then becomes how much CPU time the interrupt is using. Interrupting the application every 1.2 milliseconds could potentially affect the application. A developer will want to understand how long the interrupt will be executing every 1.2 milliseconds. Figure 3-11 shows the average UART transmit execution time for this example. The interrupt requires approximately 35 microseconds to clear the transmit-complete flag and then copy the next character into the transmit buffer.

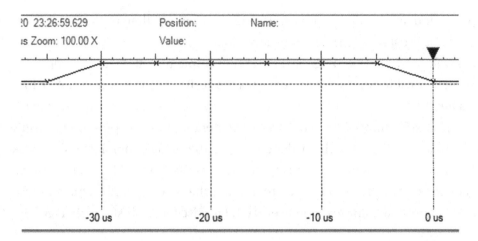

Figure 3-11. *UART transmit interrupt duration*

That is a stark difference in performance for printf between blocking and non-blocking methods! No application code executes for 12 to 21 milliseconds in the blocking implementation, while non-blocking blocks for 1 to 2 milliseconds up front and then interrupts for 35 microseconds every 1.2 milliseconds.

MODERN-DAY PRINTF IMPLEMENTATIONS

On a modern 32-bit ARM architecture, developers no longer need to be concerned with the timing required to perform printf statements. There are multiple methods available to developers that will allow even complex printf statements to be transmitted in microseconds.

These implementations include:

1. Segger real-time trace debugger capabilities

2. Utilizing the ARM ITM module

For debuggers and microcontrollers that do not include these capabilities or similar capabilities, developers will still need to be very careful with their printf statements.

Interrupts are not the only method that can be used to minimize how long a driver blocks the main application for. Developers can also use the direct memory access (DMA) controller. In a DMA implementation, a developer configures the DMA controller to interrupt and handle data movement from memory into a peripheral or from a peripheral to memory. The advantage to a DMA is that it is very fast and does not require the CPU. The CPU can be in a low-power state or executing other code while the DMA controller is moving data around the system. Considering the `printf` example, a developer could set up a memory buffer, then configure the DMA to transmit x characters from the buffer and into the UART transmit buffer. This implementation would then remove the periodic interrupt and allow the CPU to focus on the application code. An example of how a DMA setup would look can be found in Figure 3-12.

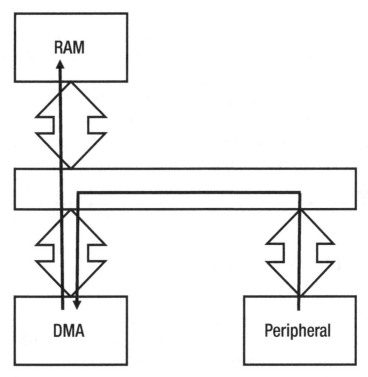

Figure 3-12. *DMA-controlled data transfer*

DMA is a powerful tool for developers but can be a complicated topic for a first-time user. Using DMA can also add unnecessary complexity to the software or result in abstractions and data movement that is not obvious from a quick look at the system. The efficiency can be well worth the trouble, however. Just don't forget: most microcontrollers have a limited number of DMA channels, so use them wisely!

CASE STUDY—USING DMA FOR ATTITUDE DETERMINATION AND CONTROL

Back when I was working on my master's degree at the University of Michigan, I was involved in the embedded-software design and implementation for a small satellite. My primary focus was the main flight-computer code that interacted with a half dozen or more subsystems and orchestrated the behavior for the entire satellite. One such subsystem was an Attitude Determination and Controls (ADACs), and it was experiencing issues retrieving and analyzing its data. Periodically, data would be lost as if the processor did not have enough throughput to handle the data stream.

As I sat down to review the firmware with the younger and less experienced engineer, I discovered that the implementation was flawless. The processor just could not keep up with the data rate, analysis, and communication simultaneously. Changing the processor was not an option. The alternative and only chance was to use the DMA to handle the data acquisition and memory storage and relieve the CPU of the responsibility. After a few short discussions and what could not have been more than an hour of updates to the drivers and software, the ADACs subsystem was operating flawlessly.

All that was needed was offloading some data handling from the CPU to the DMA controller.

Driver Component Definition

At times, it feels like there are a million different terms that float around the software development process. In some cases, these terms are used interchangeably even though there may be slight differences. In this section, we are going to explore the terms that are most often associated with drivers and framework development in the hopes that we can elucidate them while at the same time describing how to organize a driver from a high level.

A module is the fundamental unit that is used to develop a driver (or even embedded software in general). Simple drivers will contain a single module, while a complex driver such as a Wi-Fi driver may contain a dozen modules. A module is simply the combination of a header file and the source file that is associated with it. The header file contains the interface or the APIs that are used by the higher-level application code to run the module code. The source file contains the implementation details and all the details required to do the work that is exposed in the interface.

As very simple drivers, modules may sometimes even be referred to as components. A component is a collection of modules that work together to fulfill a software feature. A complex driver, like the Wi-Fi driver, is a single component that may be made up of several modules. Very simple components may simply have their header and source files added to a project. Complex components usually have a folder structure associated with them so that the component can be organized and kept separate from other code.

A driver will typically have at least three different files associated with it:

- The interface

- The source code

- A configuration module

How these three pieces are organized is completely up to the developer. In some cases, a developer may choose to create a folder for the entire component and include all these pieces together at the component's top level. In other cases, a developer may decide to create separate folders, one for each piece. There are many possibilities for how a component can be organized. A few examples can be seen in Figure 3-13.

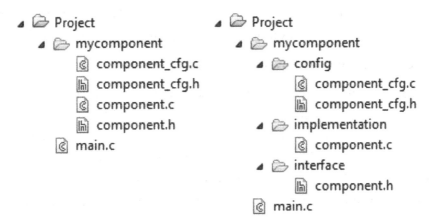

Figure 3-13. *Component organization*

DEFINITIONS

Module is part of a program that contains one or more routines. One or more independently developed modules make up a program.[3]

Component is an identifiable part of a larger program or construction. A component provides a specific function for the application. An application is divided into components that in turn are made up of modules.[4]

Interface is a boundary across which two independent systems meet and act on or communicate with each other.[5]

Naming Convention Recommendations

There are many ways that a developer can go about naming their interfaces, modules, and variables. It can be very tempting to create a new naming convention to stand out from the crowd. The problem with creating a new naming convention is that there are already great systems in existence for how a developer should name things. A great example that developers should examine can be found in the following article:

"Perfecting Naming Conventions"[6] by Jack Ganssle

Both articles provide developers with a foundation for naming that would be wise to adopt. There are a few ideas that I would like to highlight that I believe are critically important. First, developers need to use camel case. This is a widely-accepted standard within the software industry and deviating from it will dramatically affect code readability. Personally, I prefer to also capitalize the starting character in variables. That could just be the proper English showing through from doing so much writing.

---

[3]https://www.techopedia.com/definition/3843/module
[4]http://whatis.techtarget.com/definition/component
[5]www.webopedia.com/TERM/I/interface.html
[6]http://www.ganssle.com/articles/namingconventions.htm

Another convention that I highly recommend is to start with the subsystem and then work toward the specific. For example, an interface that is going to provide a read of the digital input/output peripheral would be named:

Dio_Read

The first three letters specify the subsystem followed by an underscore and then the purpose. This convention flows naturally and makes it very easy for a developer to first see the main actor and then the purpose for the interface.

Object-Oriented Programming in C

Developers should consider developing their drivers and their application code in an object-oriented manner. The C programming language is not an object-oriented programming language. C is a procedural programming language where the primary focus is to specify a series of well-structured steps and procedures within its programming context to produce a program.[7] An object-oriented programming language, on the other hand, is a programming language that focuses on the definition of and operations that are performed on data.

There are several characteristics that set an object-oriented programming language apart from a procedural language. These include:

- Abstraction

- Encapsulation

- Objects

- Classes

- Inheritance

- Polymorphism

Despite C not being object-oriented, developers can still implement some concepts in their application that will dramatically improve their software. While there are ways to create classes, inheritance, and polymorphism in C, if these features are required, developers would be better off just using C++. Applications can benefit greatly from using abstractions and encapsulation. Let's explore these concepts in detail.

---

[7]https://www.techopedia.com/definition/8982/procedural-language

---

DEFINITIONS[8]

Abstraction is revealing functionality and software features while hiding the implementation details.

Encapsulation is wrapping related data and code together into a single unit.

Objects are any entity that has a state or known behavior.

Classes are a logical software entity that is a collection of objects.

Inheritance is when a class inherits the characteristics of another class.

Abstractions and Abstract Data Types (ADTs)

An abstraction hides the underlying implementation details while making the functionality available to developers. For example, a well-implemented GPIO driver will provide an interface that tells a developer what can be done with the driver, but the developer doesn't need to know any details about how the driver is implemented or even on what hardware it runs. Abstractions hide the details from developers, creating a black box that simplifies what they need to know to use the software.

Abstractions don't only apply to component interfaces. Abstractions can just as easily be applied to data types. Abstract data types (often written as ADT for short) are data types whose implementation details are hidden from the view of the user for a data structure. There are several different methods that can be used to create an ADT in C. One method that is straightforward can be done in five easy steps. Let's look at how we can create an ADT for managing a memory stack.

First, a developer defines the abstract data type. The ADT in C is usually defined as a pointer to a structure. The ADT is declared within a header file without any underlying details, leaving it up to the implementer to fully declare the ADT in the source module. An example of an ADT would be a StackPtr_t, NodePtr_t, or QueuePtr_t, to name a few. If a developer were to define an ADT for a stack, they would start by defining the code shown in Figure 3-14 in the stack.h file. The details for the members in StackStruct_t are completely hidden from the users' perspective. Any interaction with StackPtr_t must be done using predefined operations.

---

[8]http://www.javatpoint.com/java-oops-concepts

```
typedef struct StackStruct_t * StackPtr_t;
```

Figure 3-14. *Defining an ADT*

The second step to creating an ADT is to define the operations that can be performed on the data. The operations that may be performed on an ADT are completely dependent on the purpose of the ADT. For example, an ADT for a stack might include the following operations:

- initialization
- pushing data
- popping data
- destroying the stack
- checking to see if the stack is full
- checking to see if the stack is empty

Don't forget that using an ADT is quite different from the way a developer would normally manipulate data. Typically, a developer would define the data and write code that directly manipulates the data. With an abstract data type, developers create an interface where the data is indirectly modified behind the scenes, leaving the implementation to the ADT implementer and letting the application developer simply use the data type.

Next, the ADT interface specification needs to be completed. The interface specification includes the function prototypes for all the public operations that can be performed on the ADT. The interface specification will be in the ADT header file. Considering the stack example, a developer might find that the interface specification looks something like the code shown in Figure 3-15.

```
bool Stack_Init(StackPtr_t Stack);
bool Stack_Push(StackPtr_t Stack, int Item);
bool Stack_Pop(StackPtr_t Stack, int * Item);
```

Figure 3-15. *Stack ADT interface*

Next, the ADT developer would either create the ADT implementation or a template for the implementation that would be filled in later. The ADT implementation could change from one application to the next. In fact, the ADT implementation could change during project development, and one major benefit to using an ADT is that the application that uses the ADT doesn't need to change. The implementation details are in the source module and "hidden" from the higher-level application developer. The use of an ADT provides a developer with a high degree of flexibility. An example implementation for the stack ADT can be found in Figures 3-16 through 3-19.

```
#include "stack.h"

struct StackStruct_t
{
  int Position_Current;
  int Array[STACK_SIZE];
};
```

Figure 3-16. *ADT implementation data structure*

Figure 3-16 shows the implementation for the ADT. The implementation structure uses an array with a predefined size to store the stack value and then has a position member to track where in the stack the next value will be added or removed.

```c
bool Stack_Init(StackPtr_t Stack)
{
  bool Success = false;
  Stack = malloc(sizeof(StackStruct_t));
  if(Stack != 0)
  {
    Stack->Position_Current=0;
    Success = true;
  }
  return Success;
}
```

Figure 3-17. *Stack method initialization*

The example implementation doesn't even allocate the memory for the stack until runtime. The Stack_Init function is used to dynamically allocate memory for the ADT. The user has no clue what the implementation does or how it does it and truthfully doesn't need to know or care! (Unless it could affect the real-time performance.) All the application code needs to do is create a pointer that will be used to store the location for the stack. That pointer should never even be used by the developer directly but only be used as the data object that is going to be manipulated by the operation functions.

The initialization function for the stack in this implementation is providing a robust implementation. First, it is checking the malloc return value, which will return zero if the memory could not be allocated. If everything goes as expected, the implementation will initialize the stack location member and set the return value.

```c
bool Stack_Push(StackPtr_t Stack, int Item)
{
    bool ErrorState = false;

    if(Stack->Position_Current == STACK_SIZE )
    {
            ErrorState = true;
    }
    else
    {
            Stack->Array[Stack->Position_Current] = Item;
            Stack->Position_Current++;
    }

    return ErrorState;
}
```

Figure 3-18. *Stack ADT push method*

The final step to creating the ADT is to put the ADT to the test. The ADT can be tested by writing some application code. The application code should declare an ADT and then manipulate the data through the interface specification. An example initialization and test for the stack ADT is shown in Figure 3-20. In the example, the stack.h header file is included in the application. The ADT from the user application's point of view is nothing more than a pointer. The Stack_Init function is called, which then performs the operation on the stack data to allocate memory and prepare it for use.

```c
bool Stack_Pop(StackPtr_t Stack, int * Item)
{
        bool ErrorState = false;

        if(Stack->Position_Current == 0 )
        {
                ErrorState = true;
        }
    else
    {
        Stack->Position_Current--;
        *Item = Stack->Array[Stack->Position_Current];
    }

        return ErrorState;

}
```

Figure 3-19. *Stack ADT pop method*

```c
static StackPtr_t Stack;
...
Stack_Init(Stack);
Stack_Push(Stack, 0x14);
```

Figure 3-20. *Using the stack ADT*

Finally, some data is pushed onto the stack by calling Stack_Push. Note that in the example application we are not checking the return values. This is something that a developer should do but that the author decided to not show at this point in time.

Creating an ADT is as simple as that! Using them in your software will hide the implementation details of a data structure, thus improving software maintenance, reuse, and portability. Developers who use ADTs will find that they are able to quickly adapt to changing requirements and save time by not having to dig through code searching for obscure data references.

Encapsulation and Data Hiding

Encapsulation and data hiding are an important concept that embedded-software developers should follow. Encapsulation is the idea that related data, functions, and operations should all be wrapped together into a single unit. For example, all the general-purpose input and output operations would be wrapped together in a single GPIO module. Any operations and data that involve the GPIO would be put into that module.

The idea can go even further by considering data hiding. Data hiding is where developers hide the data and the implementation from the module user. It's not important that the caller understand the implementation, only how to use the interface and what its inputs and outputs are.

Callback Functions

Callback functions are an essential and often critical concept that developers need in order to create drivers or custom libraries. A callback function is a reference to executable code that is passed as an argument to other code that allows a lower-level software layer to call a function defined in a higher-level layer.[9] A callback allows a driver or library developer to specify a behavior at a lower layer but leave the implementation definition to the application layer.

DEFINITIONS

Callback is a reference to executable code that is passed as an argument to other code that allows a lower-level software layer to call a function defined in a higher-level layer.

A callback function at its simplest is just a function pointer that is passed to another function as a parameter. In most instances, a callback will contain three pieces:

- The callback function
- A callback registration
- Callback execution

---

[9]https://en.wikipedia.org/wiki/Callback_(computer_programming)

Figure 3-21 shows how these three pieces work together in a typical callback implementation.

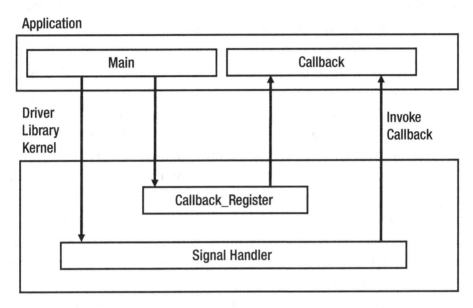

Figure 3-21. *Callback example usage*

First, a developer creates the library or module that will have an implementation element that is determined by the application developer. An example might be that a developer creates a GPIO driver that has an interrupt service routine whose code is specified by the application developer. The interrupt could handle a button press or some other functionality. The driver doesn't care about the functionality, only that at runtime it knows what function should be called when the interrupt fires. The code that will invoke the callback function within the module is often called the *signal handler*.

Next, there needs to be some way to tell the lower-level code what function should be executed. There are many ways that this can be done, but for a driver module, a recommended practice is to create a function within the module that is specifically designed to register a function as a callback. Having a separate function to register the callback function makes it very clear to the developer that the callback function is being registered to a specific signal handler. When the register function is called, the desired function that will be called is passed as a parameter into the module, and that function's address is stored.

Finally, the application developer writes their application, which includes creating the implementation for the callback and initialization code that registers that function with the library or module. When the application is executed, the low-level code has the callback function address stored, and when the feature needs to execute, it dereferences the callback function and executes it.

There are two primary examples that a developer can consider for using callbacks. First, in drivers, a developer will not know how any interrupt service routine might need to be used by the end application. If the developer is creating a library for some microcontroller's peripherals, a callback could be used to specify all the interrupts' behaviors. Using the callback would allow the developer to make sure that every interrupt had a default service routine in the event that the application developer did not register a custom callback function. When callbacks are used with interrupts, developers need to keep in mind that the best practices for interrupts need to be followed.

Second, callbacks can be used whenever there is common behavior in an application that might have implementation-specific behaviors. For example, initializing an array is a very common task that needs to be performed within an application. What if, for some applications, a developer wants to initialize array elements to all zeroes, while in another application they want the array elements initialized to random numbers? In this case, they could use a callback to initialize the arrays.

Examine Figure 3-22. The `ArrayInit` functiontakes a pointer to an array with element's size and then it also takes a pointer to a function that returns integers. The function at this point is not defined but can be defined by the application code. When `ArrayInit` is called, the developer passes in whatever function they choose to initialize the array elements. A few example functions that could be passed into `ArrayInit` can be seen in Figures 3-23 and 3-24.

```
void ArrayInit(int * Array, size_t size, int (*Function)(void))
{
  for(size_t i = 0; i < size; i++)
  {
    Array[i] = Function();
  }
}
```

Figure 3-22. *Function with callback*

```
int Zeros(void)
{
  return 0;
}
```

Figure 3-23. *Initialize elements to 0*

```
int Random(void)
{
  return rand();
}
```

Figure 3-24. *Initialize elements to random numbers*

The functions Zeros or Random are passed into ArrayInit depending on how the application developer wants to initialize the array.

Error Handling

One of the biggest problems with the C programming language is that there really is not a great way to do error handling or error trapping. Object-oriented languages have the ability to try a code block and if an error occurs to catch the error. C has no such capability. The best that C offers is the ability to check a function's return value.

The problem with checking a function's return value is that developers are really really bad at checking return values. It is not mandatory that return values are checked, so many developers will just ignore them. Ignoring return values is of course just bad discipline. In many circumstances, error handling in C is done by returning error codes or that the function completed successfully.

So, how can a developer handle errors in their drivers? The best approach that developers can take is to create a list of all the possible errors that can occur in the driver that they are creating. From that list, create an enumeration that contains all the error codes. Review the list and identify errors that the driver needs to actively manage. These errors might include transmit flag complete never sets, receive flag complete never sets, transmission is interrupted, and so forth. Do everything necessary to try to recover from an error state, and if the driver is unable to do so, don't hang there forever, but rather return an error code that can help developers debug the problem.

Leverage Design Patterns

Over time, as developers get more experience, they begin to realize that there are many design patterns in embedded software that appear frequently. A design pattern is a general reusable solution to a commonly occurring problem.[10] Using a design pattern that already exists and solves a common design problem can dramatically speed up software development and ensure a more robust solution. There are many design pattern examples that embedded software developers can utilize. A great example is the design pattern that is used to receive serial data on a UART.

The design pattern for receiving and processing serial data can be seen in Figure 3-25. An interrupt is used to receive a single character from the UART. The character is read into a buffer and then a signal is used to notify a task that there is a character that is ready to be processed. The design pattern is simple, but it does quite a few things for a developer, such as:

- Minimizes software overhead that would be associated with a polling architecture

- Minimizes processing in an ISR by only reading in the character

- Handles the hard real-time requirement (receiving a character) and signals another task to handle the soft real-time requirement (processing data)

- Provides deterministic behavior to the system

---

[10]https://en.wikipedia.org/wiki/Software_design_pattern

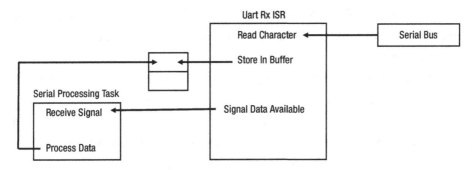

Figure 3-25. *UART Receive design pattern*

Design patterns are the puzzle pieces that can be used to quickly build an embedded system. The more that an application can leverage design patterns, the faster the software can be developed. Many drivers will adhere to very common design patterns that we've already discussed in this chapter, such as blocking and non-blocking architectures. Later in the book, as we dive into specific examples for developing different peripheral drivers, these design patterns will become clearer.

Expected Results and Recommendations

So far in this chapter, we have explored quite a few concepts that will help developers think through how they should organize and begin implementing their device drivers. There are many benefits to the techniques that we have discussed, which include a more organized, maintainable code base. There are several results related to the software that developers need to be aware of.

First, organizing the code base into components creates a very organized project. Components are easy to move from one project to the next and easy to find in the project structure. One potential drawback to organizing a project in this manner is that the more modules that are added to a project, the more files in the project, which then leads to more folder structures. The result can be:

- Slower compile times due to opening and closing so many files

- Complex include list since each component will need to be added to the compiler and linker include path

In general, these are minor issues, and developers should not let them get in their way when developing organized drivers. It's just important to recognize that it isn't all red roses and green grass.

Second, assertions are great for verifying that an assumption for inputs, pre-conditions, post-conditions, and so forth are correct, but they aren't exactly free. Every expression that is evaluated in the assertion uses up some processing time to be evaluated. While this may only be a few dozen instructions and execute very quickly, it can influence the real-time system performance. Even worse than the performance, the assertion takes up a little bit of code space on the microcontroller. Over time, a project can easily contain an assertion density approaching 3 to 5 percent, which may make the code look significantly bloated. These are reasons why assertions are often disabled before testing and production release.

Third, developers need to make sure that they are careful when they use callbacks. In many cases, callbacks register a function to an interrupt service routine. Since callbacks execute in an interrupt, they need to be short, fast, and to the point. Developers need to make sure that they follow best practices for using callbacks, which were discussed in the callback section.

Finally, developers need to be careful how far they carry the "object-oriented C" concept. It's a great idea to encapsulate data, use a few abstract data types, and so forth, but eventually a point will be reached where it may just make sense to upgrade to C++. I've had the pleasure of teaching a session once on how to create a class using the C language (not by choice). If you need full object-oriented behavior, just use an object-oriented language.

Going Further

There are several activities that readers can perform in order to consolidate the driver concepts that we have just discussed. Drivers are an important foundation in embedded systems, and it is critical to have a clear understanding of these basic concepts. Some additional activities that are recommended include:

- Find the memory map for your favorite processor. What memory regions do the following occupy?

    - Flash

    - RAM

- GPIO

- SPI

- Are there any memory-map holes that you can find? Are there any memory regions where the memory can be expanded?

- Make a list of all the inputs, outputs, pre-conditions, and post-conditions that would be associated with a GPIO driver.

- In your favorite IDE, review how to enable assertions. Create an example application with `printf` and `assert`. Create a simple function and explore the following:

    - How to use `printf` and `assert`

    - The timing to use `printf`

    - The overhead associated with `assert`

    - Practice enabling and disabling assertions. Can you measure the effect this has on your code?

- Define your own coding conventions.

    - How are you going to organize your software components?

    - What naming conventions are you going to use?

    - Identify any other conventions that you will use when developing software going forward.

- Test your skills by creating an abstract data type. Follow the stack example and implement the stack ADT. Developers interested in the Stack example source can download it here.[11]

- Create a simple callback function application that initializes an array. Create a callback to initialize an array to all zeroes and another to initialize the array to random numbers.

---

[11]http://www.beningo.com/wp-content/uploads/Downloads/ATP.zip

CHAPTER 4

Writing Reusable Drivers

"Software is like entropy. It is difficult to grasp, weighs nothing, and obeys the second law of thermodynamics; i.e., it always increases."

—Norman Ralph

Reusable Drivers

Writing a driver that can be used from one application to the next can be very helpful to embedded-software developers. Once a driver is written, developers can focus on the application code and not worry about the bits and the bytes. Driver design patterns can be reused not only on the same hardware, but also across multiple platforms with only minor changes required to adjust the driver to access the different memory regions.

In this chapter, we will examine the different methodologies that developers can use to map into peripheral memory, and then we will demonstrate how each technique can be used.

Deciphering the extern and static Keywords

The default linkage for a variable and function in the C programming language is `extern`. Having an `extern` default linkage means that *all* functions and any variables defined at the file scope are global variables and functions. In general, having global variables and making all functions available within a program is not a good programming practice. If everything in an application can be potentially touched and manipulated by any other part of the application, there is an increased probability that multiple points in the application may use a global variable without protecting its access, and this can result in

© Jacob Beningo 2017
J. Beningo, *Reusable Firmware Development*, https://doi.org/10.1007/978-1-4842-3297-2_4

a bug. These bugs are usually difficult to find and reproduce, which makes them time-consuming to fix.

One programming language best practice is to limit the scope of all variables and functions. Keep data and functions need-to-know. Keeping the scope limited will prevent another application component, or a developer, from accidentally misusing or trampling over data that they are not supposed to be using.

Junior-level embedded-software developers will often be aware that using global variables is a frowned-upon practice and will avoid using the extern keyword. The problem is that by default the extern keyword is implicitly placed before functions and variables at a file-scope level. This means that if you don't specify the linkage type, the C language toolchain will make *everything* global!

For example, look at the simple module shown in Figure 4-1. The module looks completely valid. The module would compile without errors or any warnings. However, to the compiler and linker, the application shown in Figure 4-1 looks like the program shown in Figure 4-2.

```c
#include <stdint.h>

int8_t myVariable = 0;

void myFunction(uint8_t myData);

void myFunction(uint8_t myData)
{
  myVariable = myData;
}
```

Figure 4-1. extern implicitly

```
#include <stdint.h>

extern int8_t myVariable = 0;

extern void myFunction(uint8_t myData);

extern void myFunction(uint8_t myData)
{
  myVariable = myData;
}
```

Figure 4-2. *extern explicitly*

In C, the best way to control the default external linkage in a component is to employ the static keyword. This is a storage-class specifier that tells the compiler to limit the variable's or function's scope while at the same time telling it to allocate storage for the variable that will persist throughout the application's lifetime.[1] Static overrides those implicit extern keywords that are automatically put in front of functions and variables and instead makes those variables and functions internally linked. The result: variables and functions that are only available within a single module. Figure 4-3 shows how static would work in the program that previously had external linkage.

```
#include <stdint.h>

static int8_t myVariable = 0;

static void myFunction(uint8_t myData);

static void myFunction(uint8_t myData)
{
  myVariable = myData;
}
```

Figure 4-3. *Explicitly limiting function and variable scope*

---

[1]*C in a Nutshell*, pages 156, 165

Deciphering the volatile Keyword

There are times in an embedded-software application where the application will be dependent upon changes in the physical hardware. The software will need to read a hardware flag, such as a UART transmission-complete flag. A simple example of what this code might look like can be seen in Figure 4-4. The code first defines a pointer to the location in memory where the UART_REGISTER is. The code then waits in a while loop for the UART_TX_FLAG in the UART_REGISTER to be set.

```
#define UART_TX_FLAG      0x8

uint8_t * UART_REGISTER = 0x100000;

while((UART_REGISTER & UART_TX_FLAG) != UART_TX_FLAG);
```

Figure 4-4. *Checking for the UART Tx Complete flag*

The problem with the code in Figure 4-4 is that the compiler will look at the code and realize that in the while loop, UART_REGISTER & UART_TX_FLAG is a constant expression. Nowhere in the software does that value ever change! So, the compiler will do what it is designed to do and optimize the code to something like Figure 4-5.

```
#define UART_TX_FLAG      0x8

uint8_t * UART_REGISTER = 0x100000;
while(1);
```

Figure 4-5. *The optimized UART Tx Check code*

The resulting application that is shown in Figure 4-5 is obviously not what the developer had intended, but it does teach an important lesson. When accessing hardware, developers need to reach into the C programming toolbox and pull out the volatile keyword. This instructs the compiler to reread the object's value each time it is used, even if the program itself has not changed it since the previous access.[2] A developer

---

[2] *C in a Nutshell*, pages 53, 127

can prevent the optimized code generation shown in Figure 4-5 by declaring the value being pointed to by UART_REGISTER as volatile. By doing this, the compiler will recognize that the expression in the while loop could change at any moment and the value should be reread to see if it has changed. The updated application can be found in Figure 4-6.

```
#define UART_TX_FLAG       0x8

uint8_t volatile * UART_REGISTER = 0x100000;

while((UART_REGISTER & UART_TX_FLAG) != UART_TX_FLAG);
```

Figure 4-6. *Using the volatile keyword to prevent code optimization*

Note where the volatile keyword is located in the updated code. The C statement is declaring UART_REGISTER as a pointer to a volatile uint8_t. The data is volatile, *not* the pointer. The code shown in Figure 4-7 is an example of the wrong place to put the volatile keyword. The example is showing a volatile pointer to a uint8_t. In general, having a pointer to a hardware register change is not something that we would want to have happen in an embedded system.

```
#define UART_TX_FLAG       0x8

uint8_t * volatile UART_REGISTER = 0x100000;

while((UART_REGISTER & UART_TX_FLAG) != UART_TX_FLAG);
```

Figure 4-7. *Improper volatile keyword location*

Deciphering the const Keyword

The const keyword can sometimes be deceptive in the C programming language. A developer may think that a const is a variable that is constant and cannot be modified by the application. The const keyword tells the developer that the data location that is being accessed through the identifier with the const keyword is read-only.[3] If the

---

[3]*C in a Nutshell*, page 57

variable that is being defined as const exists in RAM, a developer could conceivably create a pointer to the constant variable, typecast off the const, and then change the value. In many cases, variables declared const in an embedded system will not be stored in RAM but instead will be in flash. This prevents the constant data from being modified and really does make const data constant.

A best practice for developing embedded software is to use the const keyword as often as possible.[4] The const keyword does provide a developer some protection through the compiler if an attempt is made to change the value of an identifier. The primary places that developers should look to use the const keyword are:

- When passing data to a function that should not be modifying the data

- Pointers to hardware registers that should not change during runtime

In general, true constants such as Pi or unchanging configuration values are defined not through identifiers but through enumerations or the #define macro, with enumerations being the preferred method.

In the previous section, while looking at the volatile keyword, we saw a pointer being defined that accessed a hardware register. A variable that is being used to access hardware probably should not change during runtime. That code could be modified so that the pointer is defined as const and thus will always point to the correct place in the hardware memory map to access the UART_REGISTER. The updated code example can be seen in Figure 4-8. In the example, UART_REGISTER is a constant pointer to data located at 0x100000, which can change at any time (volatile) and is a uint8_t data type.

```
#define UART_TX_FLAG      0x8

uint8_t volatile * const UART_REGISTER = 0x100000;

while((UART_REGISTER & UART_TX_FLAG) != UART_TX_FLAG);
```

Figure 4-8. *A const pointer to a volatile uint8_t*

---

[4]Barr Group Best Practices (Embedded C Coding Standard, page 23)

Memory-Mapping Methodologies

There are several options available to developers to map their code into the microcontroller's memory regions. The technique used is going to be dependent upon an engineer's need to control:

- Code size

- Execution speed

- Efficiency

- Portability

- Configurability

The simplest techniques tend to not be reusable or portable, while the more complex techniques are. There are several memory-mapping techniques that are commonly used in driver design. These methods include the following:

- Direct memory mapping

- Using pointers

- Using structures

- Using pointer arrays

Let's examine the different methods that can be used to map a driver to memory.

Mapping Memory Directly

Once a developer has thought through the different driver models that can be used to control the microcontroller peripherals, it is time to start writing code. There are multiple techniques that a developer could use to map their driver into the peripherals' memory space, such as directly writing registers or using pointers, structures, or pointer arrays.

The simplest technique to use—and the least reusable—is to write directly to a peripheral's register. For example, let's say that a developer wants to configure GPIO Port C. In order to set up and read the port, a developer can examine the register definition file, find the correct identifier, and then write code similar to that seen in Figure 4-9.

```
PORT_C_DIRECTION = 0x14;
PORT_C_OUTPUT = 0x51;
```

Figure 4-9. *Direct register access*

Writing code in this manner is very manual and labor intensive. The code is written for a single and very specific setup. The code can be ported, but there are opportunities for the wrong values to be written, which can lead to a bug and then time spent debugging. Very simple applications that won't be reused often use this direct register write method for setting up and controlling peripherals. Directly writing to registers in this manner is also fast and efficient, and it doesn't require a lot of flash space.

Mapping Memory with Pointers

While directly writing to registers can be useful, the technique is often employed for software that will not be reused or that is written on a very resource-constrained embedded system, such as a simple 8-bit microcontroller. A technique that is commonly used when reuse is necessary is to use pointers to map into memory. An example declaration to map into the GPIO Port C register—let's say it's the data register—can be seen in Figure 4-10.

```
/* GPIO Port C is located at 0x100000 */
uint32_t * Gpio_PortC = (uint32_t *) 0x100000UL;
```

Figure 4-10. *Mapping a pointer to GPIO Port C*

Now, the code in Figure 4-10 has a problem! There is a real possibility that if we try to write code to read the port or a bit on the port the compiler will optimize out the read! The compiler will see a while loop that is checking a bit state in the register, as shown in Figure 4-11, and decide that since there is no place in the while loop that changes the values stored in the location pointed to by Gpio_PortC, there is no reason to keep reading the value, and that reading the memory location can be optimized out.

```
while((*Gpio_PortC & BIT0) == 0)
{
  /* Execute the loop code */
}
```

Figure 4-11. *Checking a register bit*

In order to resolve this issue, developers need to use the volatile keyword. Volatile essentially tells the compiler that the data being read can change out of sequence at any time without any code changing the value. There are three places that volatile is typically used:

- Variables that are being mapped to hardware registers

- Data being shared between interrupt service routines and application code

- Data being shared between multiple threads

Volatile basically tells the compiler to not optimize out the read but instead make sure that the data stored in the memory location is read every time the variable is encountered.

The location that volatile appears in the declaration is critical to properly mapping a peripheral register. Declaring a pointer to a register using the following statement tells the compiler that the *pointer* is volatile, *not* the data being pointed to. The code in Figure 4-12 is saying the pointer could change at any time when in fact it's the *data* in the register being pointed to that can change.

```
uint32_t * volatile Gpio_PortC = (uint32_t *) 0x100000UL;
```

Figure 4-12. *Incorrectly using the volatile keyword for pointer data*

The correct declaration would place the volatile keyword immediately following the data pointer and *not* immediately after the pointer, as shown in Figure 4-13.

```
uint32_t volatile * Gpio_PortC = (uint32_t *) 0x100000UL;
```

Figure 4-13. *Correctly using the volatile keyword for pointer data*

This code tells the compiler that Gpio_PortC is a pointer to a volatile uint32_t. Remember, when reading a declaration like this, start reading just to the left of the identifier and read from right to left. This will help provide clarity to the actual declaration. (I highly recommend reading the section "Complex Declarators" from the book *Expert C Programmers,*[5] which provides general advice for figuring out what a declaration means).

With the volatile keyword in the correct place, we now know the compiler won't optimize out reading the variable. However, there still is a problem with the declaration the way it has been written. Take a moment to examine the code shown in Figure 4-14.

```
/* Set the 0 bit high on PortC */
*Gpio_PortC |= 0x1;
Gpio_PortC++;
```

Figure 4-14. *Accessing memory to a non-constant pointer*

It is perfectly legal to increment our pointer Gpio_PortC. After incrementing the pointer, we could be pointed at Port D, a different register in Port C, or even an SPI or IIC peripheral. Once a pointer is mapped into memory, a developer should not be allowed to increment, decrement, or modify the location for the pointer. This is extremely dangerous! So instead, in our declaration, we should declare our pointer to be constant, as shown in Figure 4-15.

```
uint32_t volatile * const  Gpio_PortC = (uint32_t *) 0x100000UL;
```

Figure 4-15. *Constant memory-pointer declaration*

---

[5]*Expert C Programming: Deep C Secrets*, Peter Linden (Prentice Hall, 1994)

Adding the const keyword now makes it so that Port C is a constant pointer to a volatile uint32_t, and any attempts to increment or decrement the pointer in the source code will result in a compiler error. Using const in this way is critical to writing robust code, and yet if you peruse example code or the register definitions provided by microcontroller suppliers, you will find that the majority ignore this fact and allow their memory-mapped pointers to be modified within the source.

Mapping Memory with Structures

The next technique, and probably the most common technique provided by microcontroller vendors, is to use structures to map into memory. Structures provide developers with a way to create data members that directly map to a memory location. The C standard guarantees that if I create data members in a structure, they will appear in the same order without padding. The result is the ability to create structure pointers that directly map into a peripheral's memory space, as shown in Figure 4-16.

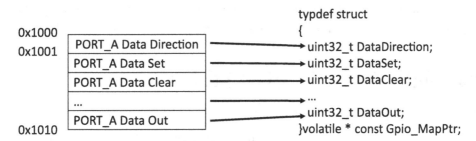

Figure 4-16. *Mapping a structure into 32-bit memory*

The structure needs to have each member match the order in order for the peripheral registers to map properly. Also notice in the declaration that the structure is abstracting the details for creating a pointer to the structure. With the structure declared in this manner, a developer could access the peripheral by using the code in Figure 4-17.

```
#define PORTC_BASE_PTR      ((GPIO_MemMapPtr)0x300000UL)

PORTC_BASE_PTR->PDIR |= (1UL << 23);
```

Figure 4-17. *Declaring a peripheral base pointer based on structure*

I'm not really a big fan of using macros in this way, although when searching through microcontroller-supplied code you will find that it is quite rampant. An alternative would be declaring PORTC_BASE_PTR as a standard identifier using the code shown in Figure 4-18.

```
GPIO_MemMapPtr PORTC_BASE_PTR =
                            ((GPIO_MemMapPtr)0x300000UL);

PORTC_BASE_PTR->PDIR |= (1UL << 23);
```

Figure 4-18. *Defining and using the memory-mapped structure*

Using structures to map memory can be efficient and provide developers with a way to start creating reusable mapped drivers. Using standards such as ARM® Cortex® Software Interface Standard (CMSIS) can provide a common and reusable method for accessing peripheral registers that improves portability. Unfortunately, as of this writing, many vendors will still use their own naming conventions, which still requires a fair amount of work to adapt to different microcontrollers.

Using Pointer Arrays in Driver Design

A unique method for mapping memory is to use a pointer array. A pointer array is an array where each array element is a pointer. For an engineer developing a driver, every element in the pointer array will point to a peripheral register for a single register type. For example, a developer would create a pointer array to set the data output on the GPIO ports by including a pointer to the data registers PORTA, PORTB, PORTC, and so forth. A second pointer array would be created to hold all the GPIO direction registers for the ports. A pointer array would be created for each register type on the peripheral, with each entry representing a channel.

There are many benefits to using pointer arrays to map memory in an embedded system. First, it allows a developer to group registers into logical channels. Second, initialization functions can be written such that they loop through each index in the array, which greatly simplifies the initialization function. Not only is the initialization simplified, but using pointer arrays also creates a design pattern that can be easily reused and ported from one application to the next and one platform to the next.

Pointer arrays also help to abstract out the hardware and convert registers into something more readable and understandable by human programmers. Developers can create easy-to-understand function names that access the pointer arrays and handle the details behind the scenes. Initialization structures can even be created that allow a table to be passed into a driver to initialize the peripheral, once again creating a common, standard framework that can be reused and easily ported.

Despite the powerful capabilities and portability that pointer arrays bring to the programming table, there are a few drawbacks that developers need to be aware of. First, creating pointer arrays will increase the program size when compared with structure or direct-access memory-mapping methods. The reason for the program increase is that there are now additional arrays that are storing pointers, and above that there is a configuration table that will be stored in flash that contains the initialization information for every peripheral and channel. The program size increase isn't terribly significant, but if a developer is limited to a microcontroller with a few thousand kilobytes of flash space then it will quickly fill with initialization data.

Second, since the peripherals are being accessed through a pointer array, there can be a performance hit a few clock cycles long when accessing low-level drivers. If a developer is using an old 8-bit microcontroller running at 8 MHz, there could be a big problem. Using a modern-day processor such as a 32-bit ARM Cortex-M, the performance difference is not noticeable in most applications. That said, a developer still needs to make sure that they monitor their system's performance.

When comparing the cost and development times to using structures or direct memory-mapping methods, pointer arrays provide developers with a flexible, reusable design pattern that is easily scalable and adaptable. Let's examine how we could map memory to a timer peripheral using the pointer array mapping technique.

Creating a Timer Driver Overview

Nearly every embedded system uses an onboard timer to keep time. A timer will often be running at one or ten milliseconds and coordinating with a scheduler to run the system. Every microcontroller will have slightly different capabilities as it pertains to the timer peripheral, but there are some commonalities among all microcontrollers. In order to determine the timer capabilities and build the infrastructure necessary to create a timer driver that can be reused and follows the pointer array memory-mapping methodology, there are several steps a developer needs to follow:

- Step #1 – Define the configuration table

- Step #2 – Define the peripheral channels

- Step #3 – Populate the configuration table

- Step #4 – Create the pointer arrays

- Step #5 – Create the initialization function

- Step #6 – Populate the driver interface

- Step #7 – Maintain and port the design pattern

These concepts can easily be applied to any peripheral driver.

Step #1: Define the Timer's Configuration Table

Before diving deep into the pointer arrays and creating the timer driver itself, it is useful to start by considering the configuration parameters that are needed to set up the timer peripheral. The reason for this is that developers need to dig through the datasheet to determine which registers exist for the timer and what the bits mean in those registers. While developers are digging through those registers, it is the perfect time to create the configuration table structure that will be used to initialize the peripheral.

For a timer module, one would expect to find registers related to the following:

- setting the mode

- enabling

- setting the clock source

- the clock pre-scaler

- and so on

The necessary information will be found by looking at each register in the timer datasheet and listing them out in a structure. After the configuration list has been created, a channel name member can be added that will be used to assign a human-readable value. Developers will also want to add a timer-interval value. The timer interval will tell the initialization function what the timer tick rate will be in microseconds. The initialization function can be written to take the configuration parameters for the clock and automatically calculate the register values necessary for the timer to behave properly so that the developer is saved the painful effort of calculating the register values.

A good practice is to place the structure definition within a header file, such as `timer_config.h`. An example timer configuration structure can be found in Figure 4-19. Keep in mind that once this structure is created the first time, it will only require minor modification to be used with another microcontroller.

```
typedef struct
{
    uint32_t TimerChannel; /**< Name of timer */
    uint32_t TimerEnable;  /**< Timer Enable State */
    uint32_t TimerMode;    /**< Counter Mode Settings */
    uint32_t ClockSource;  /**< Defines the clock source */
    uint32_t ClockMode;    /**< Clock Mode */
    uint32_t ISREnable;    /**< ISR Enable State */
    uint32_t Interval;     /**< Interval in microseconds */
}TimerConfig_t;
```

Figure 4-19. *Example timer configuration structure*

Step #2: Define the Timer's Peripheral Channels

A peripheral channel is an independent hardware module for the peripheral, such as Timer0, Timer1, and Timer2. Each timer is separate within the microcontroller but usually has the same or similar capabilities as the others. A developer can consider every register and configuration value associated with the Timer0 module to be the Timer0 channel. There are a few reasons for why a developer wants to create a channel definition within the software code base.

First, creating a channel definition allows a developer to create a human-readable value that, when included with the configuration table, makes figuring out what the configuration is associated with simpler. On a small microcontroller, this may not seem like a big deal if there are only two timers, but in a modern, high-end microcontroller there could be a dozen timers and looking at a complex configuration table can result in confusion. Confusion results in bugs, and we want to minimize bugs as much as possible.

Second, the channel definition will be used by the drivers to access the correct element in the pointer array. It is therefore critical to make sure that the channel naming order matches the pointer array order. The channels are used in the driver interface and, once again, make the code more human readable, as the timer is used throughout the application.

The channel definition is nothing more than a simple enum. It lists all the available peripheral channels that are available. For example, a microcontroller with three timers would list out TIMER0, TIMER1, and TIMER2, as shown in Figure 4-20. In addition to listing the channels, it is a good practice to create a final enum element named MAX_TIMER or NUMBER_OF_TIMERS that can then be used as a boundary-condition checker.

```
typedef enum
{
    TIMER0,          /**< Timer 0 */
    TIMER1,          /**< Timer 1 */
    TIMER2,          /**< Timer 2 */
    MAX_TIMERS       /**< Timers on the microcontroller */
}TimerRegister_t;
```

Figure 4-20. *Timer channel definition*

Step #3: Populate the Timer's Configuration Table

Once the pieces are in place to define the configuration table, developers can dive in and create it. The configuration table should be located in the timer_config.c module. The configuration table is going to be nothing more than an array where every element is of type TimerConfig_t. Since a developer probably doesn't want the initialization to be changeable during operation, the configuration table should also be declared const. The configuration table can also be declared static so that it has internal linkage. A helper function can then be created that returns a pointer to the table. The pointer to the table is what is then used in the application, and the configuration table itself stays hidden.

An example of the timer configuration table can be seen in Figure 4-21.

```
static const TmrConfig_t TmrConfig[] =
{
//   Timer      Timer       Timer       Clock           Clock Mode    Clock        Interrupt    Interrupt    Timer
//   Name       Enable      Mode        Source          Selection     Prescaler    Enable       Priority     Interval (us)
//
     {TMR0,     ENABLED,    UP_COUNT,   FLL_PLL,         MODULE_CLK,   TMR_DIV_1,   DISABLED,    3,           100     },
     {TMR1,     DISABLED,   UP_COUNT,   NOT_APPLICABLE,  STOP,         TMR_DIV_1,   DISABLED,    0,           0       },
     {TMR2,     ENABLED,    UP_COUNT,   FLL_PLL,         MODULE_CLK,   TMR_DIV_1,   DISABLED,    3,           100     },
};
```

Figure 4-21. *Example timer configuration table*

Since the configuration has internal linkage, a developer will need to create a helper function that returns a pointer to the configuration table. A simple helper function can be seen in Figure 4-22.

```
const TmrConfig_t * Tmr_ConfigGet(void)
{
    Tmr_Config;
}TimerRegister_t;
```

Figure 4-22. *Configuration table helper function*

Step #4: Create the Timer's Pointer Arrays

Creating the pointer arrays that map into the peripheral memory space is straightforward but can sometimes be confusing. The pointer arrays are going to be located within the driver module for the peripheral. For a timer, these would be the timer.h and timer.c modules. These modules would contain all the timer driver functions along with the timer driver interface.

An array will be created for every common register that exists among the timer peripherals. Each array will have a general form, which can be seen in Figure 4-23, and will be followed for nearly every memory mapping. The REG_SIZE can simply be replaced with the fixed-width integer definition for the target processor. For example, if the target is an 8-bit microcontroller, REG_SIZE would be replaced with, or defined as, uint8_t. A 32-bit processor would have REG_SIZE defined as a uint32_t.

```
static REG_SIZE volatile * const ARRAY_NAME[CHANNELS]
```

Figure 4-23. *Generic pointer array mapping pattern*

The ARRAY_NAME is simply replaced with a description for what the register type is that the array is mapping to. CHANNELS can be omitted in the array definition, but if a developer is trying to be as explicit as possible, which is always a great idea, then specifying the number of elements in the array would be necessary.

It is important to also note that the placement of const and volatile is critical. Placing them in a different location will completely change what is constant and whether the data or the pointer will be reread at each program encounter. Const is telling the compiler that the pointer in the array cannot be changed to point to anything else, keeping our pointers from changing. On most compilers, this will also force the array to be stored in flash. Volatile is telling the compiler that the data in the register may change unexpectedly, so reread the data. A developer may want to go even further by limiting the pointer-array linkage to internal by declaring the array static, which is a very good programming practice.

Using the generic definition shown in Figure 4-23, a developer will then need to use the definition pattern to create and populate an array with a pointer to the register for each peripheral channel. The register definitions are usually already created by the microcontroller manufacturer and are sometimes already in a pointer form. In most cases, just the addresses for the registers are defined, and the developer must typecast the address into a pointer when initializing the array. An example for the timer peripheral that shows a few pointer-array definitions can be seen in Figure 4-24.

```
uint32_t volatile * const tmrreg[NUM_TIMERS] =
{
  (uint32_t*)&TPM_SC, (uint32_t*)&TPM1_CNT
};
```

Figure 4-24. Example timer peripheral pointer-array initialization

Step #5: Create the Initialization Function

All the previous steps have been setting up the scaffolding that is required to map into the peripheral memory space and configure the driver. Now, it is time to write the function that will initialize the peripheral. The greatest advantage to using pointer arrays is that creating an initialization function is simple and reusable! The pointer arrays allow a developer to create a design pattern that can be reused from one application to the next with only minor modifications required to support new microcontrollers. Updating the design pattern for a new microcontroller takes just a fraction of the time that it would take to start from scratch.

The first step to creating the initialization function is to create a function stub for `Timer_Init` that takes a pointer to `TimerConfig_t`. Don't forget that `TimerConfig_t` is a structure that contains all the initialization information for the different timer channels. Developers should declare the pointer as `const` so that the initialization code can't accidentally manipulate the pointer. The configuration code is probably stored in flash anyway, so it can't easily be changed without active assistance from the flash controller, but it's a safe programming practice to declare the pointer `const` anyway.

Before a single line of code is written, it is wise to take a few minutes to develop an architectural diagram and a flowchart depicting how the initialization function is going to behave. A simple activity diagram for initializing the timers through the configuration table and pointer arrays can be found in Figure 4-25. Literally all that is done is that the code loops through the configuration table, one entry at a time, and reads the configuration setting for the peripheral. The setting is then mapped into the correct register and bits before moving on to the next parameter.

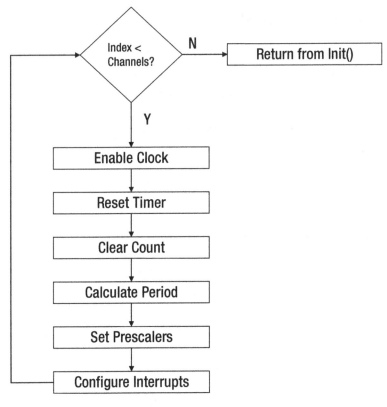

Figure 4-25. *Timer initialization flowchart*

The result is a simple initialization that just loops through the configuration table and then writes to the pointer array. A shortened initialization function example can be seen in Figure 4-26. Notice that every pointer-array access requires us to dereference the pointer in the array element. Don't forget that the full source is available with the book materials.

The initialization can be written to simplify the application developers' software as much as possible. For example, a timer module could have the desired baud rate passed into the initialization, and the driver could calculate the necessary register values based on the input configuration clock settings. The configuration table then becomes a very high-level register abstraction that allows a developer not familiar with the hardware to easily make changes to the timer without having to pull out the datasheet.

```
void Tmr_Init(const TmrConfig_t *Config)
{
    for(i=0; i < NUM_TIMERS; i++)
    {
        // Loop through the configuration table and set each
        // register
        if(Config[i].TimerEnable == ENABLED)
        {
            // Fill in the timer initialization code
        }
    }
}
```

***Figure 4-26.** Driver high-level loop initialization example*

```
// Enable the clock gate
*tmrgate[i] |= tmrpins[i];

// Reset the timer register
*tmrreg[i] = 0;

// Clear the timer counter register
*tmrcnt[i] = 0;

// Calculate and set period register for this timer
// Timer period = ((System Clock Frequency in Hz / Timer
// Divider)
// (1,000,000 / Desired Timer Interval in microseconds)) - 1
*modreg[i] = ((GetSystemClock() / Config[i].ClkPrescaler) /
(TMR_PERIOD_DIV / Config[i].Interval)) - 1;

// If the timer interrupt is set to ENABLED in the timer
// configuration table, set the interrupt enable bit, enable Irq,
// and set interrupt priority. Else, clear the enable bit.
if(Config[i].IntEnabled == ENABLED)
{
    *tmrreg[i] |= REGBIT6;
    Enable_Irq(TmrIrqValue[i]);
    Set_Irq_Priority(TmrIrqValue[i], Config[i].IntPriority);
}
```

Figure 4-27. *Timer init loop code*

Step #6: Fill in the Timer Driver Interface

After completing and testing the initialization function, the driver will require additional interfaces to control the timer. A developer may want to add interfaces to enable and disable the timer, change the counter interval, and so on. Prior to ever getting to the implementation phase, these interface features should have been identified, and with a timer initialized they can now be filled in and tested.

The details for how to design the interface will be covered in greater detail later in the book. For now, consider the following as example timer-driver functions:

- `Timer_Init`

- `Timer_Control (Enable/Disable)`

- `Timer_IntervalSet`

- `Timer_ModeSet`

Step #7: Maintain and Port the Design Pattern

Once the timer driver has been fully implemented, it is possible to use it as a design pattern. Nearly every microcontroller will have peripherals on board that have similar behaviors and functions. For example, every time module needs to have an enable, a clock source, pre-scaler, counter, and so on. The peripherals may exist in a completely different memory region and have different names, but that is why the pointer arrays come in so handy. Simply update the pointer arrays with the correct register pointers and modify the bits that are manipulated, and the driver is now ported to a new microcontroller.

Implementing a driver using pointer arrays can decrease the time required to implement and test future drivers. There is a simple procedure that a developer can follow to update the design pattern for any microcontroller.

- Step #1 – Update the configuration table definitions.

- Step #2 – Update the configuration table declarations.

- Step #3 – Update the pointer arrays.

- Step #4 – Update the initialization and driver functions.

- Step #5 – Perform regression testing.

Selecting the Right Driver Implementation

So far in this chapter, we've examined a few different methods that can be used to map a driver into the peripheral memory space. These have ranged from direct register access to the more complex pointer array mapping methods. Selecting the right method for the job can be difficult, especially if a team wants reuse but has a very resource-constrained system.

In order to make an informed decision, developers need to consider a few different factors, including:

- Code size

- Execution speed

- Efficiency

- Portability

- Configurability

Table 4-1 compares the different memory-mapping methods and where they are best deployed. Keep in mind that the table is doing a direct comparison, and while one method may be mentioned as being least efficient, a developer should take into consideration what that really means. It could be that there are a few extra instructions generated to access the register by indexing an array and dereferencing a pointer. In most applications, the additional instructions won't really affect the application performance, but performing a few experiments can be useful to wrap your mind around the best and worst cases.

***Table 4-1.** Memory Map Comparison*

Mapping Technique	Code Size	Execution Speed	Efficiency	Portability	Configurability
Direct Register Access	Smallest	Fastest	Most Efficient	Least	Least
Pointer Structure	Average	Average	Average	Average	Average
Pointer Arrays	Largest	Slowest	Least Efficient	Most	Most

In general, the direct register access technique is best used for very resource-constrained systems with less than 16 kB of code space. These systems typically are 8-bit and have clock speeds less than 48 MHz. Pointer-structure mapping is a good general technique that is often used by default by microcontroller manufacturers. Pointer arrays really require microcontrollers with at least 32 kB of code space. The main reason is that the configuration tables and the pointer arrays can take up code space, which is not available in resource-constrained devices.

Going Further

Let's examine what you can do to take the concepts we've discussed in this chapter and start to apply them to your embedded software.

- Select a code module in one of your applications. Identify all the areas where variables and functions are implicitly declared `extern`. Which ones can be changed to `static`?

- Examine the hardware register mapping file for your microcontroller. What keywords are present? `const`? `volatile`?

- Examine the hardware register mapping file for your microcontroller. What memory mapping method is it using?

- Examine the datasheet and hardware register files for your microcontroller. Write three different timer drivers using each of the following methods:

  - Directly accessing registers

  - Using structures

  - Using pointer arrays

  Answer the following questions about the drivers:

  - Which driver was the fastest to implement?

  - Which has the smallest code size? The largest?

  - Which is more human readable?

- Port each driver to a different microcontroller using the drivers just written as the starting point. Answer the following questions about the drivers:

  - Which driver was the fastest to implement?

  - Which has the smallest code size? The largest?

  - Which is more human readable?

  - Which driver was the easiest and quickest to port?

CHAPTER 5

Documenting Firmware with Doxygen

"Just because you don't like something doesn't mean that it isn't helping you."

—Tim Harford

The Importance of Good Documentation

Writing and maintaining documentation is highly important, yet it is often a neglected element of embedded-software development. Engineers typically start a project strong, keeping documentation synchronized with written code. As the project progresses, schedule and cost pressures intensify due to antsy clients and perhaps even the boss breathing down the developers' necks. The result is that the developers bury their heads in the code and just crank it out as fast as possible. Developers start to take shortcuts to save time, such as skipping documentation, telling themselves that once the software is written they'll go back and update the documentation. In reality, the code either goes undocumented or is sprinkled here and there with half-thoughts and gibberish in a rushed attempt to provide illumination into what has become chaotic.

Documentation is a tedious and unrewarding part of the embedded-software engineer's job. No one wants to do it, yet if it isn't written, maintaining and updating the code can become a nightmare for fellow developers or even for forgetful versions of our future selves. There are many benefits to having well-documented embedded software, such as:

- Having a reference to look up API and HAL calls (a software manual)

- Having a document that communicates implementation details and intent

© Jacob Beningo 2017
J. Beningo, *Reusable Firmware Development*, https://doi.org/10.1007/978-1-4842-3297-2_5

- Decreased time to train engineers (just review the documentation!)

- A clear and concise description of the standards used to develop the software, such as coding or industry standards (improved readability)

- Improved maintenance and overall costs resulting from having access to a reference rather than having to "wing it" and decode large amounts of code

- Faster speed to make updates and changes to the software

Well-documented embedded software will decrease the time and costs required to develop and maintain it, and it can even have the added benefit of decreasing the overall stress of a project.

CASE STUDY—A PROJECT WITH NO DOCUMENTATION

Documentation can mean the difference between getting to market quickly or never getting to market at all. I had a client who was working on a medical device that was inherited from another engineering company. I was called in to review the code that was available and try to make heads or tails of what features were completed and where the code stood.

The code existed as a single `main.c` file of over 100,000 lines of code, with no comments, cryptic variable names, and no documentation. After months of analysis, we finally scrapped the entire code base and started from scratch. More than six months of previously developed effort was lost because the original engineers never bothered to document their work (let alone follow any recommended coding practice).

Easing the Documentation Load

The problem with the way many developers create documentation is that they are expected to create multiple documentation sources. They create requirements documents, design documents, interface-control documents, and API references and then still must comment the source, among other documentation needs. The development of documentation that is correct and useful is time consuming. Time consuming means it's expensive too! Most companies are in a hurry to get to market and don't want to pay the documentation price. Yet, good documentation saves time and money in the long run, over the product's total lifetime. So, what can developers do to balance these needs?

There are two approaches that developers must follow in order to generate documentation that is useful and doesn't require unrealistic amounts of time. First, developers need to automatically generate their documentation. There are many tools available at freemium or even premium costs that can generate documentation based on the organization of the code and the comments associated with it. One such tool, Doxygen, will be examined in great detail in this chapter.

Second, developers need to generate all their documentation from a single source. While there is a need for requirements, design, and reference manuals, these all need to be maintained in a single source that can be used to generate the individual documents. Otherwise, if separate sources are used, developers will need to change multiple sources every time something changes in the software or in their requirements. Using a single source allows the generation tool to scan for changes and make updates to all documentation at once.

Even if developers use an automated tool to generate documentation, there is no guarantee of success without discipline. Developers must be diligent in making sure that the single source is updated as project and code changes are made. There are two factors that determine the level of quality one can expect from software documentation: whether the team is disciplined and whether they use an automated tool. Figure 5-1 demonstrates a way that we can think about documentation.

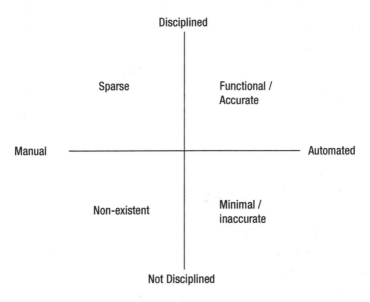

Figure 5-1. *Software documentation spectrum*

In the lower left quadrant, we have a team that is not disciplined and generates documentation manually, which will result in no documentation at all. These are teams that either are set up for failure or will require far more time and money to get their product to market and maintain it. Teams in this quadrant are not capable of creating portable and reusable firmware, but are instead functional rapid prototypers who can make something work on a bench but struggle to get anything production ready.

The lower right-hand quadrant, where we have a team that is not disciplined but has an automated tool available, we create minimal documentation that tends to be inaccurate. In this circumstance, automated tools are able to parse the general structure and flow of the code and identify variables. Something is better than nothing, but the documentation tends to be inaccurate due to developers' not updating code comments or adding any comments at all. Developers will still struggle to maintain these systems and may be frustrated by incorrect information.

The upper left-hand quadrant, where we have a disciplined team manually generating documentation, will result in accurate documentation, but it will generally be incomplete and sparse. The reason for this is that such teams need to invest large amounts of time, money, and effort to generate their documentation, which very few development teams have. The result is that we end up with great high-level documentation, but the details tend to be lacking. Many government organizations tend to fall into this category, although they happily invest the time and money.

The final quadrant, the upper right, is where developers interested in developing high-quality, reliable, portable, and reusable code should aim to find themselves. These teams are disciplined, updating code comments and design diagrams as they change. They use automated tools to scan their code base and comments to generate their documentation. They focus on the end result and generate functional and accurate documentation.

An Introduction to Doxygen

Discipline cannot be taught from the pages of a book, but how to set up and leverage automated documentation tools can be. Software tools such as JavaDocs, NaturalDocs, and Doxygen are example tools that generate documentation from the code and comments. In this book, we will focus on Doxygen, a tool that is open source and widely adopted within the software industry.

"Doxygen is a documentation system for C++, C, Java, Objective-C, Python, IDL (Corba and Microsoft flavors), Fortran, VHDL, PHP, C#, and to some extent D."[1] Doxygen offers several advantages to the software developer who is looking to keep their documentation consistent and up to date with what the source code is actually doing. Besides its free price, which is hard to beat, Doxygen allows developers to use the comments within the header, source, and other text files to generate documentation in common formats, such as HTML, RTF, or PDF. Doxygen allows the developer to show how a project was implemented by browsing files, classes, modules, variables, and other types that are used in the program in addition to generating graphs to show how they interact with each other. Doxygen can be considered a way to automatically generate a software manual for the project. Developers can even go so far as to document their tools, standards, and nearly any other piece of project documentation that might need to be generated.

CASE STUDY—SELECTING A DOCUMENTATION TOOL

A few years before I became a consultant, I was working within the defense industry for a small business that had been quite successful but had poor software processes. Despite their success, they had nearly no documentation for any of their software and had a fairly high turnover rate. One of my primary missions was to help them get their software-development process under control and develop documentation.

I developed a few criteria for selecting a documentation tool, such as:

- Accepted as an industry standard

- Low cost

- Updated multiple times per year

- Supports multiple programming languages

- Outputs HTML, RTF, and LaTeX file formats

- Supports multiple comment styles

- Strong user base and ecosystem

---

[1]Doxygen, August 2015, www.doxygen.org.

Doxygen fit these criteria, while another tool favored by a more senior engineer did not. At the time, management decided to go with the more senior engineer's recommendation, and all of the software was commented using a proprietary format. The tool was buggy and hadn't had any updates in over two years. Within a year, the tool was officially abandoned and obsolete. An expensive and time-consuming effort began to convert the comments to Doxygen.

Doxygen allows just about any kind of data to be added to the documentation, including images and equations. All the source code is available and hosted on GitHub, which allows a team to dig through the guts of the tool and modify it as needed. More important, Doxygen is widely used and supported through various software disciplines, and for more than ten years has been providing feature improvements and updates at least three times a year. There is no fear of the tool suddenly disappearing or losing its place as the standard documentation tool.

Installing Doxygen

Doxygen is a fairly simple but very configurable and powerful documentation generation tool. As developers, we can take advantage of tools such as Doxygen to generate reusable code modules that are already documented. We can use Doxygen to create templates of software for APIs or HALs that have the interface already predefined and are simply waiting for the code for the specific target to be added in order to bring it to life. Since Doxygen can be so useful for creating reusable code and interfaces, I believe it is critical to walk through the installation process and cover some of its more interesting features. You will discover that many of the HAL examples in this book were designed first by writing Doxygen comments in header and source files. The implementation of those interfaces was then filled in as needed for target applications.

The first and most important step when installing Doxygen is to locate its installation file, documentation, and any dependencies. All of the Doxygen installation and documentation can be found at `www.doxygen.org`. The installation files can be acquired from the download link located on the top left-hand side of the Doxygen website. Doxygen can be downloaded in pure source form from a GitHub repository, or individual binaries can be downloaded for one's platform of choice. While many readers may cringe, I mostly use Doxygen on Windows, but there is support for Mac OS and Linux, among others. Since I typically use Windows for my development environment, there are several additional packages required to generate PDF documents and fancy graphics for call graphs and the like. Before we get into those juicy details, download and install Doxygen for your operating system of choice.

Next, download and install Graphviz from `http://www.graphviz.org/`. Graphviz is an open source graph visualization resource provided by AT&T research. Later, we will use this package by enabling the `HAVE_DOT` function in our configuration file to allow Graphviz to generate our graphs. This results in a more visually appealing and professional result. Finally, in order to convert documentation into a PDF, install LaTex (for a Windows user, I highly recommend the use of MikTex) and Ghost Script. Together, these two packages will allow for PDF generation.

Documentation Project Setup

There are so many ways to set up a directory structure for a project. Earlier, I discussed how I like to organize a project based on the layer of firmware, such as drivers, middleware, and application. Since each of these layers could be moved from one application to the next, I find that it makes more sense to add a documents folder to each of the different layers of firmware. Depending on how you organize your software, it may even make sense to have a documents folder for each of the components in a project so that the documentation can follow that component. In any case, a documentation folder will need to have the following:

- An images folder to store any visual aids that will be included in the documentation

- An output directory for HTML-, PDF-, and RTF-generated documentation

- A configuration folder to hold the Doxygen configuration file

- A folder for additional documents, such as requirements, design, main pages, datasheets, schematics, etc.

I am a big fan of only inventing the wheel once, so as soon as a directory structure that works for you is determined, copy that folder structure (even any file starters) and save it somewhere safe for the start of each project.

One of the advantages of using Windows is that the old humdrum of command prompts and command options are a thing of the past (fine, I admit I still use the command prompt for things like ipconfig or Python scripts, but I can pretend like the old terminal days are over). Doxygen for Windows comes with a user interface called DoxyWizard that can be used to set up a Doxygen configuration file. The configuration file should be stored in the config folder of the documentation folder that was just discussed.

DoxyWizard is broken up into a tabbed user interface where each tab acts as a stepping stone for setting up the project, as can be seen in Figure 5-2. First, we have a Wizard tab that is extremely useful for configuring the initial project settings, such as project name, logo, source location, and where to store the documentation. Next, with the basics entered, the Expert tab allows the fine-tuning of Doxygen for parameters such as file extensions, messages, HTML, and many other options. Finally, the Run tab is where a developer can execute Doxygen based on the configuration-file parameters and build the documentation.

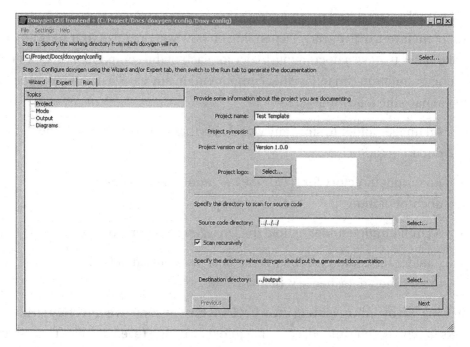

Figure 5-2. *DoxyWizard project setup*

Using the Doxygen Wizard tab is straightforward. Under Project, enter the project name, a brief description, and the version or ID for the software. If the project has a logo, the logo file can be selected, and the logo will appear on the top of each HTML documentation page in the HTML header. I usually just place my company logo, since each individual project does not have its own logo associated with it. The primary directory for source code and the destination for the documentation can also be entered. An example of the Setup page can be found in Figure 5-2.

The Mode menu provides a developer with the ability to select the programming language that is being used. An estimated 80 percent of all embedded software is developed in C, which makes the selection of optimizing for C a good guess. Obviously, if a developer is using C++ then the option for C++ optimization should be selected. Figure 5-3 shows an example of how the Mode page should look when properly configured. Note that Doxygen in this case is set to only generate documentation for documented entities. Documented entities are areas of code that have special comment blocks associated with them. For a code base without any comments, a developer could select "All Entities," and Doxygen would still parse the code and generate at least some documentation.

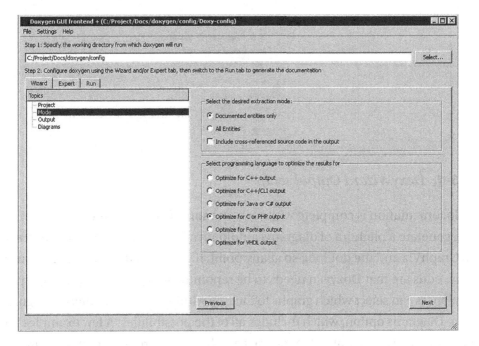

Figure 5-3. *DoxyWizard Mode setup*

The Output option provides a developer with the ability to select the types of generated documentation that should be created. Figure 5-4 reveals that the options are HTML, LaTeX, Man pages, RTF, and XML. But what about PDF? I've found that the best way to generate a PDF is to either use the LaTeX output or, better yet, to open the RTF and save it as a PDF. Sometimes it can be useful to add additional information to one of the generated files prior to creating the PDF and releasing it. The RTF also has the option of using a template so that the generated document fits a required format. Creating an RTF template is beyond the scope of this book, but be aware that templates exist if it is an area of interest.

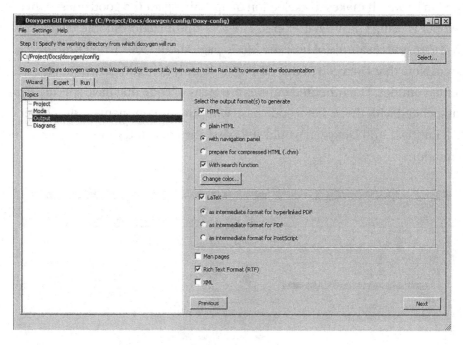

Figure 5-4. *DoxyWizard Output setup*

No documentation is complete without some sort of diagram, and Doxygen has the ability to generate a plethora of diagrams automatically for developers. The diagrams do require GraphViz and the dot tool, so at any point, if graphs in the documentation show up empty, odds are that Doxygen needs to be repointed to the GraphViz directory.

Developers can select which graphs to include within the documentation. Figure 5-5 shows the Diagrams option, which includes all of the possibilities. A few examples include class diagrams, call graphs, and dependency graphs. These are good options to include within automated documentation.

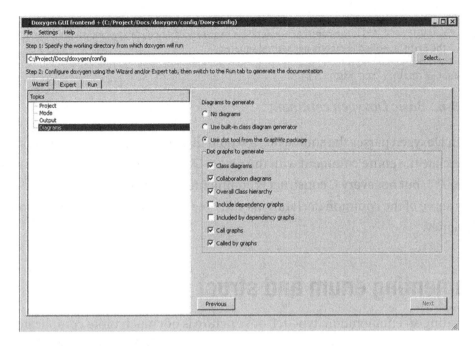

Figure 5-5. *DoxyWizard Diagrams setup*

At this point, Doxygen has enough configuration information to generate the documentation. The documentation is generated by simply moving to the Run tab and pressing the Run Doxygen button. Doxygen will chew on the configuration file for a little while and begin processing the source. When "*** Doxygen has finished" is displayed in the status window, pushing the Show HTML Output button will open the HTML document that was just generated. Any documentation that is generated from the source would be created from the functions and variables within the code and *not* from developer-generated comments. Let's examine how developers can document and customize their software for Doxygen.

Doxygen Comment Fundamentals

When it parses the source files, Doxygen looks for a specific set of characters that indicates the comment is written for Doxygen. The language selected will determine which character set is used, but for developers programming in C, we can use our standard comment blocks of /* Comment */ with a slight twist. Doxygen comments start by adding a second * character to the comment block. For example, Figure 5-6 shows how a macro or variable would be commented for Doxygen.

```
/**
 * GRAVITY_ACC_MS is the constant acceleration of gravity of a body falling near the surface of
 * the Earth, specified in meters per second squared.
 **/
#define GRAVITY_ACC_MS2    9.81
```

Figure 5-6. *Basic Doxygen comment*

When Doxygen parses the source file, it would discover the /** comment block and then associate the entire comment with the macro GRAVITY_ACC_MS. All Doxygen blocks start with /**, but not every C construct is commented in exactly the same way. Let's examine some of the common declarations and how a comment block can be formatted appropriately.

Documenting enum and struct

Documenting an enumeration, typedef, or structure is not much more complicated than a basic macro or variable, but it does have a few caveats. First, a developer must add the basic comment block above their code to provide a description for the code, such as what it is for and how to use it. Next, a developer can add a comment for every member of an enumeration or structure. Documenting the member is done by placing a comment block to the right of the member and adding the < character after the /** so that the comment becomes /**<.

The < character is used to tell Doxygen that the comment is associated with the member that was declared to the left of the comment block. If you really want, you can explicitly specify the difference between an enumeration and structure by placing an enum or struct command in front of the definition, but Doxygen does such a great job of knowing what it is documenting that it is unnecessary and not recommended. An example code snippet for documenting a structure can be found here:

```
/**
 * Defines two variables which specify the spacecraft structure.
 */
typedef struct
{
    uint8 Acceleration;    /**<Rate spacecraft is accelerating */
    uint8 Mass;                /**< The current mass of the spacecraft */
}SpaceCraft_t;
```

The most complicated code blocks to document are functions because they tend to require more information in order to be completely explicit on their purpose and how to use them. They have input and return parameters in addition to references to other functions, and even sometimes example code snippets. That is why it is extremely useful to create a function template that can be copied, pasted, and modified for each new function that is developed. Just be warned: copying and pasting a template can result in the documentation not being up to date if a developer forgets to update the pasted code.

Documenting Functions

When documenting a function, there are several important factors that a developer needs to ensure are documented to get maximum benefit. The factors include the following:

- Function name

- Function description; that is, what it does

- A list of pre-conditions that should be completed before calling the function

- A list of post-conditions that a developer can expect to occur if the pre-conditions have been met before calling the function

- Descriptions of the function's parameter list and whether the parameter is used to input and/or output data

- A description of the function return data, if there is any

- An example code snippet on how to properly use the function

- A list of related functions that would be relevant for a developer to be aware of

- A change history documenting all the changes that have been made to the function with the date, version number, developer who made the changes, and a description of the change that has been made

The preceding list might at first seem overwhelming. There is a lot of information that needs to be included. But consider what would happen if any of this information were omitted. Take, for example, omitting whether the parameters are inputs or outputs to the function. A developer looking at the function will need to take extra time to determine what the parameters are doing, and might even need to experiment to get it right. Or worse, they could just implement what they think is right and hope for the best. Hello, new bug! Such a simple piece of documentation will make it very clear what the parameters are doing. Remember, sometimes the code isn't readily available (in binary format), which means the documentation and the function prototype are the only information a developer has to go on.

A developer looking to properly document their function will need to create a function comment block that contains all this information. The first step is to provide the function name in the comment block. Documenting all the features in the preceding list will take up quite a few lines of code, and since the comment block should be above the function definition, we want to make sure that we can easily find the function name, which will follow dozens of lines later. The comment block will start with the text shown in Listing 5-1.

Listing 5-1. Function Start Block

```
/****************************************************************
* Function : Dio_Init()
*//**
```

In the preceding case, we don't want the function name to be included multiple times in a row within the generated documentation, so we leave the function name outside the Doxygen comment block. The comment block doesn't start until the /** sequence. Doxygen will automatically associate this comment block with the function that immediately follows it and associate the comment block with the function name. Including the function name in the Doxygen block would duplicate the function name in the documentation, which would make the resulting documentation confusing.

The next step is to provide a brief description of the function's purpose. Since the Doxygen comment block has already been started, we can simply start entering the text that we want for the description. An example for the description block can be seen in Listing 5-2. In this case, we want to create a heading within the comment block with the text "Description" in bold face. We can do this by placing \b before the text. The remainder of the comment should simply state the purpose of the function.

Listing 5-2. Function Description Block

```
* \b Description:
*
* This function is used to initialize the Dio based on the
* configuration table defined in dio_cfg module.
```

Next, a developer should take the time to carefully think through any of the function pre-conditions that need to be documented. For example, before making a call to a peripheral transmit function, an application should have already called the peripheral initialization function and configured the peripheral clocks. Documenting the pre-conditions is essentially a checklist for developers on what they need to make sure happens before ever using the function. An example of a pre-condition/post-condition block can be seen in Listing 5-3.

Listing 5-3. Pre-condition/Post-condition Comment Block

```
* PRE-CONDITION: Configuration table populated (sizeof > 0)
* PRE-CONDITION: NUMBER_OF_CHANNELS_PER_PORT > 0 <br>
* PRE-CONDITION: NUMBER_OF_PORTS > 0 <br>
* PRE-CONDITION: The MCU clocks configured and enabled.
* POST-CONDITION: The DIO peripheral is initialized.
```

The function parameter list and return data should be the next information listed inside the comment block. In order to document parameters in Doxygen, a developer should use the specialized Doxygen tag @param. Doxygen has several specialized tags that provide the tool with information on how to process the comment block. Refer to the latest documentation for a complete tag list. For parameters, @param can be used by itself, but it is recommended that developers follow the tag with square brackets [ ], then specify the parameter direction, such as an input [in], output [out], or both [in/out]. An example can be seen in Listing 5-4. The return parameter for the function is specified by using the @return tag followed by the type of data being returned and a description.

Listing 5-4. Function Parameter and Return Block

```
* @param [in]       Config is a pointer to the configuration table
*                   for the peripheral.
*
* @return           void
```

Developers should include at least a short example of how the function can be used. There is a mechanism within Doxygen that allows a developer to insert code snippets into the documentation. In order to show code within the documentation, two special tags are required, the @code and @endcode tags. As one might guess, the @code tag is used to tell Doxygen that the following comment block contains code, while @endcode tells Doxygen that the code block is complete. The code example can be inserted in between the tags. Doxygen will parse the code and generate a special documentation block that shows the code. An example of how to use the tags can be seen in Listing 5-5.

Listing 5-5. Function Example Code Block

```
* \b Example:
* @code
* const DioConfig_t *DioConfig = Dio_ConfigGet();
*
* Dio_Init(DioConfig);
* @endcode
```

The next critical puzzle piece is to tell Doxgyen what other functions are related to this function so that links to those functions can be generated in the documentation. The code-block format is to use the @see tag followed by the name of the function. If the function exists within the documentation, Doxygen will create a hyperlink in the HTML documentation that allows a developer to easily navigate to related functions to understand how they work. Listing 5-6 shows how to use the @see tag.

Listing 5-6. Functions Related Block

```
* @see Dio_Init
* @see Dio_ChannelRead
* @see Dio_ChannelWrite
```

Finally, our function block could contain a change history for the function. A change history isn't necessarily required, but in safety-critical systems developers may want to note at the function level the changes that were made and when they were made. Change information could be kept in a general log or at the beginning of a module, but it is up to the developer to decide how they want to track changes.

The change-history block is going to look a bit crazy at first because there is HTML formatting included so that the change list looks presentable in the final documentation. Without the HTML tags, the generated documentation would not align or look nice, which would undoubtedly drive management crazy. A developer can insert HTML tags into the documentation, such as **
** for a line break and **** to start bold-faced text and **** to end bold-faced text. In the generated documentation, a change history looks most presentable when using a table that has an 800-pixel width. An example change-history block can be seen in Figure 5-7.

```
* <br><b> - HISTORY OF CHANGES - </b>
*
* <table align="left" style="width:800px">
* <tr><td> Date         </td><td> Software Version </td><td> Initials </td><td> Description </td></tr>
* <tr><td> 09/01/2015 </td><td> 0.5.0            </td><td> JWB      </td><td> Interface Created </td></tr>
* <tr><td> 11/10/2015 </td><td> 1.0.0            </td><td> JWB      </td><td> Interface Released </td></tr>
* </table><br><br>
```

Figure 5-7. *Function Revision Log*

Each documentation block that we have discussed can be pulled together into a single block that results in a nice, legible, and reusable function template that can be used to quickly generate adequate function documentation with minimal effort and time input. A template that is fully assembled and ready to be used can be found at www.beningo.com.

Documenting Modules

Application code is going to contain a series of header and source modules that contain code comments. To generate the most consistent documentation possible, there are two additional pieces of information that developers need to add to their modules to ensure full documentation. The first is a module header. The header is something that nearly every developer already adds to their code, except in this case they are replacing general text with specialized Doxygen tags. Typical information that is included in a module header is the following:

- Module name
- Filename
- File description
- Module author

- Original file date

- Module version

- Compiler used

- Target

- Any specialized notes

- Copyright

- Licensing information

Listing 5-7 demonstrates what a typical module header would look like. Notice that the information that we would normally put in the module header simply gets an @ symbol added before it so that Doxygen can place the information in the documentation. A module header of this type would go into both header files (*.h) and source files (*.c).

Listing 5-7. Example Module Header[2]

```
/******************************************************************
* @Title        :   Digital Input / Output (DIO)
* @Filename     :   dio.c
* @Author       :   Jacob W. Beningo
* @Origin Date  :   09/01/2015
* @Version      :   1.0.0
* @Compiler     :   TBD
* @Target       :   TBD
* @Notes        :   None
*
* THIS SOFTWARE IS PROVIDED BY BENINGO EMBEDDED GROUP
* "AS IS" AND ANY EXPRESSED OR IMPLIED WARRANTIES,
* INCLUDING, BUT NOT LIMITED TO, THE IMPLIED WARRANTIES
* OF MERCHANTABILITY AND FITNESS FOR A PARTICULAR
* PURPOSE ARE DISCLAIMED. IN NO EVENT SHALL BENINGO
* EMBEDDED GROUP OR ITS CONTRIBUTORS BE LIABLE FOR ANY
* DIRECT, INDIRECT, INCIDENTAL, SPECIAL, EXEMPLARY, OR
```

---

[2]Legal wording is modified from Freescale source example code and provided as an example.

```
* CONSEQUENTIAL DAMAGES (INCLUDING, BUT NOT LIMITED TO,
* PROCUREMENT OF SUBSTITUTE GOODS OR SERVICES; LOSS OF
* USE, DATA, OR PROFITS; OR BUSINESS INTERRUPTION)
* HOWEVER CAUSED AND ON ANY THEORY OF LIABILITY,
* WHETHER IN CONTRACT, STRICT LIABILITY, OR TORT
* (INCLUDING NEGLIGENCE OR OTHERWISE) ARISING IN ANY
* WAY OUT OF THE USE OF THIS SOFTWARE, EVEN IF ADVISED OF
* THE POSSIBILITY OF SUCH DAMAGE.
******************************************************************/
```

At this point, a developer might think that is all they need to know about Doxygen to start, but there is still one more interesting feature that can be used to organize the resulting documentation. Doxygen contains an @addtogroup tag that allows the documentation to be organized by group. For example, a developer may be developing a hardware abstraction layer and wants all the modules contained within it to be shown in the documentation together under the group HAL. In this case, the developer would add the @addtogroup tag near the beginning of the module along with a curly bracket { (I like to call them squirrelly brackets). At the bottom of the module, a developer would then add one final closing squirrelly bracket. Don't forget that the squirrelly brackets must be within a comment block, otherwise the compiler will try to process them. An example of adding the contents of dio.c into a HAL group can be seen in Listing 5-8.

Listing 5-8. @Addtogroup Comment Block

```
/** @addtogroup MCU_Drivers
 *   @{
 */

Code goes here

/** @}*/
```

Creating a Reusable Template

For the most part, no developer is going to be able to remember from memory all the details thast are required to fully document a module and its contents. Remember, consistency and readability are important characteristics for software that will be ported and reused, so there must be some way to decrease the labor intensity required to document source code. The easiest way to document code is to create a header and source file template that contains generic starter information and formatting so that every time a new module is created, the template is used and contains all the Doxygen formatting and tags. The template will provide a consistent look for every module within the code base.

Figuring out all the little nuances Doxygen requires can take some time and some trial and error. I've been using Doxygen for almost a decade (if not longer), and I still periodically make adjustments and tweaks to my template. A developer could start from scratch with a blank header and source module, or they could download the templates that accompany this book and modify those templates for their own use. The resources at the end of this chapter identify where the templates can be downloaded.

Once the template has been downloaded, a developer should review each documentation section. First, review how each tag is used and the way each C language construct is documented. If the documentation does not make sense, navigate to the Doxygen website and review the user-manual entries on that tag. Run Doxygen and review what the generated HTML documentation looks like. At this point, a developer can start to make modifications to the template and then rapidly observe how the changes affect the final output.

Generating a Main Page

The fact that an application can be documented in such a way that a software manual is automatically generated is very powerful. After experimenting with Doxygen's output capabilities, a developer might eventually notice that the main HTML page is rather plain. In fact, the main page is completely blank and devoid of any useful information. As unfortunate as this may be, it is a wonderful opportunity for developers to create their own main page.

The main page should contain information about the project and code base that would be useful for anyone who is trying to get up to speed or who is developing application code. In fact, a main page would be very useful if it contained a table of contents with a series of web links that could be used to navigate to pages with important developer information. Examples for main page information include the following:

- Project introduction (what is this whole thing about?)

- Version log (which version is this and how have things changed from version to version?)

- Acronyms (what do all these funny terms mean? i.e., ADT, A2D, SPI, CAN, PWM, etc.)

- Software architecture overview

- APIs (Do we have any APIs that need to be explained?)

- HALs

- Middleware

- OS information

- Coding standards (what are our code conventions? How do we name things, etc.?)

- Documentation (how we documented things)

- Project requirements (a quick overview of what we had to do)

- Testing and validation (how did we prove that this version actually works?)

- Tools (tools that we used to develop the project, such as compiler, IDE, lint, svn, etc.)

Anything that a developer *needs* to know should be included as part of the main page. Creating the main page starts out relatively simple. There are two primary methods that can be used to populate the main page. First, a single file can be used in which the entire table of contents is added. For small projects, a single file can make a lot of sense since there probably isn't a lot of information that needs to be recorded. However, as projects grow, a single main page file can become rather large and difficult to maintain. A better approach would be to create a file for every element of the table of contents and then have Doxygen merge them into a main page. For now, we will only examine the first method, and the reader can at their own leisure investigate the more advanced technique.

Doxygen recognizes a file to be the main page by identifying the @mainpage tag at the top of the file. After the @mainpage tag has been added to the file, a developer needs to use HTML tags to create the layout and the information flow for their page. Being an expert at HTML is not required. There are a few HTML commands that a developer will find useful, which can be found in Figure 5-8. The easiest way to create links for the table is to use the HTML anchor tag. When a link is clicked that has an associated anchor, the page will jump to the anchor point, allowing the main page documentation to be easily navigated.

HTML Command	Description
<A NAME="Contents"></A>	creates an anchor
<A HREF="#Introduction">Introduction</A>	creates a link to an anchor
 	creates a carriage return on the html page
<hr>	creates a horizontal line

Figure 5-8. *HTML commands*

Each entry in the table of contents section of the main page can be considered its own separate section. Doxygen has a built-in section command that can be used to separate the content. Doxygen even provides a subsection command for the event that we need to break up our information into even smaller pieces. Sections will allow a developer to organize their main page and properly control the flow of information.

As with any document, a picture is worth a thousand words, and Doxygen even has a tag to include them. The image tag consists of the command image, a type such as html, rtf, or latex, and then the filename, such as image.jpg. Due to the way Doxygen handles images, a developer does need to include multiple image tags if more than one type of documentation is going to be created. For example, if a developer wants to create HTML, RTF, and LaTex files, an image tag needs to be added that includes the command for all three formats.

Ten Tips for Commenting C Code[3]

During the hustle and bustle of the development cycle, it isn't uncommon for commenting the code to fall to the bottom of the priority list. With the pressure to get the product out the door, discipline usually fails, and short cuts result in a poorly

---

[3] "10 Tips for Documenting C Code," originally published on EDN.com: http://www.edn.com/electronics-blogs/embedded-basics/4422388/10-Tricks-for-Documenting-Embedded-Software

commented code base. Source code that is well documented can decrease the cost and time to market by providing insights into the software that would otherwise require time and experimentation to jog the developers' memory on the what and why of the code's behavior. These insights, if lost, can increase costs and delay time to market by introducing bugs into the code base. Here are ten simple tips that can be followed to help ensure that not only does the software get documented but also that it is documented with useful information.

Tip #1: Explain the Why, Not the How

There seems to be a human tendency when developing software to want to explain what a line of code is doing rather than why the code is there in the first place. A favorite example is bit shifting a literal by x bits. The code and the comment generally look something like this:

```
// Shift bit by 8 and store in PortB
*Gpio_PortB |= (1UL<<8);
```

The comment itself leaves quite a bit to be desired. Anyone with a basic understanding of the C language knows by observation what the line of code is doing, but *why* are we shifting by 8? *Why* are we storing the shifted bit pattern in PortB? A developer who reads this line of code six months or a year after writing it will have little idea without investigation as to what this line is really doing. Something more appropriate might look something like the following:

```
// Port B bit 8 controls the motor relay that needs to be turned off
// during the emergency stop procedure. Setting bit 8 high will
// disengage the motor through a relay.
*Gpio_PortB |= (1UL<<8);
```

This comment may not be perfect, but it explains why the developer is shifting a bitwise ORing into PortB.

Tip #2: Comment Before Coding

The general wisdom of commenting code has always suggested that comments be written when the code is. This insight makes a lot of sense, because while the software is being written the *why* of it is fresh in the mind of the developer. The developer could wait until after the software is written, but the pressure of getting to market and other priorities often make it highly unlikely that the comments will convey the original intent.

An alternative to writing comments during or after the code is to instead write the comments before the software is written. This has the unique advantage of allowing the developer to think through what they are about to code and the why before ever writing a single line of code. It can be thought of as a translation of the software architecture and design phase of development into source code. This keeps the software design at the forefront of the developers' minds and allows them to think clearly about what it is they are about to write code for.

Tip #3: Use Doxygen Tags

There are many different free tools available on the web that can translate code comments into useful document formats. A tool that can scan the source and generate HTML, RTF, and/or PDF files should be a developer's dream. Why? Many development teams are forced to maintain not only their source code but also a wide variety of design documents that describe what the code is doing. These documents often trail what is happening in the program. Using a tool such as Doxygen can automatically translate the code comments into a document that fits the bill of these design documents! The result is that the developer now only has a single source and documentation chain to maintain, which should decrease the amount of time they need to spend creating "pretty" documents. (Also, hopefully this also ensures that the documentation and source code stay in synchronization with each other).

Doxygen has become widely accepted to the point that compiler and silicon vendors include Doxygen tags in their automatically generated code. They are building Doxygen into the tool chains in order to make it easier for developers to generate documentation. As developers, shouldn't we accept this free tool that makes documentation so much easier?

Tip #4: Adopt a Code Style Guide

A coding style guide contains all the information a developer would need to properly create identifiers and also how the software should be documented. A style guide helps the developer or a team of developers develop software in a uniform manner. A style guide aids the developer by removing distractions from the software that may exist due to stylistic differences, the result being that code reviews are easier because the code style is uniform and the actual code can be the focus rather than superficial details about comment locations.

Tip #5: Use a File Header

Using a version-control system is a highly recommended practice, but it can become tedious to always refer to the revision-control system regarding the changes that occur in a code base. It can sometimes be confusing or unclear what a module's purpose is. Using these reasons as a basis, it is recommended that header and source files contain a comment header describing the function and purpose of the module. There are several pieces of information that could be included in the header, but at a minimum it should include the following:

- File name
- Author
- Origin date
- Module version number
- Compiler version used to compile the code
- The intended target
- Copyright information
- Miscellaneous notes
- Revision information

Tip #6: Create a Commenting Template

One of the best methods for ensuring that code comments are consistent and that they adhere to the Doxygen syntax is to create a commenting template. There would be a need for two templates—one for header files and then another for source files. The coding templates would contain all the standard commenting blocks required to adhere to the coding style.

A commenting template would include a file header along with comment tags and commenting blocks for structures, enumerations, typedefs, and functions. An example header and source file template that can be used to develop embedded software and that uses Doxygen tags can be found at `http://www.beningo.com/162-code-templates/`.

Tip #7: Have a Consistent Comment Location

One of the most effective ways to decrease bugs and the costs associated with a software project is to perform code reviews. A developer and his peers usually perform the code review, but the process can become more difficult if the commenting structure is inconsistent. Placing comments that use different formats and putting them in different places can be distracting and detract from the code review, decreasing its effectiveness.

The use of a coding style guideline is recommended, as in the previous tip, because it would dictate not only the commenting formats that should be used but also where comments should appear. This will help keep the commenting structure uniform and allow code reviewers to focus on the code and its behavior rather than be distracted by the location or information contained within the comments.

Tip #8: Don't Comment Every Line

In all truth, developers really don't want to comment their software. It is time consuming and not enjoyable. It is much more fun to twiddle bits, control hardware, and pretty much do anything else (other than sit in a meeting, of course). Yet, what is often considered well-documented code has a comment for every single line of code.

The whole purpose of commenting code is to provide the future version of the developer or maintainer with insight as to the what and why of the software. A verbose essay is not required or wanted. Creating a block of comments that describe what the block is doing is usually completely adequate. One great advantage of commenting the block is that if the code needs to change but the block description still applies it can save development time that would otherwise be spent updating comments.

Tip #9: Start Mathematical Type Identifiers with the Type

When developing software that is performing a mathematical operation, it can be extremely useful to start the identifier with the type. For example, creating a variable named `ui8_Velocity` or `si32Acceleration` provides a developer with an instant understanding of the type.

Starting an identifier in this way has many advantages. First, there is no need to reference the variable declaration to get the type. This can save time otherwise spent continually having to refresh on the type and size of the variable and whether it needs to be cast in the calculation. Second, it makes it easier to spot casting errors, such as multiplying two 8-bit numbers without a cast.

Starting an identifier with the type is a trend that seems to come and go over time. Personally, the author has bounced back and forth on this naming convention, but it seems to prove very useful for identifiers used in mathematical calculations and can make mathematical errors much more obvious.

Tip #10: Update Comments with Code Updates

Using a template in conjunction with Doxygen can be a very powerful tool if utilized properly. Part of what is considered proper use of such templates and tools comes during software updates and maintenance. These tools are only effective if the developer is disciplined enough to update their comments as their software changes.

During the development process, requirements, design, and implementations change. As part of these changes, the developer needs to make sure that the comments are always up to date with the software that is implemented. Even if it doesn't feel like there is enough time to implement the code changes and update the comments, the developer should still take the time to do so. One reason is that over the lifetime of the product the cost will be greatly influenced by the developer's maintaining discipline despite the time pressures that may have been placed on them.

A Few Final Thoughts on Documentation

Commenting software is often delegated to being one of the lowest-priority tasks in the development cycle. The pressure to quickly implement and deploy embedded software leaves the engineer scrambling to design, implement, and deploy their firmware. The reality is that commenting code and providing clarity on the *why* can make future maintenance efforts and even the original development effort cost less, and under the right circumstances it can even decrease the time to market.

These tips are just a few simple examples of what can be done to improve the embedded-software design cycle through easing the demands that are placed on the developer by using templates, standards, automated tools, and taking the time to explain the why of the software.

Going Further

Reading about automatic documentation generation is one thing, but actually doing it is a completely different story. The following are some suggestions on next steps to improve the way your software is documented:

- Review the software documentation spectrum located in Figure 5-1. Where do you/your team currently lie within the figure?

- Identify three improvements that can be started over the next three months that can take your documentation effort from its current place on the spectrum toward where you want to be.

- Add a calendar reminder to review the progress being made in improving the documentation process monthly.

- Read "10 Tricks for Documenting Embedded Software" on Jacob's blog at EDN.com.

- Download and install Doxygen.

- Download Jacob's Doxygen templates from www.beningo.com.

- Review each template and become familiar with the different tags used.

- Select a module from an existing source project and convert it to use the Doxygen template. Generate the documentation and examine the resulting output.

- Update the template and main page for your own purposes and needs.

- Separate the main page file into separate files for each of the table of contents items. Separating the files will make them more maintainable and modular.

- Add the formatting and style of the Doxygen comment blocks to your own C style guide.

- Generate output documentation for HTML, PDF, RTF, and LaTeX. Get familiar with potential issues and workarounds that may be required to get the look and feel needed for each documentation set.

- Experiment with the advanced tabs within the DoxyWizard and learn what each feature does and how it affects the generated output.

CHAPTER 6

The Hardware Abstraction Layer Design Process

"Design is the fundamental soul of a man-made creation that ends up expressing itself in successive outer layers of the product or service."

—Steve Jobs

Why Use a HAL?

Using a HAL is a great way to develop software that can be easily reused and ported from one application and platform to the next. Why would a developer want to do such a thing? For starters, reinventing the wheel over and over again gets pretty boring. I believe most developers want to be working on cutting-edge development work instead of being stuck in a never-ending Groundhog Day[1] loop. Even for developers who prefer to do the same thing over and over and over again, development timelines are short, budgets are tight, and there is just way too much work that needs to be done on any given project. The goal is therefore to write code that can be reused, and in order to do that, developers need to create a hardware abstraction layer (HAL) to allow their middleware and application code to access the microcontroller hardware generically.

Creating a rock-solid HAL does not happen overnight. The HAL creation process is an iterative one and very well might take years. The good news is that developers can create a HAL very quickly and then with each project adjust and modify it until nearly every conceivable permutation has been encountered. We are going to walk through

---

[1] *Groundhog Day*, the 1993 comedy starring Bill Murray. If you don't understand this reference then stop now, go on Netflix, Hulu, etc., and watch the movie. An all-time classic.

149

© Jacob Beningo 2017
J. Beningo, *Reusable Firmware Development*, https://doi.org/10.1007/978-1-4842-3297-2_6

the HAL creation process, but before we do, let's take a look at the characteristics that every HAL needs to have. Keep in mind that this book examines a HAL that jumpstarts a developer's HAL needs. Rather than taking years to tweak, the readers of this book will be able develop a HAL very quickly based on the processes and accompanying materials.

A Good HAL's Characteristics

So far in this book, we've discussed several characteristics that portable and reusable software should exhibit. A well-designed and thought-out HAL will exhibit these properties, but there are a few characteristics that should be highlighted at this point. We are about to design a hardware abstraction layer—not the code that runs behind the interface, but the actual interface itself. A good HAL will contain the following characteristics:

- Human readable

- Abstracted complexities

- Well documented

- Portable

- Generic control capability

- Extensible, specific control capability

- Encapsulates data

- Reusable

- Maintainable

The hardware abstraction layer should contain a basic set of functions to control the underlying peripherals that are human readable and generic. The interface should be simple and contain fewer than a dozen functions. The more complex the interface becomes, the more difficult the interface will be to understand, port, and just simply use. Developers should only expose the need-to-know information of the interface and allow all the details to be hidden behind the interface. Developers who use the HAL don't need to be an expert in the underlying hardware and complexities, just an expert in how to use the interface!

CASE STUDY—WHEN GOOD INTENTIONS BACKFIRE

A well-designed and -executed HAL should simplify application development along with many other value-added benefits, such as faster development and decreased costs. However, when the HAL interface is designed, developers need to make sure that they provide verbose error codes and documentation that specifies what causes those errors. On numerous occasions, I've encountered vendor code that has all the dressings and appearance of being great only to discover later that when an issue occurred behind the interface, it was nearly impossible to troubleshoot and figure out what was wrong. When this happens, debugging the black box can be challenging and time consuming. Test and validate any vendor code before committing to it!

The HAL Design Process

Designing a hardware abstraction layer is a relatively straightforward process that is repeated for each microcontroller peripheral, potentially multiple times for different architectures. The general process contains seven steps:

1) Review the microcontroller peripheral datasheet.

2) Identify peripheral features.

3) Design and create the interface.

4) Create stubs and documentation templates.

5) Implement for target processor(s).

6) Test.

7) Repeat for each peripheral.

The process, while apparently simple, can require a few executions before becoming completely clear. In this chapter, we will walk through this generic process for designing a hardware abstraction layer, and then in subsequent chapters we will walk through the process again for specific peripherals and external components.

Step #1: Review the Microcontroller Peripheral Datasheet

In order to create a HAL that can be used from one application to the next, a developer must understand the microcontroller peripheral's capabilities. The only way to do this is to review the microcontroller datasheet for the peripheral. In fact, the best way to do this is to review datasheets from multiple microcontroller vendors and perform a comparison. Start by identifying microcontroller architectures that are pertinent to your particular applications. For example, select a couple of 16-bit microcontrollers from two or more suppliers and then a couple of 32-bit microcontrollers from two or more suppliers.

The first review of the datasheets should be high level. Review the descriptions and jot down notes on basic features, but don't dig into the details at this point. Collecting the datasheets and understanding the general use and purpose of each peripheral is more important at this stage.

Step #2: Identify Peripheral Features

Once the general behavior and use of a peripheral are understood, a developer needs to determine which features are common and which are uncommon to a particular microcontroller. Creating a feature matrix is a great way to identify these capabilities. Table 6-1 is an example of a feature matrix. The microcontrollers to compare are listed along the top, with the identified features in the rows of the first column. Start by creating the matrix and leaving the feature list blank. A developer will discover these as they read through the datasheets in detail. As features are added to the list, place a checkmark in each column if the microcontroller peripheral supports the feature.

Table 6-1. *Peripheral Feature Comparison List*

Peripheral Features	MCU #1	MCU #2	MCU #3	MCU #4	MCU #5
Feature #1	X	X	X	X	X
Feature #2	X	X	X	X	X
Feature #3	X		X	X	
...					

One of the best areas of the datasheet to review is the register map. The registers reveal what configuration settings are available for the peripheral. Reading the peripheral's general description can be helpful, but the details are in the registers. For example, a developer creating a HAL for a GPIO device would find the ability to multiplex the pins, set pins as inputs or outputs, and control the output of the pins. The general description may not mention these since they appear obvious to a seasoned developer. Reviewing the register map makes these capabilities obvious.

Once the feature matrix is completed, a developer should review the matrix and identify the features that are common to every microcontroller and which are attempts to differentiate the microcontroller. The common features, such as setting the pin multiplexer for a GPIO pin, will be added to the HAL interface, while non-common features such as input validation will be included through a generic interface. The common features will be the features that every single microcontroller vendor peripheral has, and those are the features to design the interface around.

Step #3: Design and Create the Interface

By this point, a developer has identified all the common and uncommon features that are associated with a particular peripheral. The developer can now create the interface. There are three key areas that a developer must take into account when designing their interface:

- A common interface
- An uncommon interface
- Callback registration

The common interface is designed to handle common peripheral features. For example, the common interface usually consists of initialization and writing and reading from the peripheral at a minimum. We will look at detailed examples in the coming chapters, but for now, Figure 6-1 provides a generic idea of what a developer would expect the common interface to look like.

```
void Dio_Init(DioConfig_t const * const Config);
DioPinState_t Dio_ChannelRead(DioChannel_t const Channel);
void Dio_ChannelWrite(DioChannel_t const Channel,
                      DioPinState_t State);
```

Figure 6-1. *Common-feature HAL interface example*

The uncommon interfaces into the peripheral have the potential to clutter up the interface and make it unwieldy. In order to handle any custom features built into the peripheral, a very simple interface can be created that allows an application developer to have full control and access to the peripheral to set up and configure those features. By keeping the HAL interface generic, the application code can extend the HAL to include those custom features. As far as the HAL is concerned, the interface is nothing more than presenting a method for reading and writing hardware registers.

Take a moment to look at the generic definition listed in Figure 6-2. Notice that even though these two interfaces are designed for uncommon peripheral features, we've managed to create a generic and reusable interface. That is a huge plus. The downside is that if a developer wants to use these customized features they need to dig into the datasheet, learn how the extended features work and how to set them up, and then extend the interface into their application code. In most circumstances though, the common interfaces are what will be used, so the downside to this technique is actually quite minimal.

```
void Dio_RegisterWrite(uint32_t const Address,
                       TYPE const Value);
TYPE Dio_RegisterRead(uint32_t const Address);
```

Figure 6-2. *Uncommon feature HAL interface*

The final piece to the HAL design puzzle is the callback registration interface. Every single peripheral has interrupts, and if we are designing a clean, reusable interface, the callback interface will provide developers with a clean way of customizing the interrupt needs without having to continually rewrite the driver when it is used in different applications. Interrupt service handlers can be written at the application level and then registered as callbacks with the specified interrupt through the callback interface.

In my experience, many developers overlook the need to have callbacks as part of their interface. Instead, every application has a slightly different version of the driver that is dependent upon the application. The ability to port this code drastically decreases and often causes confusion and issues when trying to update the drivers. The interface example is fairly simple and can be seen in Figure 6-3.

```
void Dio_CallbackRegister(DioCallback_t const Function,
                          TYPE (*CallbackFunction)(type));
```

Figure 6-3. *Callback HAL interface*

Developers may be wondering, why is there only a register function and no way to unregister a callback? The best practice for using interrupt callbacks would be to assign callbacks during the system initialization. Once registered, there shouldn't be any need to unregister or change the behavior of the system. If for some reason there is, simply register a new function with the driver. The new registration will override the old. If the developer wants nothing to be associated with the callback, simply register a default or exception handler.

Step #4: Create Stubs and Documentation Templates

At this point in the HAL design process, developers understand what features need to be included in the interface. There are two key activities that must be performed now. First, a developer must create an outline for the interface that acts as a prototype or empty implementation from which all uses of the HAL will derive. Generally, these empty interfaces are known as stubs or sometimes are referred to as scaffolding. Second, since the stubs will serve as the interface, adding documentation to the stubs can be critical to minimizing future porting and implementation efforts.

Many developers at this point will start to develop the stubs for their peripheral. I think that is a grave mistake. We understand what features go into the interface, but there currently isn't a guide as to what the stubs should look like or what they are supposed to do. Therefore, I highly recommend that developers start by documenting the work that they are about to perform. There is a simple process that developers can follow to create their documentation, which can be found here:

1) Copy the Doxygen header and source templates developed in Chapter 5.

2) Rename the copied template to the peripheral interface being designed; for example, gpio, pwm, etc.

3) Update the file header information.

4) Fill in the interface documentation by creating a function documentation block for each of the features listed back in Step #3.

5) Repeat the preceding steps until all the features for the peripheral have been documented.

Once the documentation has been developed, filling in the stubs is trivial. The documentation literally serves as our design document, and we simply read the documentation and then implement what we read. For example, take a look at the function block found in Listing 6-1, which shows the initial documentation for the Pwm_Init interface. Notice that the developer has now had time to think through the interface and identify pre-conditions and post-conditions along with the data that needs to be passed into and out of the function. At this stage, a developer can fill in the stub.

Listing 6-1. Documentation for pwm Initialization Interface

```
/**********************************************************************
* Function : Pwm_Init()
*//**
* \b Description:
*
* This function is used to initialize the pwm based on the configuration
table defined in pwm_cfg module.
*
* PRE-CONDITION: Configuration table needs to populated (sizeof > 0)
* PRE-CONDITION: The MCU clocks must be configured and enabled.
*
```

```
* POST-CONDITION: The Pwm peripheral is set up with the configuration
settings.
*
* @param[in]      Config is a pointer to the configuration table that
contains the initialization for the peripheral.
*
* @return         void
******************************************************************/
```

Filling in the stub is super easy. The function documentation is already completed, and all the developer needs to do is read the text and convert it into code. The developer can read through the documentation and simply execute these next steps:

1) Read the feature name; create a function with the same name.

2) Populate the parameter list based on the @param tags in the documentation.

3) Select appropriate types for the parameters if they have not been specified in the documentation (some interface data types may change based on the target architecture).

4) Populate the return data type.

5) For developers using C, populate the braces {} to create the function.

6) Copy the function implementation and add it to the header file for the prototype declaration.

7) Review the documentation and populate examples and the @see tags.

Before moving on to the implementation phase, developers should make sure that they save the completed template in their revision-control system. Developers will find that as they implement the HAL on multiple architectures and use it on different projects, the HAL may change slightly with time. This is perfectly normal but needs to be documented. A strict control process should be followed so that applications using different HAL versions don't run into long-term maintenance issues.

Step #5: Implement for Target Processor(s)

With the stubs and templates in place, the development team is now ready to begin implementing their HAL; that is, filling in the implementation details for a particular architecture and target microcontroller. Developers must take care at this stage that they follow proper programming techniques, use version control, perform static code analysis, and so forth.

In order to get the most out of a first pass at the HAL, developers should implement the HAL on more than a single target. Back in Step #2, the developer sifted through the datasheets for several microcontrollers in the attempt to find common and uncommon peripheral features. Ordering development kits for these same microcontrollers and implementing the HAL on all three simultaneously is a great way to flesh out issues and ensure that the HAL is on the right track.

"Wait a minute," you might say. "Implementing the HAL on three targets, perhaps only one of which will be used immediately, is wasted time and effort." Not so! Remember the reusable driver patterns that were discussed in Chapter 4? Once a pattern is implemented in code, the developer simply needs to modify the pointer arrays and make a few minor updates to the initialization. The first development kit implementation will take a while, but the remaining two or three can all be implemented and tested in less than a couple of days. Remember, the HAL will become a major building block for developers in *all* future development projects. Spending a little bit more time up front to get it right will save money and time maintaining and updating code bases.

Step #6: Test, Test, Test

A great advantage to having a well-defined hardware abstraction layer is that when porting or implementing on multiple processors it becomes possible to develop test cases that can be used for regression testing. Most of the developers that I encounter are horrible at testing. Don't get me wrong, they spot check a few things here and there, but they really have no idea if the entire code base has actually been tested or not. They just cross their fingers and ship their code, which can be downright scary sometimes. When developing a HAL that will literally form the system's foundation, testing is not optional.

When testing a HAL, there are a few tips and tricks that developers should keep in mind to minimize the stress and pain. These include the following:

- Create a testing interface.

- Develop a formal set of test cases.

- Use regression testing.

- Automate the testing.

A single peripheral could potentially have thousands of possible initialization states. Verifying every single possible configuration value would be time consuming and nearly impossible if a developer were to not automate testing. Developing automated testing for a HAL takes some time, but the peace of mind and the quality of the software that comes from it is well worth it. In order to perform automated tests, a developer will need to do the following:

- Create a test interface into each of the peripherals.

- Develop an external testing application.

- Set up a test communication protocol to drive testing.

- Use an external application that runs the peripheral through its possible initializations and behaviors.

Figure 6-4 shows an example setup for testing a HAL. A developer could use a code test harness, but to really test an embedded system the tests should be run on live hardware. Figure 6-4 shows the use of an external test bench that stimulates the HAL and peripheral to perform its different functions. Developers can make testing as simple or as complicated as is needed. A very robust check of the implementation would transmit the different possible configuration tables to the HAL and then verify that all registers are set up as expected.

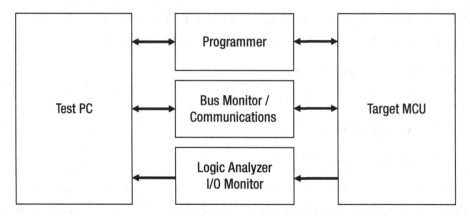

Figure 6-4. *HAL test setup*

Testing can be a very time-consuming process, especially in the early stages of the HAL design. Keep in mind that once the tests and the interface are created, they are designed once and used forever. The investment in most cases is well worth it, especially when one considers the typical cost to resolve a software bug.

Step #7: Repeat for the Next Peripheral

Once a developer has successfully walked through these steps for a single peripheral, they are ready to repeat them and develop a HAL for every peripheral and device that will be used in their projects. Some development teams find it useful to dedicate an engineer or two for creating HALs for every possible device up front. Others simply create new HALs as the project requires. There is no right or wrong way to go about doing this.

In my own development efforts, I typically design a new HAL as the need arises. Once designed though, I can reuse the HAL from one project to the next with little to no effort. Application code becomes easily reusable because the interface doesn't change! I use configuration tables to initialize the peripherals, and once the common features are identified, the initialization structure doesn't change. A typical peripheral driver using the HAL interface takes less than a day to implement in most circumstances.

So, if this is your first time reaching Step #7, congratulations! I look forward to seeing you here again shortly. As you repeat the process over and over again, you may discover that you feel like Bill Murray's character in *Groundhog Day*. Don't worry! Eventually you will move on to bigger and better things and have a well-developed, robust HAL on which to build all your cool application code.

10 Tips for Designing a HAL[2]

Now that we have examined the seven major steps required to develop a HAL, let's discuss ten tips that are critical to this process. These tips may not all be new to the reader since we have already discussed a few in this book. Repetition is sometimes the key to the success so we will review them again.

Tip #1: Identify Core Features

A HAL needs to be a consistent and standard set of functions that can be used across multiple hardware platforms. Microcontrollers come with a standard set of peripherals, all of which serve a particular purpose in an embedded system. When developing a HAL, examine each of the standard microcontroller peripherals and identify their core features. A few core features that would be needed for a communication device, for example, would be initialization, transmit, and receive functions. These are basic must-have functions that would be needed in nearly any application. An example of a core HAL for a UART can be found in Figure 6-5.

```
void Uart_Init(const UartConfig_t * Config);
uint8_t Uart_CharRx(UartChannel_t Channel);
void Uart_CharTx(uint8_t *Char, UartChannel_t Channel);
```

***Figure 6-5.** Example core UART features*

Tip #2: Avoid an All-Encompassing HAL

Engineers sometimes fall into the "one ring to rule them all" trap. The trap is that engineers start with something simple and elegant and then grow the solution to cover the universe. HAL designers should avoid trying to create an all-encompassing or singular HAL to rule every microcontroller device and peripheral. The reason to avoid an all-encompassing HAL is that complexity, cost, and the potential for bugs will drastically increase if you try to create one. Every microcontroller has niche features, so it would just be impossible to create a standard and elegant HAL for them all.

---

[2]Originally published on June 2, 2015 @ EDN.com: http://www.edn.com/electronics-blogs/embedded-basics/4439613/10-Tips-for-designing-a-HAL

Tip #3: Add Register-Access Hooks

What can a developer do to handle niche peripheral features that aren't handled by the HAL? The answer is to build register-access functions into the HAL. A HAL can expose the fact that it doesn't cover every possible use and state of the peripheral and instead provide write and read access to select registers within the driver. The register-access functions would be considered "expert"-mode HAL functions that should be used only by developers who are familiar with the inner workings of the microcontroller. An example of how the register-access functions might look can be seen in Figure 6-6.

```
void Dio_RegisterWrite(uint32_t const Address,
                       TYPE const Value);
TYPE Dio_RegisterRead(uint32_t const Address);
```

Figure 6-6. *Register-access HAL example*

Tip #4: Use Doxygen to Outline the HAL

A great way to plan and develop documentation for a HAL is to outline it using Doxygen. There are several advantages to using Doxygen to plan the HAL. First, Doxygen uses code comments to generate HTML, RTF, and PDF documents, which means the developer already has source comments on what the different functions are supposed to do. Second, since the comments for the HAL are automatically developed, the HAL source files become a blank template in which developers can fill in the HAL functions per the software architecture and requirements. Finally, any updates that are made to the HAL over time can be made in one place, the source files, and then the updates easily propagate to the documentation.

Tip #5: Get a Second Set of Eyes

Getting a second set of eyes on the HAL is a wonderful way to get a fresh perspective. In fact, one of the best things to do during any development cycle is to get multiple eyes on the design. Every engineer has his or her own views and experiences that can contribute to the HAL. Feedback from multiple parties, especially those that may have to use the HAL, is a great way to minimize how many changes will need to be made to the HAL and helps to ensure that the HAL will survive long term to maximize code reuse and minimize cost.

Tip #6: Don't Be Afraid to Iterate

During the first release of a HAL, there are going to be minor problems and discoveries that were overlooked during its design and review. Don't sweat it! Designing a perfect HAL is unrealistic, and the goal should be to develop one that is good enough to start using. Gather feedback from the users of the HAL and then make minor iterative updates. Make sure that the changes are well documented so that legacy HAL users can easily update to the latest revision. After a few iterations, a developer will find that their HAL has become a very well-oiled machine that saves precious development time.

CASE STUDY—ITERATING TO PERFECTION

No one gets a perfect HAL on the first try. The HAL that I use in my own development efforts and with my clients is a HAL that I developed over the course of five to seven years. The first iteration worked with a single microcontroller, a PIC24. After the first project, the HAL was ported to a Freescale Kinetis-L component, which revealed numerous flaws and holes in the HAL. The next port proved to require only minor cosmetic changes.

Every iteration afterward didn't change the existing HAL at all but instead added additional features, such as handling callbacks and the ability to extend the interface easily. The most important aspect was that with each iteration, the documentation became clearer and included more examples. Eventually, the HAL matured to the point where porting it to a new microcontroller requires nearly no changes whatsoever! Start simple and use the time available wisely, and before you know it you will have a robust and portable HAL.

Tip #7: Keep the View at 30,000 Feet

Remember that one of the HAL's purposes is to provide a standard and consistent interface that abstracts the hardware functionality. Keep the interface simple and the level of detail about how the hardware works at the 30,000 feet view. A great test is to have a manager or a software newbie review the HAL and ensure that they can understand how it works.

Keeping the HAL at a high abstraction level will not only help to maximize its use but it will also eliminate misunderstandings that can result from long debugging sessions, increased costs, or missed deadlines. Also keep in mind that the HAL should allow enough leeway so that a developer can implement the HAL functions in way that fits their requirements and application needs. The API or HAL should allow for different low-level implementation strategies to be implemented and supported.

Tip #8: Use Appropriate Naming Conventions

A safe bet when developing a HAL is to use an interface that is ANSI-C compliant. An ANSI-C-compliant HAL will ensure portability across multiple compilers and tool chains. An example of an ANSI-C-compliant requirement would be to limit the function name length to 31 significant characters. Additional considerations would be to use standard portable types and avoid compiler intrinsics. Another quick tip is to define a short coding standard with naming and coding standard best practices on how the HAL interface should be written.

Tip #9: Include a Parameter for Initialization

One of the most common mistakes encountered when designing a HAL is to have a peripheral initialization function take no parameters. In essence, the initialization is hard coded for every application. A parameter-less initialization greatly limits the HAL's portability. An initialization function would be better served passing a pointer to a configuration table. The simplest implementation would just have an empty void table. A more complex implementation would use the pointer to loop through the table and configure the peripheral. Either way, passing a pointer provides greater portability and reuse to the HAL.

Tip #10: Deploy on Multiple Development Kits

A simple and effective way to test out a HAL is to deploy it on multiple microcontrollers from different silicon vendors. Developing simple test code will help to shake out the HAL and elucidate any portability issues up front. Development kits are a great way to cheaply get hardware to test HALs on. Most microcontroller development kits cost less than $20.

Going Further

We've examined a fair amount of information on how to create a HAL from a generic point of view. In the next chapters, we will walk through the process again for a number of microcontroller peripherals. The following are ideas on how you can take the concepts in this chapter a bit further:

- Download the Doxygen header and source modules from
  `https://www.beningo.com/162-code-templates/`.

- Select three microcontroller development kits to test a HAL on.

- Walk through the process in this chapter and design a HAL for the GPIO peripheral.

- Review any existing HALs and list updates and changes that need to be made to them.

- Set up a revision-control repository in which to store your microcontroller HALs.

- Identify two team members to participate in HAL design and schedule regular weekly meetings for HAL reviews and development.

CHAPTER 7

HAL Design for GPIO

"Insufficient facts always invite danger."

—Spock, *Star Trek*, Season 1, Episode 25 ("Space Seed," 1968)

GPIO Peripherals Overview

The general-purpose input/output peripheral (GPIO), also commonly known as
the digital input/output peripheral (DIO), is the most commonly used peripheral
in all embedded systems. The obvious reason is that the GPIO peripheral is how a
microcontroller interacts with the external world around it. Whether the goal is to blink
a simple LED by changing the voltage on the pin or to perform a more complex task such
as multiplexing the pin to an internal peripheral to communicate with a device on the
SPI bus, a developer needs to understand the ins and outs of the GPIO peripheral.

In general, the GPIO peripheral is the gatekeeper for the microcontroller pins. Digital
information can be received and transmitted to the pins. Each pin is connected to a
multiplexer, which in some cases provides limits to the possible peripheral connections
to the pins. The GPIO peripheral will commonly tri-state during start-up until the
peripheral has been configured to set its pins to input or outputs. Some microcontrollers
may have a default input/output setting. The best recommendation if you want to
understand the full peripheral capabilities is to examine the datasheet in detail.

Step #1: Review the GPIO Peripheral Datasheet

In order to develop a successful hardware abstraction layer that will withstand the
tests of time, a development team should review the microcontroller datasheet for
several different part families and manufacturers. By examining multiple datasheets,

© Jacob Beningo 2017
J. Beningo, *Reusable Firmware Development*, https://doi.org/10.1007/978-1-4842-3297-2_7

the developer will quickly learn which features are common and which are meant to be product differentiators.

Before jumping right into the datasheet and getting to work, a team should identify at least three different microcontrollers that will be used for comparison. Since each microcontroller vendor and architecture can vary drastically in capabilities, selecting from the broadest parts range will help ensure that the largest possible combinations are examined. For the examples in this book, we will examine the following microcontrollers:

- NXP Kinetis-L KL25Z family (32-bit ARM Cortex-M0+)[1]

- STMicroelectronics STM32F4 family (32-bit ARM Cortex-M4)[2]

- Microchip PIC24F family (16-bit proprietary core)[3]

- Microchip PIC18F family (8-bit proprietary core)[4]

From reviewing the preceding list, the reader can see that we have a sampling of 8-, 16-, and 32-bit cores along with selections from different silicon vendors that contain ARM cores. While we will not see every possible permutation for the peripherals, using just these four microcontrollers will allow for a complete HAL to be developed.

During the initial datasheet review, developers should be attempting to get a general feel for how the peripherals work and its general capabilities. Lower-level details such as the register mappings will be examined in depth during the feature-identification step. Most microcontroller datasheets are thousands of pages of technical details. In this step, just finding the right datasheet and identifying the correct pages and sections in those manuals will prepare developers for the real work that follows.

Step #2: GPIO Peripheral Features

With a basic understanding of the peripheral's function—in this case, mapping the internal peripheral to the pins and controlling the input and outputs to the microcontroller—a developer can dive into the details and identify specific peripheral

---

[1]NXP KL25Z Sub-Family Reference Manual

[2]ST Microelectronics STM32F427xx Datasheet

[3]Microchip PIC24FJ128GA010 Family Datasheet

[4]Microchip PIC18F2455 Datasheet

features. The easiest way to record the different features is to use an Excel spreadsheet. By using a spreadsheet, a developer can list each microcontroller along the spreadsheet's top row, the features down the first column as they are discovered, and then also provide a mark to indicate whether the microcontroller under review supports the feature.

Examining each microcontroller's GPIO datasheet results in a table like Table 7-1.

Table 7-1. *GPIO Feature Comparison*

Feature	NXP KL25Z	STM32F4	PIC24F	PIC18F
Pin Output	X	X	X	X
Pin Input	X	X	X	X
Pin Toggle	X	X	X	X
Port Output	X	X	X	X
Port Input	X	X	X	X
Port Data Direction	X	X	X	X
Multiplexing	X	X	X	X
Pull-up/down Resistors		X		X

The table is very useful because at a quick glance developers can see what features for the peripheral are common across any microcontroller and which ones are specialized. They can also see where the differences are. Take, for example, the STM32F4 and the PIC18F. Both microcontrollers have internal pull-up resistors, while the other microcontrollers don't have this feature. These minor differences will potentially come into play when the HAL is designed or could be critical when the configuration table for the peripheral is developed. For GPIO, the differences seem minor, but as we will see with other peripherals, the differences can become quite large.

Step #3: Design and Create the GPIO HAL Interface

Defining the HAL interface is really the most exciting part of the entire process. As the reader will discover, once the process is done a few times, a commonality will begin to reveal itself and designing the interfaces will eventually become nearly second nature. For now, the table that was created in Step #2 is going to prove very important to us.

Table 7-1 provides a developer with some functional details that the HAL is going to need to exhibit in order to give the application developer enough control over the hardware. After all, we want our HAL to abstract the low-level hardware and make it easier for the application developer to interact with the microcontroller.

Every HAL interface is going to require, at a minimum, the following:

- Initialization

- Input/output

- Low-level register access

- Callbacks

The easiest place to start designing is the initialization. Every peripheral initialization will follow a simple design. The initialization will start with a peripheral identifier, such as Dio or Gpio, followed by an underscore (_), and then the function that the interface will provide. When creating your first HAL, the initialization should return void until the interface has become mature enough to return error codes. The choice is completely up to the implementer though, if you want to leave the hooks in for errors from the start.

The initialization function should take a pointer to a configuration table that will tell the initialization function how to initialize all the Gpio registers. The configuration table in systems that are small could contain nearly no information at all, whereas sophisticated systems could contain hundreds of entries. Just keep in mind, the larger the table is, the larger the amount of flash space is that will be used for that configuration. The benefit is that using a configuration table will ease firmware maintenance and improve readability and reusability. On very resource-constrained systems where a configuration table would use too much flash space, the initialization can be hard coded behind the interface, and the interface can be left the same. An example for the Dio_Init function can be seen here:

```
void Dio_Init(const DioConfig_t * const Confit);
```

The next critical interface for the GPIO HAL is to determine the necessary inputs and outputs required by the peripheral. For GPIO, the number of input and output interfaces has the potential to get out of control very quickly. A developer could act on individual pins, entire ports, adjust modes, and validate inputs, just to name a few. When developing an interface, a developer should attempt to minimize it so that it doesn't become too large and unwieldy.

My personal preference is to operate on the GPIO interface at only the pin level. I view every single pin as an individual channel for the peripheral interface and design my HAL accordingly. For example, I include `ChannelRead`, `ChannelWrite`, and `ChannelToggle` functions within my HAL. `ChannelRead` is used to read the input state for a pin. `ChannelWrite` is used to write a desired state to an individual pin. `ChannelToggle` will simply toggle the state for the desired pin. I keep each function separate, but if the interface were to get too large, these three could be combined into a single function that takes a parameter for the pin operation that will be performed on the peripheral.

The input/output interface might not just contain read and write functions. There could be times when the pin mode or direction need to be changed during program execution. During such a circumstance, a developer may decide that having `ChannelModeSet` and `ChannelDirectionSet` functions as part of the interface would be appropriate.

The next major functions that should be included in the HAL are generic register-access functions. These functions are designed to handle "extra" peripheral features that are NOT common in all microcontrollers. The `RegisterWrite` and `RegisterRead` functions are meant to allow a developer to access the peripheral functions and then extend the HAL into the board support package (BSP) or the application code. By extending the HAL in this manner, a HAL can remain constant no matter what special features a microcontroller feature may have.

BEST PRACTICE—INTERFACE SIZE

Keep any module interface to a dozen or fewer functions. The more functions there are, the more difficult it can be for developers to remember and even find the function call they are looking for.

Finally, a developer needs to consider functionality that may need to be set at the application layer but that is hidden behind the veil of the HAL. An example might be to have generic interrupt service routines that are defined in the driver but whose functionality is determined during runtime or at compile time. Once a driver is developed, we don't want to have to change the code from one application to the next. Instead, we prefer to use a callback function.

A callback function allows us to register a custom function during runtime that will handle the behavior we are interested in without the need to change the code. It's completely possible that we would not use a callback function in an application but still would want to include it as an option in the HAL. In many situations, the callback function is used to register higher-level application code within the lower-level code. A perfect example is using a callback to register interrupts within the driver code. The exact code that is required for the interrupt service routine (ISR) may be unknown at the time the drivers are designed and may change from one application to the next. Using a callback keeps the driver code flexible so that it can adapt easily to the application code's needs.

The resulting interface for the GPIO HAL would look something along the lines of Figure 7-1.

```
void Dio_Init(const DioConfig_t * const Confit);
DioPinState_t Dio_ChannelRead(DioChannel_t Channel);
void Dio_ChannelWrite(DioChannel_t Channel,
                            DioPinState_t State);
void Dio_ChannelToggle(DioChannel_t Channel);
void Dio_ChannelModeSet(DioChannel_t Channel,
                            DioMode_t Mode);
void Dio_ChannelDirectionSet(DioChannel_t Channel,
                                PinModeEnum_t Mode);
void Dio_RegisterWrite(uint32_t Address, TYPE Value);
TYPE Dio_RegisterRead(uint32_t Address);
void Dio_CallbackRegister(DioCallback_t Function,
                            TYPE (*CallbackFunction)(type));
```

Figure 7-1. *GPIO HAL interface*

Step #4: Create GPIO Stubs and Documentation Templates

A well-designed HAL will be used from one project to the next and for multiple microcontrollers. Once the interface has been designed, a developer can create a generic header and source file that can be quickly adapted to any architecture. The

172

template must contain a few simple components, fully defined interface stubs, and documentation.

The interface stubs are the declarations contained in a header file and the definitions for the interface found in the source file. One recommendation for the template file is to use the word TYPE where a developer would normally put the C language type. The reason for doing this is that a team may be working with an 8-bit, 16-bit, or 32-bit microcontroller whose registers will vary in size based on the architecture. When the template is used to create real code, the template is copied and then each TYPE is updated to the appropriate architecture bus width.

Each interface designed into the HAL should be documented. In an earlier chapter, we examined how Doxygen can be used to document a header and source file along with how to document functions and declarations. These skills will be essential to properly documenting the HAL. In fact, the example templates that were developed earlier will be directly applied to create the HAL template.

The template is designed to contain common interfaces and documentation but can also contain common code! For example, earlier we examined how to create configuration tables, and since the HAL is designed for common peripheral features, a configuration template file can also be created that contains the default configuration for *any* microcontroller. We can add any other code, such as the ability to read and write GPIO pins, that will not change with the architecture. The ability to leverage code in this manner can be very powerful and allows a developer to create drivers based on the HAL template in a few hours rather than days or weeks.

During the template-development stage, a team should also examine each interface and document all the pre-conditions and post-conditions that are expected for the interface. For example, calling the Dio_Init function on an ARM-based microcontroller before enabling the GPIO clock will result in a failed initialization. Somewhere within the interface template the documentation needs to state that a pre-condition for executing the Dio_Init HAL is that the GPIO peripheral clock has been enabled. A simple problem could occur if the configuration table has not been fully populated. For that reason, another pre-condition would be that the configuration table has a size greater than zero.

The idea of defining pre-conditions and post-conditions is not new to us, since we have already discussed the concept for design-by-contract. In this case, a developer uses Doxygen to document the contract between any user for the interface and what the interface will do for the caller. The assert macro can even be used in the template to ensure that the pre-conditions and post-conditions are adhered to in any subsequent software.

For the GPIO HAL, Figure 7-2 shows an overview of the interface and how it is organized into different files. The HAL contains header and source modules for configuration data that is used to initialize the peripheral on startup and then header and source modules that contain the behavior functions for the HAL.

Dio_config.h
Dio_config.c
Dio.h
Dio.c

Figure 7-2. *GPIO HAL organization*

So far, we have discussed every aspect required to develop our template and application stubs. Let's now examine the documentation for each interface in the GPIO HAL. Listings 7-1 to 7-4 provide the documentation for each HAL GPIO interface. The documentation is detailed and fully self-explanatory, so I leave it up to the reader to examine each figure before catching back up with me in Step #5.

Listing 7-1. Code Listing for Dio_Config.h

```
/** @file dio_cfg.h
 *  @brief This module contains interface definitions for the
 * Dio configuration. This is the header file for the definition of the
 * interface for retrieving the digital input/output configuration table.
 */
#ifndef DIO_H_
#define DIO_H_


/*****************************************************************
 * Includes
 *****************************************************************/


/*****************************************************************
 * Preprocessor Constants
 *****************************************************************/
/**
```

```
 * Defines the number of pins on each processor port.
 */
#define NUMBER_OF_CHANNELS_PER_PORT            8U


/**
 *   Defines the number of ports on the processor.
 */
#define NUMBER_OF_PORTS                 8U


/***********************************************************************
* Typedefs
***********************************************************************/
/**
 * Defines the possible states for a digital output pin.
 */
 typedef enum
 {
    DIO_LOW,                                /** Defines digital state
ground */
    DIO_HIGH,                               /** Defines digital state
power */
    DIO_PIN_STATE_MAX                       /** Defines the maximum
digital state */
 }DioPinState_t;


/**
 * Defines an enumerated list of all the channels (pins) on the MCU
 * device. The last element is used to specify the maximum number of
 * enumerated labels.
 */
typedef enum
{
    /* TODO: Populate this list based on available MCU pins */
    FCPU_HB,               /**< PORT1_0 */
    PORT1_1,               /**< PORT1_1 */
```

```
    PORT1_2,                    /**< PORT1_2 */
    PORT1_3,                    /**< PORT1_3 */
    UHF_SEL,                    /**< PORT1_4 */
    PORT1_5,                    /**< PORT1_5 */
    PORT1_6,                    /**< PORT1_6 */
    PORT1_7,                    /**< PORT1_7 */
    DIO_MAX_PIN_NUMBER     /**< MAX CHANNELS */
}DioChannel_t;

/**
 * Defines the possible DIO pin multiplexing values. The datasheet
 * should be reviewed for proper muxing options.
 */
typedef enum
{
    /* TODO: Populate with possible mode options */
    DIO_MAX_MODE
}DioMode_t;

/**
 * Defines the possible states of the channel pull-ups
 */
typedef enum
{
    DIO_PULLUP_DISABLED,     /*< Used to disable the internal pull-ups */
    DIO_PULLUP_ENABLED,      /*< Used to enable the internal pull-ups */
    DIO_MAX_RESISTOR         /*< Resistor states should be below this value
*/
}DioResistor_t;

/**
 * Defines the digital input/output configuration table's elements that are
used
 * by Dio_Init to configure the Dio peripheral.
 */
```

```c
typedef struct
{
    /* TODO: Add additional members for the MCU peripheral */
    DioChannel_t Channel;           /**< The I/O pin           */
    DioResistor_t Resistor;          /**< ENABLED or DISABLED      */
    DioDirection_t Direction;     /**< OUTPUT or INPUT                */
    DioPinState_t Data;               /**<HIGH or LOW           */
    DioMode_t Function;               /**< Mux Function  - Dio_Peri_Select*/
}DioConfig_t;

/**
 * Defines the slew rate settings available
 */
typedef enum
{
  FAST,       /**< Fast slew rate is configured on the corresponding pin, */
  SLOW       /**< Slow slew rate is configured on the corresponding pin, */
}DioSlew_t;


/***********************************************************************
* Function Prototypes
***********************************************************************/
#ifdef __cplusplus
extern "C"{
#endif

const DioConfig_t * const Dio_ConfigGet(void);

#ifdef __cplusplus
} // extern "C"
#endif

#endif /*DIO_H_*/

/***End of File***************************************************/
```

Listing 7-2. Code Listing for Dio_Config.c

```c
/** @file dio_cfg.c
 *  @brief This module contains the implementation for the digital
 * input/output peripheral configuration
 */
/**********************************************************************
 * Includes
 **********************************************************************/
#include "dio_cfg.h"                    /* For this modules definitions */


/**********************************************************************
 * Module Preprocessor Constants
 **********************************************************************/


/**********************************************************************
 * Module Preprocessor Macros
 **********************************************************************/


/**********************************************************************
 * Module Typedefs
 **********************************************************************/


/**********************************************************************
 * Module Variable Definitions
 **********************************************************************/
/**
 * The following array contains the configuration data for each
 * digital input/output peripheral channel (pin). Each row represents a *
 single pin. Each column is representing a member of the DioConfig_t
 * structure. This table is read in by Dio_Init, where each channel is then
 * set up based on this table.
 */
```

```
const DioConfig_t DioConfig[] =
{
/*                      Resistor                                    Initial      */
/* Channel             Enabled       Direction      Pin            Function      */
/*                                                                               */
{ PORT1_0,             DISABLED,     OUTPUT,        HIGH,          FCN_GPIO      },
{ PORT1_1,             DISABLED,     OUTPUT,        HIGH,          FCN_GPIO      },
{ PORT1_2,             DISABLED,     OUTPUT,        HIGH,          FCN_GPIO      },
{ PORT1_3,             DISABLED,     OUTPUT,        HIGH,          FCN_GPIO      },
{ PORT1_4,             DISABLED,     OUTPUT,        HIGH,          FCN_GPIO      },
{ PORT1_5,             DISABLED,     OUTPUT,        HIGH,          FCN_GPIO      },
{ PORT1_6,             DISABLED,     OUTPUT,        HIGH,          FCN_GPIO      },
{ PORT1_7,             DISABLED,     OUTPUT,        HIGH,          FCN_GPIO      },
};


/****************************************************************
* Function Prototypes
****************************************************************/


/****************************************************************
* Function Definitions
****************************************************************/
/****************************************************************
* Function : Dio_Init()
*//**
* \b Description:
*
* This function is used to initialize the Dio based on the configuration
* table defined in dio_cfg module.
*
* PRE-CONDITION: Configuration table needs to populated (sizeof > 0)
*
* POST-CONDITION: A constant pointer to the first member of the
* configuration table will be returned.
*
```

```
* @return                 A pointer to the configuration table.
*
* \b Example Example:
* @code
* const Dio_ConfigType *DioConfig = Dio_GetConfig();
*
* Dio_Init(DioConfig);
* @endcode
*
* @see Dio_Init
* @see Dio_ChannelRead
* @see Dio_ChannelWrite
* @see Dio_ChannelToggle
* @see Dio_RegisterWrite
* @see Dio_RegisterRead
*
*************************************************************************/
const DioConfig_t * const Dio_ConfigGet(void)
{
/*
* The cast is performed to ensure that the address of the first element
*  of configuration table is returned as a constant pointer and NOT a
* pointer that can be modified.
*/
    return (const *)DioConfig[0];
}

/************** END OF FUNCTIONS ******************************/
```

Listing 7-3. Listing for Dio.h

```
/** @file dio.h
 *   @brief The interface definition for the dio.
 *
 *   This is the header file for the definition of the interface for a digital
 *   input/output peripheral on a standard microcontroller.
 */
```

```c
#ifndef DIO_H_
#define DIO_H_

/*******************************************************************
* Includes
*******************************************************************/
#include <stdint.h>             /* For standard type definitions */
#include "dio_cfg.h"            /* For dio configuration */
#include "constants.h"          /* For HIGH, LOW, etc */


/*******************************************************************
* Preprocessor Constants
*******************************************************************/


/*******************************************************************
* Configuration Constants
*******************************************************************/


/*******************************************************************
* Macros
*******************************************************************/
/*******************************************************************
* Typedefs
*******************************************************************/


/*******************************************************************
* Variables
*******************************************************************/


/*******************************************************************
* Function Prototypes
*******************************************************************/
#ifdef __cplusplus
extern "C"{
#endif
```

```
void Dio_Init(const DioConfig_t * const Config);
DioPinState_t Dio_ChannelRead(DioChannel_t Channel);
void Dio_ChannelWrite(DioChannel_t Channel, DioPinState_t State);
void Dio_ChannelToggle(DioChannel_t Channel);
void Dio_RegisterWrite(uint32_t Address, TYPE Value);
TYPE Dio_RegisterRead(uint32_t Address);
void Dio_CallbackRegister(DioCallback_t Function,
TYPE (*CallbackFunction)(type));


#ifdef __cplusplus
} // extern "C"
#endif


#endif /*DIO_H_*/


/*** End of File **************************************************/
```

Listing 7-4. Listing for Dio.c

```
/** @file dio.c
 *   @brief The implementation for the dio.
 */
/**************************************************************************
* Includes
**************************************************************************/
#include "dio.h"                    /* For this modules definitions */
#include <xxx.h>                        /* For Hardware definitions      */
/**************************************************************************
* Module Preprocessor Constants
**************************************************************************/


/**************************************************************************
* Module Preprocessor Macros
**************************************************************************/
```

```
/********************************************************************
* Module Typedefs
*********************************************************************/
/********************************************************************
* Module Variable Definitions
*********************************************************************/
/**
*  Defines a table of pointers to the peripheral input register on the
* microcontroller.
*/
static TYPE volatile * const DataIn[NUM_PORTS] =
{
        (TYPE*)&REGISTER1, (TYPE*)&REGISTER2,
};


/**
 *  Defines a table of pointers to the peripheral data direction register
on
* the microcontroller.
 */
static TYPE volatile * const DataDirectin[NUM_PORTS] =
{
        (TYPE*)&REGISTER1, (TYPE*)&REGISTER2,
};


/**
 *  Defines a table of pointers to the peripheral latch register on the
 *  microcontroller
 */
static TYPE volatile * const DataOut[NUM_PORTS] =
{
        (TYPE*)&REGISTER1, (TYPE*)&REGISTER2,
};


/**
```

```
 *   Defines a table of pointers to the peripheral resistor enable register
 *   on the microcontroller
 */
static TYPE volatile * const Resistor[NUM_PORTS] =
{
        (TYPE*)&REGISTER1, (TYPE*)&REGISTER2,
};

/**
 *   Defines a table of pointers to the port's function select register
 *   on the microcontroller
 */
static TYPE volatile * const Function[NUM_PORTS] =
{
        (TYPE*)&REGISTER1, (TYPE*)&REGISTER2,
};


/**********************************************************************
* Function Prototypes
**********************************************************************/
/**********************************************************************
* Function Definitions
**********************************************************************/
/**********************************************************************
* Function : Dio_Init()
*//**
* \b Description:
*
* This function is used to initialize the Dio based on the configuration
* table defined in dio_cfg module.
*
* PRE-CONDITION: Configuration table needs to populated (sizeof > 0) <br>
* PRE-CONDITION: NUMBER_OF_CHANNELS_PER_PORT > 0 <br>
* PRE-CONDITION: NUMBER_OF_PORTS > 0 <br>
* PRE-CONDITION: The MCU clocks must be configured and enabled.
*
```

```
* POST-CONDITION: The DIO peripheral is set up with the configuration
* settings.
*
* @param                 Config is a pointer to the configuration table that
*                                 contains the initialization for the
peripheral.
*
* @return                void
*
* \b Example:
* @code
* const DioConfig_t *DioConfig = Dio_ConfigGet();
*
* Dio_Init(DioConfig);
* @endcode
*
* @see Dio_Init
* @see Dio_ChannelRead
* @see Dio_ChannelWrite
* @see Dio_ChannelToggle
* @see Dio_RegisterWrite
* @see Dio_RegisterRead
* @see Dio_CallbackRegister
*
*****************************************************************/
void Dio_Init(const DioConfig_t * Config)
{
        /* TODO: Define implementation */
}


/*****************************************************************
* Function : Dio_ChannelRead()
*//**
* \b Description:
*
```

```
*   This function is used to read the state of a dio channel (pin)
*
* PRE-CONDITION: The channel is configured as INPUT <br>
* PRE-CONDITION: The channel is configured as GPIO <br>
* PRE-CONDITION: The channel is within the maximum DioChannel_t
* definition
*
* POST-CONDITION: The channel state is returned.
*
* @param                  Channel is the DioChannel_t that represents a pin
*
* @return                 The state of the channel as HIGH or LOW
*
* \b Example:
* @code
*    uint8_t pin = Dio_ReadChannel(PORT1_0);
* @endcode
*
* @see Dio_Init
* @see Dio_ChannelRead
* @see Dio_ChannelWrite
* @see Dio_ChannelToggle
* @see Dio_RegisterWrite
* @see Dio_RegisterRead
* @see Dio_CallbackRegister
*
**********************************************************************/
DioPinState_t Dio_ChannelRead(DioChannel_t Channel)
{

}

/**********************************************************************
* Function : Dio_ChannelWrite()
*//**
```

```
* \b Description:
*
*  This function is used to write the state of a channel (pin) as either
* logic high or low through the use of the DioChannel_t enum to select
* the channel and the DioPinState_t to define the desired state.
*
* PRE-CONDITION: The channel is configured as OUTPUT <br>
* PRE-CONDITION: The channel is configured as GPIO <br>
* PRE-CONDITION: The channel is within the maximum DioChannel_t definition
*
* POST-CONDITION: The channel state will be State
*
* @param                 Channel is the pin to write using the DioChannel_t
*                                   enum definition
* @param                 State is HIGH or LOW as defined in the
*                                   DioPinState_t enum
*
* @return                void
*
* \b Example:
* @code
*   Dio_WriteChannel(PORT1_0, LOW);      // Set the PORT1_0 pin low
*   Dio_WriteChannel(PORT1_0, HIGH);     // Set the PORT1_0 pin high
* @endcode
*
* @see Dio_Init
* @see Dio_ChannelRead
* @see Dio_ChannelWrite
* @see Dio_ChannelToggle
* @see Dio_RegisterWrite
* @see Dio_RegisterRead
* @see Dio_CallbackRegister
*
```

```
**********************************************************************/
void Dio_ChannelWrite(DioChannel_t Channel, DioPinState_t State)
{

}

/*********************************************************************
* Function : Dio_ChannelToggle()
*//**
* \b Description:
*
*   This function is used to toggle the current state of a channel (pin).
*
* PRE-CONDITION: The channel is configured as OUTPUT <br>
* PRE-CONDITION: The channel is configured as GPIO <br>
* PRE-CONDITION: The channel is within the maximum DioChannel_t definition
*
* POST-CONDITION:
*
* @param                   Channel is the pin from the DioChannel_t that is
*                                       to be modified.
*
* @return              void
*
* \b Example:
* @code
*     Dio_ChannelToggle(PORTA_1);
* @endcode
*
* @see Dio_Init
* @see Dio_ChannelRead
* @see Dio_ChannelWrite
* @see Dio_ChannelToggle
* @see Dio_RegisterWrite
* @see Dio_RegisterRead
* @see Dio_CallbackRegister
```

```
*
* <br><b> - HISTORY OF CHANGES - </b>
*
******************************************************************/
void Dio_ChannelToggle(DioChannel_t Channel)
{

}
/*************************************************************************
* Function : Dio_RegisterWrite()
*//**
* \b Description:
*
*   This function is used to directly address and modify a Dio register.
* The function should be used to access specialied functionality in the
* Dio peripheral that is not exposed by any other function of the
* interface.
*
* PRE-CONDITION: Address is within the boundaries of the Dio register
* addresss space
*
* POST-CONDITION: The register located at Address with be updated
* with Value
*
* @param                    Address is a register address within the Dio
*                                     peripheral map
* @param                    Value is the value to set the Dio register to
*
* @return           void
*
* \b Example:
* @code
*    Dio_RegisterWrite(0x1000, 0x15);
* @endcode
*
```

```
* @see Dio_Init
* @see Dio_ChannelRead
* @see Dio_ChannelWrite
* @see Dio_ChannelToggle
* @see Dio_RegisterWrite
* @see Dio_RegisterRead
* @see Dio_CallbackRegister
*
*******************************************************************/
void Dio_RegisterWrite(uint32_t Address, TYPE Value)
{

}


/********************************************************************
* Function : Dio_RegisterRead()
*//**
* \b Description:
*
*   This function is used to directly address a Dio register. The function
*   should be used to access specialied functionality in the Dio peripheral
*   that is not exposed by any other function of the interface.
*
* PRE-CONDITION: Address is within the boundaries of the Dio register
* addresss space
*
* POST-CONDITION: The value stored in the register is returned to the
* caller
*
* @param               Address is the address of the Dio register to read
*
* @return              The current value of the Dio register.
*
* \b Example:
* @code
```

```
*       DioValue = Dio_RegisterRead(0x1000);
* @endcode
*
* @see Dio_Init
* @see Dio_ChannelRead
* @see Dio_ChannelWrite
* @see Dio_ChannelToggle
* @see Dio_RegisterWrite
* @see Dio_RegisterRead
* @see Dio_CallbackRegister
*
*
**********************************************************************/
TYPE Dio_RegisterRead(uint32_t Address)
{

}
/**********************************************************************
* Function : Dio_CallbackRegister()
*//**
* \b Description:
*
* This function is used to set the callback functions of the dio driver. By
* default, the callbacks are initialized to a NULL pointer. The driver may
* contain more than one possible callback, so the function will take a
* parameter to configure the specified callback.
*
* PRE-CONDITION: The DioCallback_t has been populated
* PRE-CONDITION: The callback function exists within memory.
*
* POST-CONDITION: The specified callback function will be registered
* with the driver.
*
```

```
* @param       Function is the callback function that will be registered
* @param       CallbackFunction is a function pointer to the desired
*                       function
*
* @return      None.
*
* \b Example:
* @code
*     DioCallback_t Dio_Function = DIO_SAMPLE_COMPLETE;
*
*     Dio_CallbackRegister(Dio_Function, Dio_SampleAverage);
* @endcode
*
* @see Dio_Init
* @see Dio_ChannelRead
* @see Dio_ChannelWrite
* @see Dio_ChannelToggle
* @see Dio_RegisterWrite
* @see Dio_RegisterRead
* @see Dio_CallbackRegister
*
*********************************************************************/
void Dio_CallbackRegister(DioCallback_t Function,
TYPE (*CallbackFunction)(type))
{

}


/************** END OF FUNCTIONS *****************************/
```

Step #5: Implement GPIO HAL for Target Processor

To many developers, Step #5 is the most exciting part for the development process—porting the HAL to a real target. In the following example, the GPIO HAL is implemented for the NXP KL25Z Freedom Board, which contains an ARM Cortex-M microcontroller.

In the examples that follow, I've stripped out the function documentation and focused just on the executable code.

Let's start by examining the pointer arrays. Listing 7-5 shows how the GPIO registers can be organized into similar groupings and mapped to memory. A pointer array is created for each register type within the GPIO peripherals. A pointer to the register is then added to the array, which will later allow the initialization and application code to simply loop through the array to access the register.

Listing 7-5. Pointer Array Memory Map Example for Kinetis-L KL25Z

```
/**
 * Defines a table of pointers to the Port Data Input Register
 */
uint32 volatile * const portsin[NUM_PORTS] =
{
        (uint32*)&GPIOA_PDIR, (uint32*)&GPIOB_PDIR,
};


/**
 * Defines a table of pointers to the port's data-direction register
 */
uint32 volatile * const portsddr[NUM_PORTS] =
{
        (uint32*)&GPIOA_PDDR, (uint32*)&GPIOB_PDDR
};


/**
 * Defines a table of pointers to the Port Data Output Register
 */
uint32 volatile * const ports[NUM_PORTS] =
{
        (uint32*)&GPIOA_PDOR, (uint32*)&GPIOB_PDOR,
};
```

```
/**
 *  Defines a table of pointers to the Port Data Toggle Register
 */
uint32 volatile * const ptoggle[NUM_PORTS] =
{
        (uint32*)&GPIOA_PTOR, (uint32*)&GPIOB_PTOR
};

/**
 *  Defines a table of pointers to the Pin Control Registers
 */
uint32 volatile * const pinctl[NUM_PORTS] =
{
        (uint32*)&PORTA_PCR0, (uint32*)&PORTB_PCR0
};
```

Let's start examining the Dio_Init code, which can be found in Listing 7-6. The initialization is straightforward. A pointer to the configuration table is passed into the interface, and a for loop is used to read each element one row at a time. Based on the information stored in the configuration register, the appropriate register is accessed through the pointer array and the correct bits within the register are set based on the configuration.

Listing 7-6. GPIO Initialization Example for Kinetis-L KL25Z

```
void Dio_Init(const Dio_ConfigType * Config)
{
  uint8 i = 0;                       // Loop counter variable
  uint8 number = 0;                  // Port Number
  uint8 position = 0;                // Pin Number

  // Loop through all pins, set the data register bit and the data-direction
  // register bit according to the dio configuration table values
    for (i = 0; i < NUM_DIGITAL_PINS; i++)
    {
    number   = Config[i].Channel / NUM_PINS_PER_PORT;
    position = Config[i].Channel % NUM_PINS_PER_PORT;
```

194

```
   // Set the Data-Direction register bit for this channel
if (Config[i].Direction == OUTPUT)
{
 *portsddr[number] |= (1UL<<(position));
 }
 else
 {
  *portsddr[number] &=~ (1UL<<(position));
  }

// Set the Data register bit for this channel
if (Config[i].Data == HIGH)
{
*ports[number] |= (1UL<<(position));
}
else
{
*ports[number] &= ~(1UL<<(position));
}
   }
}
```

Once the initialization code is created, the remaining HAL functions are relatively simple to implement. They simply access the pointer array and either set or retrieve register data. For example, the Dio_ChannelRead code, which can be seen in Listing 7-7, reads in the state for the input register, shifts the data, and determines whether the bit is set high or low.

Listing 7-7. GPIO ChannelRead Example for Kinetis-L KL25Z

```
DioPinState_t Dio_ChannelRead(DioChannel_t Channel)
{
   /* Read the port associated with the desired pin */
   DioPinState_t PortState =
      (DioPinState_t)*portsin[Channel/NUM_PINS_PER_PORT];
```

```
    /* Determine the port bit associated with this channel */
  DioPinState_t PinMask =
    (DioPinState_t)(1UL<<(Channel%NUM_PINS_PER_PORT));

    /* Mask the port state with the pin and return the DioPinState */
    return (( PortState & PinMask) ? DIO_HIGH : DIO_LOW);
}
```

The Dio_ChannelWrite function needs to determine which GPIO register to access and then which bits to set in order to set the state for the GPIO pin. This is done through calculating the correct pointer array element to access and then setting the bit within the register that corresponds to the pin. An example can be seen in Listing 7-8.

Listing 7-8. GPIO ChannelWrite Example for Kinetis-L KL25Z

```
void Dio_ChannelWrite(DioChannel_t Channel, DioPinState_t State)
{
    if (State == DIO_HIGH)
    {
      *ports[Channel/NUM_PINS_PER_PORT] |=
                    (1UL<<(Channel%NUM_PINS_PER_PORT));
    }
    else
    {
      *ports[Channel/NUM_PINS_PER_PORT] &=
              ~ (1UL<<(Channel%NUM_PINS_PER_PORT));
    }
}
```

The Dio_ChannelToggle function does the exact same thing as Dio_ChannelWrite except that rather than accessing the output register, the toggle register is used. Listing 7-9 shows the implementation for the toggle function.

Listing 7-9. GPIO ChannelToggle Example for Kinetis-L KL25Z

```
void Dio_ChannelToggle(DioChannel_t Channel)
{
    *ptoggle[Channel/NUM_PINS_PER_PORT] |=
(1UL<<(Channel%NUM_PINS_PER_PORT));
}
```

In earlier chapters, we discussed the need to extend the HAL interface. The extension for the interface is to handle custom peripheral behaviors that are not common to every peripheral on every processor. In these applications, the ability to write to and read from a generic register is very useful. The great part about implementing generic register read and write functions is that once written they can be used repeatedly with only minor modifications needed. The recommendation is that good programming practices are followed by verifying the address and data that you are trying to access. Listings 7-10 and 7-11 show an example of what these functions might look like, excluding the defensive checks.

Listing 7-10. GPIO RegisterWrite Example for Kinetis-L KL25Z

```
void Dio_RegisterWrite(uint32_t Address, TYPE Value)
{
    uint32_t volatile * const RegisterPointer = (uint32_t *) Address;

    *RegisterPointer = Value;
}
```

Listing 7-11. GPIO RegisterRead Example for Kinetis-L KL25Z

```
TYPE Dio_RegisterRead(uint32_t Address)
{
    uint32_t volatile * const RegisterPointer = (uint32_t *) Address;

    return *RegisterPointer;
}
```

Step #6: Test, Test, Test

Setting up and creating test harnesses that can also perform regression testing is beyond the scope of this book. Let's briefly discuss the GPIO peripheral in general and a few tests that should be performed after implementation to ensure that the driver is working as expected.

First, the initialization function is the most complicated function within the HAL interface. The maximum test case number is going to directly depend on the following:

- How many registers are included in the peripheral

- Maximum possible number of states those registers can have

- Maximum combination of states within the registers

In previous chapters, we examined how cyclomatic complexity can serve as an indicator of the minimum number of test cases required to prove that a function behaves as expected. At the lowest driver layers, cyclomatic complexity will not be much help for the configuration code. The registers are really the primary dictator of the number of test cases required. Cyclomatic complexity can only help a developer ensure there are enough test cases to test their driver functions.

The best place to start is at the configuration table. The configuration table lists the primary features of the driver that need to be configured at startup. Manipulating and automating this table and its configuration is the best bet for testing the initialization code.

A developer will want to make sure that they develop at least enough test cases to test all the linearly independent paths within their driver functions as well. Developers may even want to consider getting logic analyzers to directly connect to their boards; the analyzers can then be read through a script to verify that the input and output states on the GPIO pins are correctly controlled. A simple script that uses a UART can also be created that will also read in all the register settings and verify that they match what is expected.

Step #7: Repeat for the Next Peripheral

At this point, the GPIO HAL is designed, templated, and documented, and a test example has even been implemented for the NXP KL25Z. After running through a few basic test cases to verify that the implementation works as expected, a developer is now ready to move on to the next peripheral and begin designing the next HAL. In the next chapter, we will examine the SPI peripheral and how we can design a basic HAL for it using the techniques that we have been discussing in this book.

Going Further

The GPIO peripheral is a foundational module that developers need to take the utmost care when developing to ensure that their software scales. The following are some ideas on how a developer can take the concepts discussed in this chapter and immediately apply them to their own development cycle.

- Identify at least three different microcontrollers that you are currently working with or interested in working with. Collect the GPIO peripheral's datasheets for each microcontroller.

- Review the datasheets in detail and generate a peripheral feature list like the one shown in Table 7-1. How do the results compare? Are they the same or have new peripheral features such as input validation been discovered?

- Review the table and identify the features that belong in a standard HAL interface. Create an initial HAL interface list and identify the input and output features for the interfaces.

- Create a documented template using the skills learned in Chapter 5 on Doxygen and create the GPIO stubs. An alternative to creating the template yourself is to visit `www.beningo.com` and purchase the templates developed by Jacob Beningo.

- Identify the development board that the first port will be performed on. Use the examples in this chapter to fill in the implementation for the target. If the reader is interested in a working example that can be used for educational purposes, examples for the NXP KL25Z development board are available on `www.beningo.com` under Insights ➤ Toolkits.

- Develop basic test cases based on the configuration table and HAL input and output features. Verify that the ported code behaves as expected.

- Consider developing test-case document templates that will be used to test ported GPIO code.

- Investigate how regression testing could be used to automatically verify that the HAL is working as expected. Inject an error into the code and verify that the regression testing is able to catch the issue.

CHAPTER 8

HAL Design for SPI

"No sensible decision can be made any longer without taking into account not only the world as it is, but the world as it will be."

—Isaac Asimov

An Overview of SPI Peripherals

The Serial Peripheral Interface bus (SPI) is a high-speed serial bus that is commonly used to interface with external memory, sensors, and many other devices. The SPI bus at the hardware level requires the following:

- a Master Output Slave Input (MOSI) line

- a Master Input Slave Output line (MISO) line

- a clock (CLK) line

- at least a single slave select (SS) line

Every slave device that communicates with the master, typically the microcontroller, has a slave select line that asserts which slave device is being communicated with. The SPI bus can support as many slave devices as there are GPIO pins available to communicate with them. The fact that a slave select pin is required for every device is one disadvantage to using the SPI peripheral.

There are many advantages though. First, SPI is a very simple serial interface. For every clock pulse, a master output bit and a slave output bit are clocked out simultaneously on the bus. This behavior makes it so that bi-directional communication can occur very quickly. Second, the SPI bus typically can communicate at 1 Mbps to 16 Mbps, which makes it an extremely fast communication channel. There are many other advantages to using the SPI bus, but the last one that I will mention is that the SPI peripheral is very easy to set up and use.

201

© Jacob Beningo 2017
J. Beningo, *Reusable Firmware Development*, https://doi.org/10.1007/978-1-4842-3297-2_8

Figure 8-1 shows an example of how slave devices would be connected to a microcontroller using the SPI bus. As you can see, the more slave devices there are, the more GPIO pins that are required for the slave select.

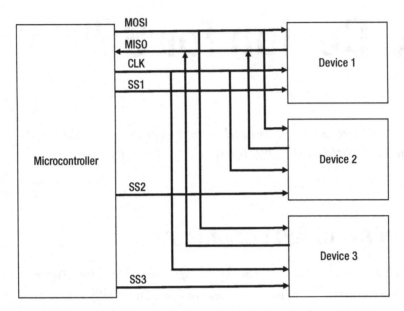

Figure 8-1. *Example SPI hardware architecture*

Step #1: Review the SPI Peripheral Datasheet

Just as we discussed before, a developer should gather several different microcontroller datasheets in order to perform a comparison between the different peripherals' capabilities. In the previous chapter, we created a simple feature-comparison table for the GPIO peripheral, and this is exactly what we will do again for the SPI peripheral. Since the SPI peripheral adheres to a strict standard, there will be far fewer differences in feature sets than with GPIO.

During the initial datasheet review, developers should be attempting to get a general feel for how the peripherals work and their general capabilities. The lower-level details, such as the register mappings, are examined closely during the feature-identification step. Most microcontroller datasheets contain thousands of pages of technical details. In this step, just finding the right datasheet and identifying the correct pages and sections in those manuals will prepare the developer for the real work that follows.

Step #2: SPI Peripheral Features

My personal preference is to always visualize data. I completely agree with the old saying, "A picture is worth a thousand words". Developers that are pulling together a comparison can do so using a simple feature matrix. Using the same microcontrollers as we discussed in the last chapter results in a table like Table 8-1.

Table 8-1. *SPI Feature Comparison*

Feature	NXP KL25Z[1]	STM32F4[2]	PIC24F[3]	PIC18F[4]
Master/Slave	X	X	X	X
Tx/Rx	X	X	X	X
Wait mode	X	X		
Bi-directional	X	X		
High-speed dual output	X	X		
MSB/LSB	X	X	X	X
DMA	X	X		
CRC		X		

The table can be used by developers to quickly determine the common and uncommon features in the peripheral that later either will be placed into the HAL or will require a HAL extension. When the reader walks through their own SPI peripherals, they may find that they have significantly more features available than I've listed. The goal here is to provide an example and leave some work to the reader.

---

[1]NXP KL25Z Sub-Family Reference Manual
[2]ST Microelectronics STM32F427xx Datasheet
[3]Microchip PIC24FJ128GA010 Family Datasheet
[4]Microchip PIC18F2455 Datasheet

Step #3: Design and Create the SPI HAL Interface

Just as we did before, the next step is to create the SPI HAL interface. Table 8-1 provides a developer with some functional details that the HAL is going to need to exhibit in order to give the application developer enough control over the hardware. What's interesting about most SPI peripherals is that most of the features can simply be controlled by the way we initialize the peripheral. The interface itself only requires a few very simple functions. For SPI, the required interfaces will be the following:

- Initialization

- Data transmit and receive

- Low-level register access

- Callbacks

You will notice a similarity between these interface needs and the GPIO. The only difference is that instead of an Input/Output feature there is a Data Transmit and Receive, which could still be considered Input/Output. Most peripherals will have a very similar outline for their interface.

A developer will want to decide what the major inputs and outputs required to configure and run the SPI bus are and decide on the operations that need to be performed on the bus. The operations go in the interface, and the inputs and outputs will be used by the operations in some way. For example, a configuration table that is used to initialize the SPI peripheral will contain all the data required to set up the peripheral and will be passed into the Spi_Init function.

The resulting interface for the SPI HAL would look something along the lines of Figure 8-2. Notice how the interface follows a very similar pattern to the GPIO HAL and that it is easily readable and extendable.

```
void Spi_Init(SpiConfig_t const * const Config);
void Spi_Transfer(SpiTransfer_t const * const Config);
void Spi_RegisterWrite(uint32_t const Address,
                       uint32_t const Value);
uint32_t Spi_RegisterRead(uint32_t const Address);
void Spi_CallbackRegister(SpiCallback_t const Function,
                          TYPE (*CallbackFunction)(type));
```

Figure 8-2. *SPI HAL interface*

Step #4: Create SPI Stubs and Documentation Templates

Once again, get out your template-making hat! It's time to create the documentation and the function stubs that will be used for the SPI HAL. When the stubs and documentation are complete, don't forget to save these templates. They represent the stand-alone SPI interface without any implementation details in the modules. It's always a good idea to save a clean template, and then if specific design patterns will be implemented behind the scenes, save those separately.

CASE STUDY—DESIGN PATTERNS AND TEMPLATES

Design patterns are a solution to a common problem that exists in software engineering. There are many different design patterns, such as using a circular buffer for receiving UART data.

As you develop your own interfaces, drivers, and application code, keep an eye open for repeating patterns. These patterns should be captured and saved into a template so that they can be reapplied to future applications.

For example, transmitting and receiving data on the SPI bus will use a design pattern for how the HAL is designed, but a design pattern can also be used also behind the scenes in the implementation,. Design patterns save time by avoiding your having to reinvent the wheel. Instead, a better wheel can be made.

The SPI HAL will require several files in order to contain all the operations necessary to communicate with an external device on the SPI bus. The modules that are necessary can be found in Figure 8-3.

```
spi_config.h
spi_config.c
spi.h
spi.c
```

Figure 8-3. *SPI HAL module files*

Once each file has been created, the generic Doxygen template can be used to fill in the modules. A quick pass through to update for SPI would then be necessary. There are several functions that will need to be added to the modules. In order to save the reader time and effort, Listings 8-1 and 8-2 show an example of what is needed. Don't forget that each function should have its inputs and outputs documented as well as provide a detailed example of how to use the interface. It also wouldn't hurt to set up the assertions at this point to validate the preconditions and post-conditions.

Listing 8-1. SPI Init Function Template

```
/*****************************************************************
* Function : Spi_Init()
*//**
* \b Description:
*
* This function is used to initialize the Spi based on the configuration
table
*   defined in spi_cfg module.
*
* PRE-CONDITION: Configuration table needs to populated (sizeof > 0)
* PRE-CONDITION: The MCU clocks must be configured and enabled.
*
* POST-CONDITION: The peripheral is set up with the configuration
*
```

```
* @param[in] Config is a pointer to the configuration table that contains
*                         the initialization for the peripheral.
*
* @return           void
*
* \b Example:
* @code
*       const SpiConfig_t *SpiConfig = Spi_ConfigGet();
*
*       Spi_Init(SpiConfig);
* @endcode
*
* @see Spi_ConfigGet
* @see Spi_Init
* @see Spi_Transfer
* @see Spi_RegisterWrite
* @see Spi_RegisterRead
* @see Spi_CallbackRegister
*
**************************************************************/
void Spi_Init(SpiConfig_t const * const Config)
{

}
```

Listing 8-2. SPI Transfer Function Template

```
/*********************************************************************
* Function : Spi_Transfer()
*//**
* \b Description:
*
* This function is used to initialize a data transfer on the SPI bus.
*
```

```
* PRE-CONDITION: Spi_Init must be called with valid configuration data
* PRE-CONDITION: SpiTransfer_t must be configured for the device
* PRE-CONDITION: The MCU clocks must be configured and enabled.
*
* POST-CONDITION: Data transferred based on configuration
*
* @param[in]      Config is a configured structure describing the data
*                 transfer that occurs.
*
* @return         void
*
* \b Example:
* @code
*        const SpiConfig_t *SpiConfig = Spi_ConfigGet();
*
*        Spi_Init(SpiConfig);
*            Spi_Transfer(AccelerometerConfig);
*
* @endcode
*
* @see Spi_ConfigGet
* @see Spi_Init
* @see Spi_Transfer
* @see Spi_RegisterWrite
* @see Spi_RegisterRead
* @see Spi_CallbackRegister
*
*********************************************************************/
void Spi_Transfer(SpiTransfer_t const * const  Config)
{

}
```

In order to save the reader time and also muscle fatigue from having to carry around a giant and heavy book, the templates for the helper functions and the common RegisterRead, RegisterWrite, and callback functions have been left out. They are included in the example templates that go with this book. If needed, refer to Chapter 7 on GPIO Hals and review how these function stubs are set up. The only difference between the SPI and DIO setups is that the functions are preceded with Spi instead of Dio.

Step #5: Implement SPI HAL for Target Processor

At this point, a template for the HAL is ready to go. There are several different ways the implementation can be done, which we discussed earlier in the book. My personal favorite is to use pointer arrays to map memory. This technique is very portable and can very quickly be adapted for nearly any microcontroller. For this reason, I'll show an example how I implement SPI using this technique.

In the following example, the SPI HAL is implemented for the NXP KL25Z Freedom Board, which contains an ARM Cortex-M microcontroller. I've stripped out the function documentation and focused just on the executable code since we have already examined the documentation that should precede these functions.

Let's start by examining the pointer arrays. Listing 8-3 shows how the SPI registers can be organized into similar groupings and mapped to memory. A pointer array is created for each register type within the SPI peripherals. A pointer to the register is then added to the array, which will later allow the initialization and application code to simply loop through the array to access the register.

Each microcontroller will have different registers and register types. In this example, only a few registers are shown to demonstrate the general flow of how a developer would implement their driver.

Listing 8-3. Example SPI Pointer-Array Mapping

```
/**
 *  Defines a pointer table to the spi control 0 registers.
 */
uint8_t volatile * const spicon1[NUM_SPI_CHANNELS] =
{
        (uint8_t*)&SPI0_C1, (uint8_t*)&SPI1_C1
};
```

```
/**
 * Defines a pointer table to the spi control 1 registers.
 */
uint8_t volatile * const spicon2[NUM_SPI_CHANNELS] =
{
        (uint8_t*)&SPI0_C2, (uint8_t*)&SPI1_C2
};


/**
 * Defines a pointer table to the spi status registers.
 */
uint8_t volatile * const spistat[NUM_SPI_CHANNELS] =
{
        (uint8_t*)&SPI0_S, (uint8_t*)&SPI1_S
};


/**
 * Defines a pointer table to the spi bit-rate control registers.
 */
uint8_t volatile * const spibr[NUM_SPI_CHANNELS] =
{
        (uint8_t*)&SPI0_BR, (uint8_t*)&SPI1_BR
};
```

Just like before, setting up these pointers is a great way to access memory and set up initialization functions that easily loop through a configuration table and then set the bit values in the registers. An example initialization function can be found in Listing 8-4.

Listing 8-4. Example SPI Initialization Function

```
void Spi_Init(Spi_ConfigType const * const Config)
{
    uint8_t Index = 0;          // Loop index variable

    for(Index=0; Index < NUM_SPI_CHANNELS; Index++)
    {
            if(Config[Index].SpiEnable == ENABLED)
```

```
{
            // Enable clock gate for spi channel
            *spigate |= spipins[Index];

            // Disable the SPI channel
            *spicon1[Index] &= ~REGBIT6;

    // Set the MASTER/SLAVE mode
    if(Config[Index].MasterMode == MASTER)
    {
            *spicon1[Index] |= REGBIT4;
    }
    else
    {
            *spicon1[Index] &= ~REGBIT4;
    }

    // Set SPI clock frequency
    Spi_SetBaud(Config[Index]);

    // Set Wait mode
    if(Config[Index].WaitMode == DISABLED)
    {
            *spicon2[Index] |= REGBIT1;
    }
    else
    {
            *spicon2[Index] &= ~REGBIT1;
    }

    // Set Bidirectional mode
    if(Config[Index].Bidirection == ENABLED)
    {
            *spicon2[Index] |= REGBIT0 + REGBIT3;
    }
```

```
                    else
                    {
                            *spicon2[Index] &= ~(REGBIT0 + REGBIT3);
                    }

                    // Set slave select mode
                    Spi_SetSS(Config[Index]);

                    // Calculate transfer delay using clock frequency
                    Spi_CalcDelay(Config[Index]);

                    // Re-enable the SPI channel
                    *spicon1[Index] |= REGBIT6;
            }
        }
}
```

In order to save space, the configuration structure is not shown, but from reviewing the initialization function, you can easily see the information that is being stored there.

The SPI bus is a unique communication interface in that it receives data while it transmits data. This makes the SPI bus very efficient. We can use the transmit buffer to store the receive data, which limits how much RAM we need to allocate to communicate with slave devices.

Creating a robust Spi_Transfer function isn't trivial or something that should be attempted without first thinking through the design and process. The SPI bus, while simple, does require that certain steps be followed in order to successfully handle all the possible cases. Figure 8-4 shows the steps the driver must go through to transfer data. In many cases, each step can be placed into a separate helper function to keep the code readable and maintainable. The function overhead will slightly affect the performance unless the functions are in-lined.

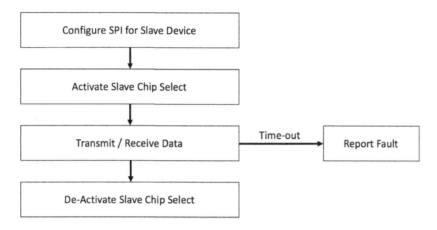

Figure 8-4. SPI Transfer Function Flow Chart

The flow chart looks simple, but there is an important consideration that developers need to look at that I often see overlooked. If something goes wrong, the driver needs to be able to detect that the communication timed out. Most drivers I review assume that everything will always work as expected and end up hanging up because a device at some point fails to respond or something happens that prevents the "transmission complete" flag from being set. Make sure that you think through the potential failure points and how the higher-level application will be notified that a device is not responding.

The Spi_Transfer implementation can be found in Listing 8-5.

Listing 8-5. Example Spi_Transfer Function

```
void Spi_Transfer(const Spi_TransferType * const Config)
{
        uint16_t i = 0;
        uint16_t j = 0;
        uint32_t x = 0;

        // Setup the spi registers with the spi device settings
        Spi_Setup(Config);

        // Initialize the chip select
        Spi_SetCs(Config);
```

```
/**************************************************************
* Transmit (and receive) the data one byte at a time.
**************************************************************/
for(i = 0; i < Config->NumBytes; i++)
{
/**************************************************************
* Check the shift direction. If it is LSBit first, reverse the order
* in which we transmit each byte (last byte first) as well.
**************************************************************/
if (Config->Direction == LSB_FIRST)
{
        j = Config->NumBytes - i - 1;
}
else
{
        j=i;
}

  Mcu_TimeoutStart(INTERVAL_10MS);

  // Check transmit buffer empty flag
  while(*spistat[Config->SpiChannel] & REGBIT5 == 0)
  {
     if(Mcu_TimeoutCheck() == 1)
     {
        Fault_StateSet(FAULT_SPI_TXFLAG);

        break;
     }
  }

  *spibuf[Config->SpiChannel] = (*(Config->TxRxData + j));

  for(x = 0; x < TransferDelay[Config->SpiChannel]; x++);

  Mcu_TimeoutStart(INTERVAL_10MS);
```

```
while(*spistat[Config->SpiChannel] & REGBIT7 == 0)
{
    if(Mcu_TimeoutCheck() == 1)
    {
        Fault_StateSet(FAULT_SPI_RECEIVE);

        break;
    }

}

*(Config->TxRxData + j) = *spibuf[Config->SpiChannel];

} // End for


/****************************************************************
 * Latch the data into the slave by de-selecting the chip select.
 ****************************************************************/
// In some cases the chip select will de-select the device
// before the last bit is transmitted.  This is due to the flag
// options of this peripheral.  In order to transmit properly, a
// slight delay is included before deselection.
for(x = 0; x < TransferDelay[Config->SpiChannel]; x++);

    Spi_ClearCs(Config);
}
```

Step #6: Test, Test, Test

It is very easy for development teams to overlook having a robust and automated test system. The time and effort required to create such a system can potentially be daunting, especially for small- to medium-size businesses. Don't let that discourage you from developing an automated test harness. The time and cost investment decreases the overall software life costs with the ability to easily verify that changes and updates haven't broken code.

Take the time to implement a test harness at this early development stage and reap the rewards for the entire development cycle.

Step #7: Repeat for the Next Peripheral

At this point, a developer would continue to follow this process and develop a HAL for every microcontroller peripheral. This would include peripherals such as analog-to-digital converters, pulse-width modulators, UARTs, SPI buses, and so on. Since the process remains very similar for each peripheral, we will now explore how we can take the HAL that we have already started to create and build higher-level APIs that use the HALs to perform a more abstract function.

In the next chapter, we will develop a HAL for EEPROM and memory devices that can be used to access both internal and external devices. If you are still interested in seeing how the HAL might look for other peripherals, "API Standard for MCUs" includes a full API listing along with templates. It can be found at `www.beningo.com`.

Going Further

The SPI peripheral is a foundational module that developers need to take the utmost care developing to ensure that their software scales. The following are some ideas on how a developer can take the concepts discussed in this chapter and immediately apply them to their own development cycle.

- Identify at least three different microcontrollers that you are currently working with or are interested in working with. Collect the SPI peripheral datasheets for each microcontroller.

- Review the datasheets in detail and generate a peripheral feature list like the one shown in Table 8-1. How do the results compare? Are they the same or do they have new peripheral features beyond what we discussed in this chapter?

- Review the table and identify the features that belong in a standard HAL interface. Create an initial HAL interface list and identify the input and output features for the interfaces

- Create a document template using the skills learned in Chapter 5 on Doxygen and create the SPI stubs. An alternative to creating the template yourself is to visit www.beningo.com and purchase the templates developed by Jacob Beningo.

- Identify the development board that the first port will be performed on. Use the examples in this chapter to fill in the implementation for the target. If the reader is interested in a working example that can be used for educational purposes, examples for the NXP KL25Z development board are available on www.beningo.com.

- Develop basic test cases based on the configuration table and HAL input and output features. Verify that the ported code behaves as expected.

- Consider developing test-case document templates that will be used to test ported SPI code.

- Create automated test cases that can be executed daily to verify that the HAL is working as expected. Don't forget to inject errors to verify that the regression tests are correct.

CHAPTER 9

HAL Design for EEPROM and Memory Devices

"Before software can be reusable, it must first be usable."

—Ralph Johnson

An Overview of Memory Devices

Nearly every embedded system requires non-volatile data storage in one form or another. Whether a developer needs to store a simple system state or a complex set of calibration data, there are several potential non-volatile storage devices that are available, such as the following:

- Internal flash

- Internal EEPROM

- External EEPROM

- Externa flash

Using internal flash and EEPROM devices can be useful when you want to limit external devices, product size, complexity, and cost. There can be several potential issues with using internal memory storage, however. First, internal flash and EEPROM devices tend to be more complex to set up and use than external devices. Developers must grapple with setting internal clocks perfectly to ensure that the internal memory devices are not damaged. Second, application code is stored either in or near the

© Jacob Beningo 2017
J. Beningo, *Reusable Firmware Development*, https://doi.org/10.1007/978-1-4842-3297-2_9

internal memory devices. Manipulating these devices during runtime in a production system could result in something going wrong and the application code or calibration information being removed from the system.

Throughout my career, I've never had any issues using internal flash and EEPROM devices. Every time that I have used one though it has required extra upfront care to make sure that the implementation was correct. When using internal flash, there are several additional issues that need to be addressed, as follows:

- How is the internal flash controller affected by a brownout event? (I've seen the entire flash get erased in this situation when it was enabled to erase/write)

- What is the maximum number of erase/write cycles? (Internal memory is usually less than an external device)

- Does a circular buffer-type implementation need to be created in order to minimize wear and tear on the flash?

- How much drift will there be in the clock at various voltages and temperature ranges? Is it enough to cause an erase or write cycle to fail?

The worst-case analysis on what can go wrong always seems to bring up more potential issues than if you were using an external device. This doesn't mean that developers should avoid internal memory but simply that they need to be careful with how they implement it.

In this section, we are going to develop a hardware abstraction layer that can be used to govern both internal and external memory devices, with our primary focus being on external EEPROM devices. The nice thing about the HAL is that it abstracts out these devices so that the underlying details are completely hidden. The device could be an internal or external device, on a SPI or I2C bus, or even be for different memories, such as EEPROM, Flash, or some other architecture. A properly designed HAL doesn't care about the underlying implementation or architecture, which means that if we do our job right, we can design an interface for memory devices once and use it for any memory device in any project indefinitely.

Just as we did in the last several chapters, we will continue to follow our simple seven-step process to design our memory HAL. In this case, we are going to focus primarily on external EEPROM devices, but the HAL can easily be used with any memory device on nearly any interface, as we mentioned before.

Step #1: Review the EEPROM Peripheral Datasheet

Before a developer can start to design their HAL for memory devices, they need to review the datasheets for several devices and determine what the common and uncommon features are. If you take a moment to hop on Digikey.com, Mouser.com, or whatever your favorite electronic part supplier is, you will notice that there are hundreds of potential memory devices that are available, ranging in memory capabilities and interfaces. At this first glance, it may seem slightly overwhelming how any developer could create a standard interface that covers all those devices, let alone a subset. Don't be discouraged! It turns out that all memory devices have very similar capabilities and that the major difference is interface and size. In fact, all these memory devices are managed by a JEDEC standard, which not only makes the interface we will develop easy, but even makes the underlying code reusable.

At this point, the goal is not to dig into any technical details but rather to identify several different devices that the HAL will be based on. Select a few devices from manufacturers that you are comfortable with and download the datasheets for a closer and more detailed review. In this chapter, I'm going to examine the following memory devices:

- Microchip 25AA160D, 16 kb EEPROM[1]

- Microchip 25AA1024, 1 Mb EEPROM[2]

- Rohm BR25L640-W, 64 kb EEPROM[3]

- STMicroelectronics M95512-DR, 512 kB EEPROM[4]

- ONSemi CAT25128, 128 kb EEPROM[5]

---

[1]Microchip 25AA160D, 16 kb EEPROM, https://www.digikey.com/product-detail/en/ microchip-technology/25AA160D-I-ST/25AA160D-I-ST-ND/2125495

[2]Microchip 25AA1024, https://www.digikey.com/product-detail/en/ microchip-technology/25AA1024T-I-SM/25AA1024T-I-SMTR-ND/1228443

[3]Rohm BR25L640-W, 64 kb EEPROM

[4]STMicroelectronics M95512-DR, 512 kB EEPROM, https://www.digikey.com/product-detail/ en/stmicroelectronics/M95512-DRDW3TP-K/497-14457-1-ND/4729165

[5]ONSemi CAT25128, 128 kb EEPROM, https://www.digikey.com/product-detail/en/ on-semiconductor/CAT25128VI-GT3/CAT25128VI-GT3OSTR-ND/2063309

These devices provide a basic sampling that we can use to develop our HAL, but nearly any device could be selected.

CASE STUDY—MEMORY DÉJÀ VU

I was creating a driver for another external memory device when I started to get the feeling that I had written the exact same code before. The memory device that I was working with was completely different from the one we had used on the last project, yet I kept getting a feeling of déjà vu.

Finally, I couldn't take it any longer and went back to review the code from the previous project. Sure enough, despite being a completely different memory device, the basic commands were identical! Further investigation revealed that there was a standard that the devices were following.

The moral of the story is that we need to always be on the lookout for repeating patterns in the work that we do and leverage anything that already exists that we can. After this realization, I created a reusable interface that I still use to this day.

Step #2: EEPROM Peripheral Features

Once the datasheets have been gathered and a developer has had a chance to peruse them briefly, it is time to dig into the details and start comparing the different devices. Just as before, the easiest way to compare the different features is to create a basic spreadsheet and list each device and feature on the axes and then place a checkmark where a feature is present on the device. Table 9-1 shows a basic summary of the features that I found in the devices I mentioned previously.

Table 9-1. *EEPROM Device Feature Comparison*

Feature	Microchip 25AA160D	Microchip 25AA1024	Rohm BR25L640-W	STM M95512-DR
Write Enable	X	X	X	X
Write Disable	X	X	X	X
Write	X	X	X	X
Read	X	X	X	X
Read Status	X	X	X	X
Write Status	X	X	X	X
Page Erase		X		
Sector Erase		X		
Power Down		X		
Read ID				X
Write ID				X
Lock Status				X

The JEDEC standard can be easily seen in Table 9-1. These are the features that are supported by every device, such as the Write Enable and Disable features. Just like with a microcontroller peripheral, many memory manufacturers will include the JEDEC standard features but also attempt to differentiate themselves by adding additional features that developers might find useful. For example, the Microchip 25AA1024 includes a Page Erase feature, which would typically be present in a flash controller rather than an EEPROM controller. The feature gives developers an easy method for quickly erasing large amounts of data. Such a feature could be very useful but also very dangerous if not properly used and protected in source code.

Step #3: Design and Create the EEPROM HAL Interface

Once again, Table 9-1 is our guide for creating the features and functions that we need in our HAL. The functions we create to control our memory devices should be looked at as operations to perform on data. The memory locations are the data, and the operations might be things such as the following:

- Initialization

- Writing data

- Reading data

- Writing and reading the status register

Creating a HAL for EEPROM is just like any other peripheral except in this example we are not going to include a callback function. A callback might exist if the EEPROM or memory device is internal to the microcontroller. In this example though, the EEPROM device is external to the microcontroller, which does not have any way to trigger an internal interrupt on the microcontroller. For this reason, a callback is not included. If a developer wanted to create an all-encompassing HAL that covered both internal and external devices, they could include the callback and then just populate the code depending on the circumstances.

An interface example can be seen in Figure 9-1. Notice that this HAL still follows the standard pattern we have seen with microcontroller peripherals. There is still an initialization function, a read/write function, and then register-access functions. The primary difference here is that we have added an additional `WriteStateSet` function that is used to control the write state of the memory. This easily could have been pulled into the `RegisterWrite` capability, but in this example we want to explicitly create it in the interface so that application users see that there may be extra steps necessary to work with the memory device. If that detail were abstracted into the general `RegisterWrite` capability, it might be easily overlooked. How a developer chooses to handle these types of issues is dependent on their needs and preferences. There is *not* a right or wrong answer.

```
void Eeprom_Init(const EepromConfig_t * Config);
void Eeprom_Read(uint8_t * Dest, uint32_t Src, uint8_t Size);
void Eeprom_Write(uint32_t Dest, uint8_t * Src, uint8_t Size);
void Eeprom_WriteStateSet(EepromWriteState_t State);
void Eeprom_RegisterWrite(EepromRegister_t Register,
                          uint8_t Value);
uint8_t Eeprom_RegisterRead(EepromRegister_t Register);
```

Figure 9-1. Example EEPROM HAL interface

The HAL for the memory interface doesn't look too bad. It could be much worse. The first HAL version I created originally had more than a dozen different interfaces! I had created the following:

- StatusRegisterWriteEnable

- StatusRegisterWriteDisable

- DataWriteEnable

- DataWriteDisable

Then, I had even extended the interface in the original HAL to include custom features, such as the following:

- EraseChip

- EraseSector

- ErasePage

- PowerDown

- ReadID

The result was a HAL that had more than a dozen functions and was very difficult to navigate and understand. In time, as I realized that the interface was too large, I refactored the HAL so that it represented a much smaller and more manageable function set. Everything related to custom features is now extended into a separate module that is specific to the device, including all the erase functionality, identification, and energy-savings modes. The main HAL was also refactored into the final version, shown in Figure 9-1.

The HAL does include some custom datatypes. The primary HAL includes an EepromWriteState_t. This allowed the original WriteEnable and WriteDisable functions to be refactored from two separate functions to a single function that is controlled by its parameters. The control is created by declaring a typedef enum with the possible states, as shown in Figure 9-2.

```
typedef enum
{
   EEPROM_DISABLE,
   EEPROM_ENABLE,
   EEPROM_MAX_STATE
}EepromWriteState_t;
```

Figure 9-2. *EEPROM write state enumeration*

Developers also will need to consider the different registers that can be accessed through the interface and will make up the EepromRegister_t. In general, this won't be done until the coding stage simply because the registers available will vary from one part to the next. Just for fun though, we will get ahead of ourselves and show an example of what the EepromRegister_t might look like in Figure 9-3.

```
typedef enum
{
   EEPROM_STATUS_REG,
   EEPROM_PWR_REG,
   EEPROM_MAX_REG
}EepromRegister_t;
```

Figure 9-3. *Example EepromRegister_t definition*

At this point, the base HAL is in place and we are ready to start building the documentation and software stubs.

Step #4: Create EEPROM Stubs and Documentation Templates

It is now time to build out the documentation templates and empty function stubs that will be used to create the EEPROM HAL. At this point, the reader has gone through this process several times and probably doesn't need to see an example stub for every EEPROM function. For this reason, we will focus on providing an example stub for just the following functions:

- `Eeprom_Init`

- `Eeprom_Write`

- `Eeprom_Read`

The remaining documentation requirements will be very similar to what we have already seen in previous chapters.

The first function to document is the `Eeprom_Init` function. `Eeprom_Init` is just like every other initialization function that we have seen so far in this book except for one crucial fact: the `EepromConfig_t` needs to contain a member that tells the driver what communication port is being used to interact with the EEPROM device. EEPROM could be internal to the microcontroller or on an I2C bus, SPI bus, or some other yet to be invented interface. My earliest HAL implementations required an `SpiTransfer_t` or `I2cTransfer_t` to be passed into the initialization function. That version required two different HAL sets to be maintained, and, over time, they were refactored into a single function that abstracts the communication interface into a configuration parameter.

When the documentation template is created, it is important not to forget about determining the pre-conditions and post-conditions that are required in order for the operation that will take place to be successful. In the chapter on Doxygen, we discussed in detail what developers should be including in their documentation along with example templates. Listing 9-1 through Listing 9-3 show how to create the documentation stubs for the EEPROM HAL. Don't forget that there would be other functions along with additional source and header documentation.

Listing 9-1. Example EEPROM Init HAL Documentation

```
/************************************************************************
* Function : Eeprom_Init()
*//**
* \b Description:
*
* This function is used to initialize the eeprom. There are several
* operations that this function performs. First, it configures the
* communication channel that is used to interface with the EEPROM.
* Second, it enables write protection and disables the HOLD hardware
* feature.
*
* PRE-CONDITION: Dio driver initialized
* PRE-CONDITION: Communication driver initialized
*
* POST-CONDITION: The EEPROM device is initialized and write
* protected.
*
* @param      Config is a pointer to a CommBus_t that contains the
* communication bus configuration information for interfacing to the
* EEPROM.
*
* @return     void
*
* \b Example:
* @code
*    const DioConfig_t *DioConfig = Dio_ConfigGet();
*    const SpiConfig_t *SpiConfig = Spi_ConfigGet();
*    const EepromConfig_t *EepromConfig = Eeprom_ConfigGet();
*
*    Dio_Init(DioConfig);
*    Spi_Init(SpiConfig);
*    Eeprom_Init(EepromConfig);
* @endcode
*
```

```
* @see Eeprom_ConfigGet
* @see Eeprom_Init
* @see Eeprom_Read
* @see Eeprom_Write
* @see Eeprom_RegisterWrite
* @see Eeprom_RegisterRead
**********************************************************************/
void Eeprom_Init(const EepromConfig_t * Config)
{
        // Initialization code goes here!
}
```

Listing 9-2. Example EEPROM Read HAL Documentation

```
/*********************************************************************
* Function : Eeprom_Read()
*//**
* \b Description:
*
* This function is used to initialize the eeprom. It currents enables write
* protection and disables the HOLD hardware feature.
*
* PRE-CONDITION: Dio driver initialized
* PRE-CONDITION: Spi driver initialized
* PRE-CONDITION: Eep_Init called
*
* POST-CONDITION: Size bytes are read from location Src into Dest.
*
* @param  Dest - pointer to the location where data will be stored.
* @param  Src  - the starting address that is to be read
* @param  Size - the number of bytes that are going to be read.
*
* @return      void
*
* \b Example:
* @code
```

```
*    const DioConfig_t *DioConfig = Dio_ConfigGet();
*    const SpiConfig_t *SpiConfig = Spi_ConfigGet();
*    const EepromConfig_t *EepromConfig = Eeprom_ConfigGet();
*
*    Dio_Init(DioConfig);
*    Spi_Init(SpiConfig);
*    Eeprom_Init(EepromConfig);
*    Eeprom_Read(Buffer, 0x0, 8);
* @endcode
*
* @see Eeprom_ConfigGet
* @see Eeprom_Init
* @see Eeprom_Read
* @see Eeprom_Write
* @see Eeprom_RegisterWrite
* @see Eeprom_RegisterRead
**************************************************************************/
void Eeprom_Read(uint8_t *Dest, uint32_t Src, uint32_t Size)
{
        // Enter Read code here!
}
```

Listing 9-3. Example EEPROM Write HAL Documentation

```
/**********************************************************************
* Function : Eeprom_Write()
*//**
* \b Description:
*
* This function is used to write data to the eeprom device. There is a
limit
* of being able to only write 256 bytes of data to the eeprom at a time!
*
* PRE-CONDITION: Dio driver initialized
* PRE-CONDITION: Spi driver initialized
* PRE-CONDITION: Eep_Init called
```

```
 *
 * POST-CONDITION: Size bytes are written from location Src into Dest.
 *
 * @param  Dest - Address where the data will be stored in eeprom.
 * @param  Src  - pointer to the data to be stored
 * @param  Size - the size of the data that is going to be written.
 *
 * @return     void
 *
 * \b Example:
 * @code
 *   const DioConfig_t *DioConfig = Dio_ConfigGet();
 *   const SpiConfig_t *SpiConfig = Spi_ConfigGet();
 *   const EepromConfig_t *EepromConfig = Eeprom_ConfigGet();
 *
 *   Dio_Init(DioConfig);
 *   Spi_Init(SpiConfig);
 *   Eeprom_Init(EepromConfig);
 *   Eeprom_Write(0x0, Buffer, 8);
 * @endcode
 *
 * @see Eeprom_ConfigGet
 * @see Eeprom_Init
 * @see Eeprom_Read
 * @see Eeprom_Write
 * @see Eeprom_RegisterWrite
 * @see Eeprom_RegisterRead
 **********************************************************************/
```

Step #5: Implement EEPROM HAL for Target Processor

Implementing the HAL for an external EEPROM device is a little bit more exciting than implementing a microcontroller peripheral driver. The reason is that the external EEPROM device follows a standard and uses a communication interface on the microcontroller, which means once we implement the base HAL we can literally reuse the implementation without having to make any modifications. The only changes that need to be made will be in the configuration files for the EEPROM setup or in the extended HAL if we want to implement a non-standard feature.

This is exciting because we are finally at a point where we are writing code once and reaping the benefits for every project thereafter. The other HALs certainly can be reused, but if a team is moving from one microcontroller to the next, a little more work is required, whereas with the external devices this code can be completely reused.

In this section, we are going to look through the implementation for the EEPROM HAL, but we are only going to examine a minimum feature set. The EEPROM device will also be an external SPI device. We will examine the following functions:

- Eeprom_Init

- Eeprom_Write

- Eeprom_Read

From these implementation details, readers should be able to create and fill in the remaining HAL features on their own. Let's start by examining the Eeprom_Init function in Listing 9-4.

Listing 9-4. Example EEPROM Initialization Function

```
void Eeprom_Init(const EepromConfig_t *Config)
{
  uint8_t Value;

  // Set up the internal configuration pointer
  EepromConfig = Config;

  // Disable HOLD pin in hardware. We will not be using this function.
  Dio_ChannelWrite(EEPROM_HOLD, HIGH);

  // Read status register
  Value = Eeprom_RegisterRead(EEPROM_READ_STATUS_REG);
```

```
// Bits 2 and 3 of the status register are the block write protection, so
// if (Value & 0x0C) is not zero, block write protection is enabled.
if((Value & 0x0C))
{
  // Disable write protection
  Eeprom_WriteProtection(EEPROM_WP_DISABLE);

  // Disable block write protection in status register
  Eeprom_RegisterWrite(EEPROM_WRITE_STATUS_REG, 0x00);
}
}
```

Notice that the initialization function is simple and could be used with any standard EEPROM device. The function starts by assigning the external EEPROM configuration pointer to a local, module-defined variable. The hardware write protection is configured, followed by the internal write protection. This initialization by default disables the write protection, but a developer could create their own initialization that makes this feature configuration defined. That would allow the default values to change based on the application needs. (I leave that as an exercise for the reader to perform).

The next function that a developer would create is the Eeprom_Write function. An example for this function can be seen in Listing 9-5.

Listing 9-5. Example EEPROM Write Function

```
void Eeprom_Write(uint32_t Dest, uint8_t *Src,  uint32_t Size)
{
  uint8_t status;

  // Setup Command
  EepromConfig.TxRxData[0] = EEPROM_WRITE;
  EepromConfig.TxRxData[1] = ((Dest & 0xFFFFFF) >> 16);
  EepromConfig.TxRxData[2] = ((Dest & 0xFFFF) >> 8);
  EepromConfig.TxRxData[3] = (Dest & 0xFF);

  // Fill the tx buffer with the data
  for(Index = 0; Index < Size; Index++)
```

```
    {
            EepromConfig.TxRxData[Index + 4] = Src[Index];
    }


    // Change transfer Size. Command, Address, Data
    EepromConfig.NumBytes = Size + 4;


    // Disable the write protection
    Dio_ChannelWrite(EEPROM_WP, DIO_HIGH);


    // Transmit the data command
    Spi_Transfer(&EepromConfig);


    status = Eeprom_RegisterRead(EEPROM_READ_STATUS_REG);
    // Poll the busy bit in status register
    while(status & 0x01)
    {
        status = Eeprom_RegisterRead(EEPROM_READ_STATUS_REG);
    }


    // Set the transfer size back to 2
    EepromConfig.NumBytes = 2;


    // Enable the write protection
    Dio_ChannelWrite(EEPROM_WP, DIO_LOW);
}
```

The code shown in Listing 9-5 is basic example code that does *not* perform any safety checks on the data size that is coming in or performing any checks to verify that the data written was done so successfully. However, it does demonstrate how this code could be used with any EEPROM device. In a production-intent implementation, a developer would make sure that at least the following cases are considered and handled:

- Source address is valid.

- Destination address is valid.

- Data size is valid.

- Check for write errors.

- Verify the written data by reading it back out and comparing it.

The write function starts out by defining the first four bytes in the data stream as the command and the address that the data will be written to. Following this setup, the data is copied into the transmit buffer. Once again, for production, there should be some safety checks to make sure that the transmit buffer does not overflow. If the data cannot fit within a single transaction then the code would need to set up multiple write actions. To keep things simple, I've removed all these details.

With the transmit buffer set up, a developer updates the number of bytes to transmit and then initiates the communication transfer. This example shows an explicit call to the Spi_Transfer function, but a developer could implement this in such a way that the transaction could occur on any bus. To do this, the function call would dereference a function pointer to the desired transmit function. Before transmitting and writing the data, the function also disables any write protection that might be enabled on the chip.

The write function will not be instantaneous. This driver uses a polled monitoring technique to watch the status register for the "write complete" flag to be set. Once the write has completed successfully, the write protection is enabled and the local variables are reset to their default values.

The EEPROM read function turns out to be just as simple if not more so than the write function. The read function can be found in Listing 9-6.

Listing 9-6. Example EEPROM Read Function

```
void Eeprom_Read(uint8_t *Dest, uint32_t Src, uint32_t Size)
{
  uint16_t Index = 0;

    // Prepare the command
    EepromConfig.TxRxData[0] = EEPROM_READ;
    EepromConfig.TxRxData[1] = ((Src & 0xFFFFFF) >> 16);
    EepromConfig.TxRxData[2] = ((Src & 0xFFFF) >> 8);
    EepromConfig.TxRxData[3] = (Src & 0xFF);

    // Fill the output buffer with dummy data
    for(Index = 4; Index < Size + 4; Index++)
```

```
    {
        EepromConfig.TxRxData[Index] = 0xAA;
    }


    // Change the number of bytes being transmitted.
    // Command, Address, Dummy Data
    EepromConfig.NumBytes = Size + 4;


    // Transmit the data command
    Spi_Transfer(&EepromConfig);


    // Store the returned data
    for(Index = 0; Index < Size; Index++)
    {
        Dest[Index] = EepromConfig.TxRxData[Index + 4];
    }


    // Set the transfer size back to 2
    EepromConfig.NumBytes = 2;
}
```

Just like with the write function, the read function starts by configuring the command and the address that will be read from. Once this is done, the Spi_Transfer function is called to perform the transaction. When all the data has been read into the buffer, the function copies the received data into the desired destination. Copying the data could cause a slight performance hit on the EEPROM functionality. A developer could also create their function so that the data is placed directly into the destination location rather than in an intermediary buffer or use a pointer to directly access the data.

Don't forget that the read function is just an example! Production code should include assertion and runtime checks to make sure that the buffers do not overflow and that all error conditions and use cases are covered appropriately. It should also take into account the efficiency, performance, and memory usage.

Step #6: Test, Test, Test

After discussing this step three times previously, I don't think I have much more to add. Testing the HAL is critical and having an automated way to do so will dramatically simplify a developer's life. Early in my career, most companies that I worked for simply checked basic functionality and hoped for the best. As I grew as an engineer, I realized how important not just full testing is but also automated testing. Early on, there were quite a few projects I inherited where even minor changes to the code base would break something somewhere in the code.

When something broke, there was no way to truly test the system to make sure that everything was still working. Weeks or months later we would discover a bug that, after tremendous effort, was traced back to a minor change. (Tracing back to the change was only possible because I had forced these companies to start using revision-control systems). I can't stress enough how important testing and automated testing is to software that will be reused and ported to multiple products and platforms.

Step #7: Repeat for the Next Peripheral

At this point, the reader has seen several different examples of how this process can be followed to develop a HAL for internal and external peripherals. If the reader were developing their own HAL, they would now select their next-highest-priority peripheral and begin the process all over again.

Don't forget that the HAL will not be perfect on the first iteration. Undoubtedly, there will be adjustments as new parts are integrated and as products evolve. Don't worry about getting it perfect the first time through.

So far, we have looked at how we can create a base HAL for different devices. Let's now look at how we can extend a HAL using the EEPROM device as an example.

Extending the EEPROM HAL

So far in this book, we have discussed the fact that we can extend a HAL for custom features on a peripheral or device, but we have never examined one! Extending the HAL is not difficult, but it is still a good idea to see how it can be done. In this section, that is exactly what we are going do.

Going back to Table 9-1, there are several custom features that do not belong in the primary HAL. These features include the following:

- Erase modes

- Reading chip identification

- Low-power modes

While these are all useful features that a developer probably wants to implement, they are not supported in every device. They are instead a manufacturer's custom implementation designed to differentiate their product from the competition. A developer would add a separate module that would handle these customizations. The module name could be anything, but the following are a few suggestions:

- hal_device_ext

- device_ext

- device_hal_ext

As the reader can see, my personal preference is to indicate in some way that the HAL is an extension. Some HALs include the word *hal* in their naming conventions, but I typically do not do this. My preference is to specify the device with the assumption that the device module contains the HAL functions to control the device. If a developer were working with the 25AA1024, they would end up with the following files:

- eeprom_25aaxxxx.h

- eeprom_25aaxxxx.c

- eeprom_25aaxxxx_ext.h

- eeprom_25aaxxxx_ext.c

- eeprom_25aaxxxx_cfg.h

- eeprom_25aaxxxx_cfg.c

Everything required to use a 25AA device would be included in these files. Notice that in this example I am putting EEPROM in front of the part number. I do this because without it a developer could easily get confused as to the purpose or function that part number is associated with. They may find themselves wasting time trying to remember which of these ten different part numbers was EEPROM.

The HAL extension functions will vary depending on the extra features that are available on the device. For example, Figure 9-4 shows several new HAL functions that are added to the EEPROM module through the _ext file.

```
void Eeprom_Erase(EepromErase_t EraseMode);
uint8_t Eeprom_ReadID(void);
void Eeprom_PowerDown(void);
```

Figure 9-4. *Extending the EEPROM HAL*

The HAL extensions may require additional type definitions in order to constrain and define the possible parameters that can be used to control the interface. Earlier, we discussed how in my earliest HALs I had a separate function for every erase function on the EEPROM device. Having multiple functions to control this behavior can complicate the interface and make readability and maintainability worse. For that reason, a single function that is then controlled by the parameter is preferred. Figure 9-5 shows an example enumeration that would be used to control the erase functions on an EEPROM chip. Keep in mind that this is specific to a single chip since most EEPROM devices do not require a mass erase function.

```
typedef enum
{
   EEPROM_CHIP,
   EEPROM_SECTOR,
   EEPROM_PAGE
}EepromErase_t;
```

Figure 9-5. *Example EepromErase_t for the extended HAL*

As you can see, extending an interface isn't complicated. Extending an interface is just adding additional functionality to an existing HAL. In many instances, the extension implementation will use the base HAL's `RegisterWrite` and `RegisterRead` functions to access the device's registers. In this way, the extension is dependent upon the base HAL in the implementation. This is not required, but it can simplify the implementation.

Going Further

Developing a HAL for an external device such as an EEPROM device is no different than creating a HAL for an internal device. The implementation will require accessing a communication peripheral such as I2C or SPI, but the HAL design is the same. Now is a great time to apply these techniques yourself. The following are some ideas of how a developer can take the concepts discussed in this chapter and immediately apply them their own development cycle.

- Identify at least three EEPROM devices that you are interested in working with. Collect the datasheets and begin following the seven HAL design steps that we have been discussing. If you want to make things interesting, select devices in the following categories:

  - three external EEPROM and at least one microcontroller with internal EEPROM

  - three external Flash devices and at least three microcontrollers that have internal flash controllers

- Review the datasheets in detail and generate a peripheral feature list like the one shown in Table 9-1. How do the results compare? Are they the same or do they have new peripheral features beyond what we discussed in this chapter?

- Review the table and identify the features that belong in a standard HAL interface. Create an initial HAL interface list and identify the input and output features for the interfaces.

- Create a documented template using the skills learned in Chapter 5 on Doxygen and create the EEPROM and flash stubs. An alternative to creating the template yourself is to visit www.beningo.com and purchase the templates developed by Jacob Beningo.

- Identify the development board that the first port will be performed on. Use the examples in this chapter to fill in the implementation for the target.

- Develop basic test cases based on the configuration table and HAL input and output features. Verify that the ported code behaves as expected.

- Consider developing test-case document templates that will be used to test ported EEPROM and flash code.

- Create automated test cases that can be executed daily to verify that the HAL is working as expected. Don't forget to inject errors to verify that the regression tests are correct.

CHAPTER 10

API Design for Embedded Applications

".. . the purpose of abstraction is not to be vague, but to create a new semantic level in which one can be absolutely precise."

—Edsger W. Dijkstra, The Humble Programmer

Applications Made Easier

Having a well-defined hardware abstraction layer can go a long way in improving firmware reusability. Abstracting out the hardware layer is not the only abstraction layer available to embedded-software developers. Developers can also make use of APIs, which will provide high-level abstractions within the application code and can have just as dramatic an effect on code reusability and the overall development cycle as HALs can. For all intents and purposes, an API is really just a HAL that doesn't touch any hardware. It's meant to provide a developer with an abstraction that can be used to simplify and speed up application implementation.

APIs make implementing application software easier and faster. A developer that needs access to an SD card library doesn't need to write from scratch the code necessary to interact with one. They can use a library that contains a well-defined set of APIs that can then perform the necessary operations of the communication channel and talk with

243

© Jacob Beningo 2017
J. Beningo, *Reusable Firmware Development*, https://doi.org/10.1007/978-1-4842-3297-2_10

the SD card to get the desired result. APIs provide developers with several advantages, such as the following:

- Creates a black box that performs the desired operation with little to no knowledge of how it does it

- Increases and improves reusability

- Speeds up development

- Improves code readability

Creating and using APIs for embedded software in today's environment really is a no-brainer. Developers should be creating APIs to produce more modular and reusable code. The benefits have been proven time and time again. However, as developers go about creating their APIs, there are several disadvantages that should be kept in mind. These include the following:

- Each API level will have a minor performance hit when storing the function return address on the stack unless the functions are in-lined by the compiler.

- Libraries from third-party sources could have hidden issues related to security, performance, code size, and robustness. Developers should carefully study the code that they are using and analyze it.

SOFTWARE TERMINOLOGY

An **application framework** is a collection of different components, a set of APIs, that are interrelated and assist a developer in rapidly developing an application.

In most cases, the benefits far outweigh the disadvantages, and if developers are aware of the disadvantages, they can mitigate any potential issues that might arise from them.

Designing APIs

Creating an API for an embedded application is not much different than the process that we have been using throughout this book to create a HAL. The major differences are that we are working at a higher abstraction level, removed from the hardware. This makes life easier on the developer. We no longer need to compare datasheets for multiple microcontroller devices and carefully craft an interface that supports them all. The same process used to design a HAL can be used to make an API, with a few minor modifications. The modified process for designing an API is as follows:

1) Identify the features and operations that the API will perform.

2) Design and create the API.

3) Create the stubs and documentation templates.

4) Implement the API.

5) Test the implementation.

That's it! The process is shortened by two steps since we don't have to review a bunch of datasheets. The nice part about the API level is that we implement once and only need to maintain the interface. The APIs should be usable across platforms, and only HAL dependencies would ever need to be updated.

Every best practice that we have discussed related to HALs in this book also applies to the API level. For example, developers should try to keep their APIs manageable and limited to no more than a dozen per component. A developer should break up and organize their component so that it contains four different modules, as follows:

- The component header definition file

- The component source implementation file

- The component configuration header file

- The component configuration source file

Keeping a component organized in this fashion will help maximize reuse and will also help keep the APIs associated with it organized and easily navigable.

Application Frameworks

An application framework is a collection of different components, or set of APIs, that are interrelated and assist a developer in rapidly developing an application. Application frameworks have been around for PC developers for decades, but embedded-software developers really haven't had application frameworks available to them until recently. The reason why is that embedded developers only focused on one-off applications and had no reason to create reusable code and application frameworks to help them speed up development.

Developers have started to move to 32-bit ARM-based microcontrollers. With this transition, the hardware has become so complicated that microcontroller manufacturers such as Microchip, Renesas, and ST Microelectronics have started to develop application frameworks for their parts. Application frameworks help their customers speed up development and abstract out the hardware. Developers therefore don't need to become experts on every register in the microcontroller and how each works. These frameworks include not only a HAL but often high-level APIs to implement features such as SD card, RTOS, command consoles, and much more. An example application framework from Renesas can be found in Figure 10-1. Notice how it includes everything from the board support package and HAL to several different application-level functions.

When you are thinking about creating your own APIs and collecting them into a framework, take some time to review what has already been done in the industry. You might find that you are able to use something that already exists or at least leverage the best practices from other teams that have already made progress in developing useful reusable firmware.

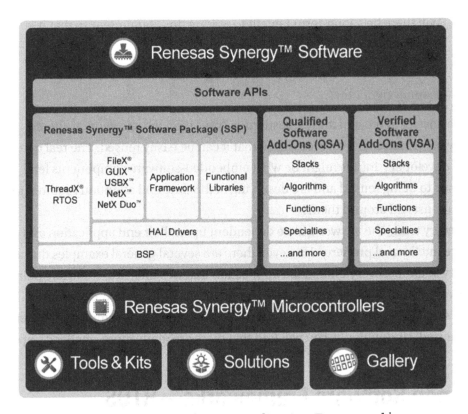

Figure 10-1. *Renesas Synergy™ Software Application Framework[1]*

Creating Your Own APIs

Now that we have examined some general APIs and how they can be used with an embedded system, it's time to start carefully considering what the reader should be doing to create their own APIs. We don't necessarily need to create the perfect solution or convert every piece of code we write into a masterpiece for reusable software. A developer needs to reasonably identify the core application components that offer the greatest benefit to being reused in multiple applications. There are several questions that a developer should ask themselves as they consider whether a feature should be designed so that it can be reused. These include:

- Is this component going to be used in more than one application?

- Will this component be ported to another hardware platform in the future?

[1]https://www.renesas.com/en-us/products/synergy/features.html

- Will there be a long-term benefit to writing this component so that it is reusable?

- Is there available time and budget to write this code in a reusable manner right now?

If the answer to most of these questions is "yes," then the component should probably be written to have a nice API so that it can be easily reused. The real question in many developers' minds might be what embedded-software components lend themselves to being reused and are deserving of the time and attention required to create a robust API around them?

For every team, the answer will be dependent upon their end application and their core intellectual property. However, there are several general examples that are necessary in almost every embedded application that we can use as a starting point to provide an example for how a developer should design and create their own APIs.[2] The examples that I am about to provide are major components in an embedded system that can be reused. Undoubtedly, you will find that there are many more smaller components.

Common Software Frameworks—RTOS and Schedulers

An obvious component that is present in every embedded system is a scheduler. The scheduler might be a simple cooperative scheduler or it very well might be a full-blown RTOS. As fun as creating an RTOS might be, scheduling algorithms have been beaten to death, and there is no reason to professionally develop yet another RTOS or scheduling algorithm. Since most systems have some scheduling element to them, an RTOS is a perfect example of a reusable component that can be ported to multiple applications and platforms.

The obvious challenge with an RTOS is its API. There is no standard! Every developer and their brother who has written their own RTOS has a completely different API than everyone else. This can create a huge issue for reuse if a development team might possibly swap out RTOSes in the future or wants that component to be modular. In an

---

[2]http://www.webopedia.com/TERM/L/library.html

earlier chapter, we discussed how a developer might need to create a wrapper layer in their software so that an RTOS can easily be swapped in and out. The wrapper layer, shown in Figure 10-2, provides a well-known interface through which to access the features available in any RTOS and allows the RTOS to easily be swapped out.

Using a wrapper for the RTOS layer has immediate advantages, such as the following:

- Swapping out the RTOS

- Consistent application interface for any scheduler

- Being highly portable

The only real downside to having a wrapper layer around the RTOS is that there is a slight performance hit due to making a function call to get into the wrapper, which then must call the associated RTOS function. This disadvantage can be overcome by function in-lining and enabling compiler optimizations.

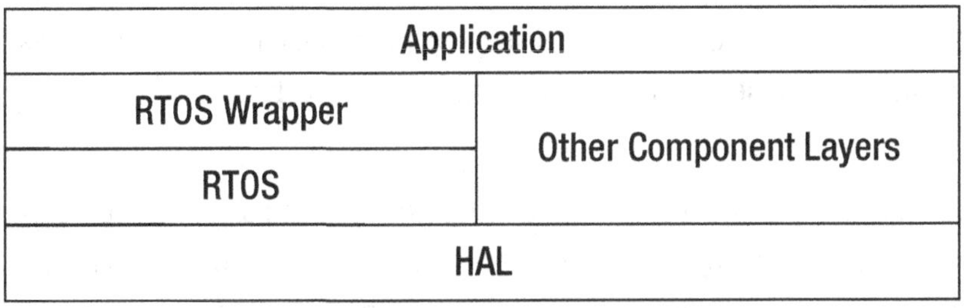

Figure 10-2. *RTOS wrapper layer*

Using a wrapper to allow any RTOS to be used in an application is interesting, but does anyone in the industry actually do this? Besides an engineering firm that is scattered here or there, one major player that *does* use an RTOS wrapper is Microchip. Microchip has its MPLAB® Harmony software, which "adds in the flexibility to use a Real-Time Operating System (RTOS) or work without one."[3] They have literally designed an RTOS wrapper that allows RTOSes such as

- ThreadX;

- FreeRTOS;

- Micrium OS2 or 3;

---

[3]http://www.microchip.com/mplab/mplab-harmony

to be swapped into and out of their software platform. The application code makes calls to the same API calls, but the API is populated with the specific RTOS feature's API call.

That is definitely something that a developer who is working on a reusable software framework or trying to maximize firmware reuse should take into consideration.

CASE STUDY—YET ANOTHER RTOS

Embedded-software developers love to get down into the bits and bytes and work at the hardware level. Real-time developers especially take pride in being able to fine-tune and control not just the hardware but also the deterministic timed behavior of the system. These developers have always loved to write scheduling algorithms. The problem with writing your own scheduler or RTOS is that it has been done a million times by a million engineers.

There are currently over a hundred different real-time operating systems and scheduling algorithms commercially available. Designing and getting a basic scheduler up and running isn't a big deal, but creating one that is robust and correct all the time and that is designed under a certified development cycle starts to push the time and budgetary constraints available on projects today.

The advice I can give is to use a proven scheduling algorithm and only write your own on your own free time if it is something that you are passionate about. Writing a scheduler can provide great insights into how a real-time scheduler works. Examining and modifying one that already exists can be far more efficient, however, and you can learn just as much.

Common Software Frameworks— Console Applications

Console applications are a core component that is included in many embedded applications. The console application has its `printf` functionality, which can help a developer see the code's status, but far more important is the command-handling piece. Embedded systems often accept commands externally, whether they are from a host PC or a device located through a network across the world.

The components required to implement a console application are standard. A developer needs a communication interface such as a UART or USB that is connected to a command parsing and response module. This is standard, and it makes a lot of sense to package these components in such a way that they can be reused and integrated in a single framework. Figure 10-3 shows an example stack-up. In the example, the communication interface is a generic interface that is shared among all communication devices. The input module contains the command parser, which would be configurable for the application.

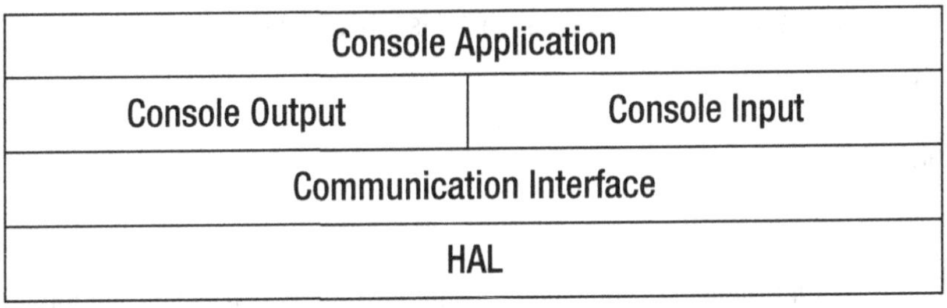

Figure 10-3. *Software layer stack-up for a console application*

The Renesas Synergy Platform does something very similar to this. While their platform offers a wide variety of components, one component that I have found to be very useful is their console-application module. This module can be added to any Synergy project and be connected to USB, a UART, or any communication channel that is available on the microcontroller! Once in the project, a developer creates a command list and the function that should be executed if the command is received.

These components aren't just reusable; they also drastically decrease the time required to create a console feature on an embedded system. Once again, why reinvent the wheel when one already exists? It's far better to instead invent something that builds upon it!

CASE STUDY—COMMAND PARSERS

Since so many systems have a need to transmit a command, after the third or fourth time having to implement one, I designed a configurable and reusable command parser that became a necessary element in my bag of tricks. The parser I designed contains several elements:

- An enum that defines available commands

- A function for each command

- A configuration table that lists each available command and has a function pointer to the command function

- A search algorithm that can find the matching command and execute the associated function

This may seem complicated, but I've found that once a switch statement grows to more than a dozen or so cases, it becomes difficult to manage and maintain. I've worked on applications that had hundreds of commands and have seen this implemented in a massive, nearly unsearchable switch statement.

Using a command parser with the elements I just described can improve

- readability;

- maintainability; and

- portability.

The best part is that it is simple to copy the template into a new application, list the new commands, and in a few minutes have a command parser up and running in the system.

Common Software Frameworks—Bootloaders

One of my all-time favorite frameworks is the bootloader framework that I put together and have been using on my own projects and my clients' projects for the last half a decade or so. The ability to update firmware in the field is so important, and yet it's usually the last software piece that any development team thinks to add to their system. This leaves developers scrambling at the end of a project to add firmware update capabilities to their system.

I quickly found that the problem my clients were facing was multi-fold and included the following:

- They didn't know how to write a bootloader.

- Microcontroller-vendor bootloaders were example code and did not meet production software requirements.

- The time required to learn, build, and debug a bootloader on average was three months.

- Developing a solution in-house could easily cost a company $40,000 to $60,000 depending on the requirements.

These were big problems for the clients, especially the timing and robustness requirements. So, how do you solve a problem that is common to nearly every embedded system and can be time-consuming to build? You create a reusable firmware framework that can be ported to multiple hardware platforms!

That is exactly what I did. I took many of the lessons and discussions that we have had in this book and applied them to creating a software framework that could be used to easily adapt bootloaders to any microcontroller. The framework was not done in a single shot, but rather started out with basic capabilities and APIs and then, over the course of a half-dozen or so bootloaders, took full shape. This required creating low-level HAL drivers and higher-level APIs. The basic, simplified results can be seen in Figure 10-4.

Bootloader Application			
HAL	Communication Interface	Memory Interface	Scheduling Interface	Watchdog Interface
Drivers			

Figure 10-4. *Beningo Microcontroller Bootloader Solution (Micro-boot, MCU-Boot)*

Every bootloader requires access to a communication interface, whether it's an SD card, UART, USB, I2C, and so on. The bootloader must access memory in some way. At a minimum, it needs to access the internal flash controller, but it may also need to access a file system or an external EEPROM device. Bootloaders may require scheduling or basic timing in order to detect if an operation has timed out. There is so much more associated with a bootloader, but I think the reader gets the idea.

The big question is: how has such a framework helped? The very first bootloader I ever wrote took three months of calendar time and approximately eight weeks of active development time. (When you take on an activity like this internally, regular development must continue, so it is never just the straight workload). The second bootloader, now that I had experience under my belt, still took six to eight weeks' development time.

After the second bootloader experience, I realized that I was probably going to be creating these throughout my career and should think about designing one that I could reuse and port to different applications. I designed a first-pass framework, and the third bootloader I wrote took less than four weeks. Adjustments to the framework were made, additional features were added, and the next one took two weeks. With time and a reusable framework, bootloader implementation has become extremely easy and fast. Table 10-1 shows the progression and the effect that the bootloader framework had on the development activity. Obviously, the development effort has greatly benefited from the availability of a reusable framework.

Table 10-1. *Bootloader Development Times and Estimated Costs*

Bootloader Iteration	Framework Available?	Estimated Dev. Time	Comments
1	No	8 Weeks	
2	No	8 Weeks	
3	Yes	4 Weeks	Framework 0.5
4	Yes	3 Weeks	Framework 0.8
5	Yes	2 Weeks	Framework 1.0
6	Yes	2 Weeks	Framework 1.1
7	Yes	2 Weeks	Framework 1.2

After examining the data, keep in mind that this is the time necessary to get the bootloader up and running. Integrating a user application and updating it to work with the bootloader can sometimes be considerable work, depending on how they designed their application and the tools that they used.

Common Software Frameworks—FAT File System

Another component that a developer can leverage and that they probably wouldn't want to create themselves is a FAT file-system component. FAT file systems are often used on embedded systems to store log data or files on either an SD card, an external memory device, or sometimes even on internal flash memory. There are many different FAT file-system components available if one does a quick internet search. One particular component that has gained traction and a big following in the embedded space is FatFS.[4]

---

[4]http://elm-chan.org/fsw/ff/00index_e.html

FatFs has a great API set. The APIs are all easy to remember and very simple. A short listing can be seen in Listing 10-1. You might notice that all the APIs start with the same prefix so as to identify that it is a file API, and then the function immediately follows. The API is clean and easy to read and remember. One could complain that there are more than a dozen functions in the API, but the APIs are so simple and straightforward that it wouldn't make any sense to reduce their number! The dozen functions are a rule of thumb, not a law.

Listing 10-1. FatFs File Access API's[4]

```
f_open - Open/create a file
f_close - Close an open file
f_read - Read data from the file
f_write - Write data to the file
f_lseek - Move read/write pointer, expand size
f_truncate - Truncate file size
f_sync - Flush cached data
f_forward - Forward data to the stream
f_expand - Allocate a contiguous block to the file
f_gets - Read a string
f_putc - Write a character
f_puts - Write a string
f_printf - Write a formatted string
f_tell - Get current read/write pointer
f_eof - Test for end-of-file
f_size - Get size
f_error - Test for an error
```

What is great about FatFs is that even the file organization is clean and has been well thought out. The framework is layered so that a developer only needs to provide some low-level access into the hardware, and the higher-level API calls will function on the hardware as expected. This is a great example of how to architect software that has a clean API and is modular enough to be used on multiple platforms.

Open source software, though, doesn't always have the greatest implementation. A quick analysis shows that there are many functions with a cyclomatic complexity greater than 10. In fact, there are several with values greater than 20, and even a few in the 30s and 40s. These functions obviously have probably never been fully tested and could potentially be harboring unknown bugs just waiting to strike. That doesn't stop engineers from using them. In all honesty, I've never had any obvious issues that I've found when I use them, but still, "buyer" beware.

Going Further

APIs are the foundation that most modern software is built upon. They nicely abstract out and hide the implementation details, allowing developers to focus on their application rather than on common software features. The following are several thoughts on where you can go from here to improve and get up to speed on creating your own APIs:

- Review the best practices for HALs. These best practices also apply to APIs.

- Go online and review some common open source software. Evaluate how well that software provides the following:

    - Appropriate APIs

    - Software architecture

    - Speed that support is provided for

    - Software-development process

    - Testing procedures

- Review the APIs from different RTOS suppliers. Which APIs seem to be the easiest to use and remember?

- Review your own software and identify common software features that could easily be converted into their own separate reusable software governed by a simple set of APIs.

- Implement those features as a reusable component and start building your own libraries and frameworks.

- Examine the software components that are open source and microcontroller-vendor-specific that we discussed in this chapter. Then do the following:

    - Identify the best practices used in each.

    - Determine what could be done better.

CHAPTER 11

Testing Portable Embedded Software

"Program testing can be used to show the presence of bugs, but never to show their absence!"

—Edsger W. Dijkstra

"Defect-free software does not exist."

—Wietse Venema

Cross Your Fingers and Pray

Testing an embedded system is critical to ensure that it not only meets requirements but also has a minimum bug count. Developers can rarely prove that their application has no bugs in it, but they can develop extensive test cases that minimize the chances that a bug is hiding in their application. Testing strategies can vary from manual system-level testing to sophisticated automated tests that are performed on a continuous-integration server and reported on a nightly basis.

SOFTWARE TERMINOLOGY

Regression testing is the ability to automatically run test cases that were previously executed to verify that they still pass after the software has been modified.

257

J. Beningo, *Reusable Firmware Development*, https://doi.org/10.1007/978-1-4842-3297-2_11

The worst testing strategy that a development team can have, and unfortunately one that I have seen implemented on numerous occasions, is the "cross your fingers and pray" strategy. In this implementation, developers spot-check their code and the system to make sure that they don't notice any major system defects. The spot-checking has minimal code coverage and is a highly manual procedure. When the product ships, developers mostly just cross their fingers and pray that they don't run into any major issues.

In order to have a consistent test strategy, developers need two key features in their tests: automation and regression. Automated tests are necessary because there is no way that a developer or a team can dedicate the time and effort necessary to manually check that every line of code is executed and behaves as expected. The only way to perform these checks is to automate testing so that it can be executed without human interaction.

Once tests are automated, developers can employ regression testing, which is the ability to rerun tests that were previously executed to verify that they still pass. Regression testing is an amazing tool that, if executed periodically, can show developers where feature additions or changes in the code base may have broken the application code. Debugging is far more efficient if a developer can be alerted immediately when the problem arises in the system rather than weeks or months later.

Development teams that want to reuse their firmware and port it from one hardware platform to the next need the ability to automatically test that their ported code is working as expected—without requiring significant time. To do so, there are several key test areas that need to be developed, as follows:

- Unit tests

- Functional tests

- Regression tests

- Integration tests

In this chapter, we will review best practices and considerations that developers should look at when developing a test strategy for their reusable firmware.

Unit Testing

The most basic testing that every developer should be performing on their embedded systems is unit testing. Unit testing is a software-development process in which the smallest testable parts of an application are individually and independently scrutinized for proper operation.[1] For firmware engineers, a unit is an individual function. As engineers develop their functions, they should also be developing test cases that will validate the functions work as expected.

A unit test should test the function by validating that the range of possible inputs to the function produce known and expected outputs. Unit tests should also include inputs that are known to be invalid to ensure that the function can handle errors appropriately. Figure 11-1 shows at a high level how a function would be tested.

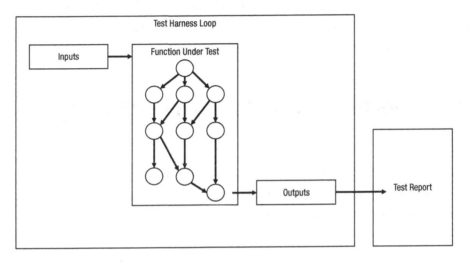

Figure 11-1. *A test harness running unit tests*

First, a test harness would be set up that could automatically run the function under all the input conditions that are required to test the function. Next, these inputs should allow the function to follow all possible branches through the function, which can be seen as the connected circles in the "Function Under Test" block. We will discuss how we can ensure we have the minimum number of test cases required in the next section. Finally, the function will produce an output that results in the work that it performed, which can then be recorded in a test report.

SOFTWARE TERMINOLOGY

Unit testing is a software-development process in which the smallest testable parts of an application are individually and independently scrutinized for proper operation.[1]

---

[1]http://searchsoftwarequality.techtarget.com/definition/unit-testing

Unit tests can be performed manually, but they are far more effective if they can be automated. Running any test case manually is a very time-consuming process. Always try to find a way to automate the process. I don't enjoy spending my time testing or debugging, so the more automated these processes are, the better!

Embedded-software developers often struggle with determining the correct number of test cases that they should have in order to fully test a function. Developers can easily define the inputs to enter a function, but they also need to make sure that every line of code is executed and that every code branch is traversed. Thankfully, there is a tool developers can utilize that will save them from having to manually determine how many test cases they need to create. That tool is *cyclomatic complexity*.

Taking Advantage of Cyclomatic Complexity for Unit Testing

Cyclomatic complexity is probably one of my favorite topics to discuss because it has so many benefits for embedded-software developers. The first benefit, which we have already discussed, is that cyclomatic complexity can be used to minimize function complexity. The cyclomatic complexity measurement results in a finite number that is assigned to a function and sets the reliability risk for bugs and testing. Table 11-1 shows a basic summary of the various complexity measurements and the software's reliability risk.

Table 11-1. *Cyclomatic Complexity Effect on Reliability Risk*[2]

Complexity	Reliability Risk
1 – 10	A simple function, little risk
11 – 20	More complex, moderate risk
21 – 50	Complex, high risk
51+	Untestable, very high risk

[2]McCabe, Thomas Jr. "Software Quality Metrics to Identify Risk." Presentation to the Department of Homeland Security Software Assurance Working Group, 2008. (http://www.mccabe.com/ppt/SoftwareQualityMetricsToIdentifyRisk.ppt#36); and Laird, Linda, and M. Carol Brennan (2006). *Software Measurement and Estimation: A Practical Approach*. Los Alamitos, CA: IEEE Computer Society.

The second benefit that developers can leverage from the cyclomatic complexity measurement is that it provides a value for the minimum number of test cases that need to be defined and executed in order to fully test a function. This is because cyclomatic complexity measures the number of linearly independent paths through the function. A linearly independent path is any path through a program that introduces at least one new edge that is not included in any other linearly independent path.[3] Let's look at a few quick examples.

The first example will be a function that takes two parameters and contains a simple if/else statement. The code can be seen in Listing 11-1. In this example, we have two linearly independent paths. The first path is where var1 is equal to var2. The second path is if var1 and var2 are not equal. Using the M-squared RSM tool on this code, the cyclomatic complexity result is two, which is what we would expect. We have two linearly independent paths through the function.

In this example, we know that we should have two test cases to ensure that each linearly independent path gets tested. A developer would also want to test the possible values for var1 and var2 if it would impact the behavior of the function. There would be no point in testing every possible combination if it would not impact how the function behaves.

Listing 11-1. Function with a Cyclomatic Complexity Equal to 2

```
int MyFunction(int var1, int var2)
{
   if(var1 == var2)
   {
      var1++;
   }
   else
   {
      var2++;
   }
}
```

---

[3]http://www.ironiacorp.com/

An interesting example is one where a developer has two if/else statements that occur one after the other. Each if/else statement calls a function. The code can be seen in Listing 11-2. If a developer were counting possible paths through the code, they would notice the following function combinations would be executed and count the following:

1) Foo() Bar()

2) Foo() Code()

3) Dead() Bar()

4) Dead() Code()

What is interesting is that the cyclomatic complexity measurement is three for this function despite there being four possible paths! Was the cyclomatic complexity wrong? No, it wasn't! Cyclomatic complexity measures linearly independent paths. The last path is not linearly independent of the first three paths because it does not introduce any new nodes (program statements) that were not included in the first three paths.[4] This is a great example of how cyclomatic complexity provides the minimum number and not the actual number of test cases required to test a function.

Listing 11-2. Cyclomatic Complexity, Three Functions with Four Paths

```
int MyFunction(int var1, int var2)
{
    if(var1)
    {
            Foo();
    }
    else
    {
            Dead();
    }

    if(var2)
    {
            Bar();
    }
}
```

---

[4]https://stackoverflow.com/questions/24191174/cyclomatic-complexity-1-if-statements

```
    else
    {
        Code();
    }
}
```

There are several different tools that developers can use to measure cyclomatic complexity. A few that I have used in the past include the following:

- GMetrics[5]

- M-squared's RSM[6]

- LDRA[7]

- Visual Studio IDE (built-in)

- Understand IDE (built-in)

Standard Interface . . . Standard Tests

The nice thing about reusable software is that once unit tests are developed for the HALs and the APIs, the tests can also be reused. A carefully crafted HAL becomes a standard interface that is used from one application to the next. That standard interface will then have standard tests associated with it that can always be run to make sure that any ported or reused code still behaves the way it is expected to on the new system.

A developer can easily see the advantages of having a standard test suite that is executed on their drivers and their application code. These include:

- Writing the test once

- Reusing the tests for years or possibly a decade or more

- Quick and easy verification of changes to the software

- Speedy verification of new ports

- Decreased costs

---

[5]http://gmetrics.sourceforge.net/gmetrics-CyclomaticComplexityMetric.html
[6]https://msquaredtechnologies.com/
[7]http://www.ldra.com/en/

There are also several disadvantages that developers need to be aware of concerning standard tests. These concerns include:

- A hole in the tests will be propagated to all software that follows.

- The upfront time necessary to design and implement the tests

- The potential cost to purchase tools and implement the tests

The advantages of using standard tests obviously outweigh the disadvantages. Developers can easily mitigate the disadvantages by

- periodically reviewing the standard tests to make sure that they still completely cover the code;

- updating the tests as the underlying APIs change; and

- performing periodic test reviews internally and with a third party to make sure that nothing has been overlooked.

By doing these three things, developers can make sure that they always have standard tests that can be executed on their standard APIs.

Functional Testing

Functional testing is a testing process that is used to verify that the software conforms with all its requirements.[8] In most instances, it's a testing method that is used to verify that the business needs or the end-user needs are being met. Functional testing is most often executed at the application level to verify that the end users' inputs provide expected outputs.

Functional testing often follows black-box or white-box testing methods. In black-box testing, the tests are created with little to no knowledge of how the system's inner workings were created. The test simply knows that pressing button A should result in output A.

When the developer who designed the system gets involved in creating the tests, the testing is known as white-box testing. Since the developer has intricate knowledge of the inner workings of the device, they can devise tests that not only verify the inputs/outputs for the system but also test corner cases and specific internal actions.

---

[8]Grenning, James (2011). *Test-Driven Development for Embedded C*, The Pragmatic Programmers.

Functional testing can go beyond simply verifying the inputs and outputs for the system. They can also include unit testing. For embedded developers, we have an interesting problem in that most of our code touches hardware. Registers get manipulated that affect the output on a physical pin. There can be multiple configurations, and it can be difficult and time consuming to verify that all the combinations are correct and function as expected. This is where two different tools come into play to help embedded-systems developers: test-driven development and hardware in-loop testing.

Test-Driven Development

In James Grenning's book *Test-Driven Development for Embedded C*, he defines test-driven development as "a technique for building software incrementally where no production code is written without first writing a failing unit test."[8,9] The idea behind TDD is that a developer first writes their test case, makes it fail, and then writes the code necessary to make the test case pass. Once the test case passes, they write another test case that fails, and then they write the code that resolves that test case. It then continues in this manner until the entire software is completed.

There are several obvious advantages to using TDD, including the following:

- It is verified that every test case can detect a failed state.

- Test cases are created incrementally for every piece of code that is written.

- Adding new code that breaks previously written code is immediately detected.

- A test harness is used that allows for easy regression testing.

When one considers the advantages of thinking through the tests first and then writing the code, it's quite brilliant and counterintuitive to the way that embedded-software developers write software, so much so that if you read the book and try it out, you may find yourself struggling to accept a TDD mindset.

---

[9]https://www.techopedia.com/definition/19509/functional-testing

TDD is not without its own headaches and issues. There are several disadvantages to TDD that can affect embedded-software developers, such as the following:

- Needing to create mocks to simulate hardware accesses

- Setting up the development environment is time-consuming and tricky

- Adopting the mindset and truly following TDD is difficult

- The process can feel very time-consuming

Despite these disadvantages, developers may still want to investigate TDD and determine which pieces could work best for their reusable firmware.

Hardware In-Loop Testing

Hardware in-loop (HIL) testing runs the test case code on the target microcontroller rather than using a mocked software layer to act as the hardware. HIL testing can be extremely useful for verifying that hardware accesses from a HAL are working as expected and even for testing that all outputs from the system work as expected. Figure 11-2 shows an example of what a HIL setup might look like.

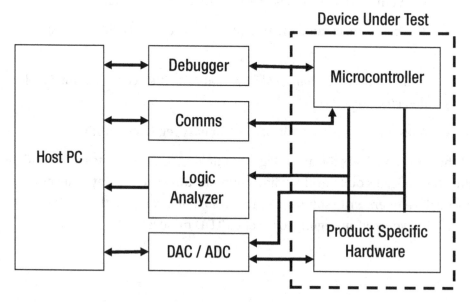

Figure 11-2. *Hardware in-loop testing*

HIL testing can contain several different components. First, there is the device under test, which is commonly referred to as the DUT. The DUT will have information that it is critical to access in order to verify the system is working, such as the following:

- Microcontroller register values

- Pin I/O states

- Communication channels

- Product relates signals from sensors, actuators, etc.

Now, a developer could go through and manually monitor these signals, but that would be a very time-consuming process. Instead, a developer can build out their HIL test harness to include tools that can automatically sample desired states.

This brings us to our second component, the debugger. The debugger is used by the test controller to load applications and test code onto the target microcontroller, and also to control those tests through the debugger communications port. Most modern debuggers act as a virtual communication port, and with minimal software a developer can create a test command-control channel to manage the microcontroller. The controller can request telemetry, register values, and even monitor the software trace and event history.

Next, a developer will normally have a communication channel via which to talk with the product. For example, if the product is an automotive product, there may be CAN messages that the product responds to that need to be tested. Another example would be a device that has a COMM port. Whatever the communication interface is, there needs to be a tool that can convert that communication to a COMM port that the test scripts can control.

Another useful tool to include in the HIL, and one that is very useful for verifying the HAL and configuration tables, is a logic analyzer. Each GPIO pin on the microcontroller can be connected to the logic analyzer and then sampled at either a predetermined rate or when events occur in the system. For low–pin count parts, this is straightforward and doesn't require expensive hardware. However, if the microcontroller being used has a hundred pins or more, logic-analyzer hardware could be expensive. The same processor's development kit, which probably has a header for every pin anyway, can be used as a logic analyzer with a little bit of software.

Developers may also find that their system requires an analog or digital input or that their system outputs an analog or digital signal. In these cases, using an ADC or DAC will give the test harness access to these signals so that they can be recorded while executing the test cases.

Finally, this brings us to the host computer that runs the test suite and must monitor and control the entire testing process. There are several different test harnesses from companies such as LDRA, but it is also possible for developers to write their own Python scripts to test and validate their system. In many cases, the direction a team will go will depend upon several factors, such as the following:

- Available budget

- Available time

- Team members available for the project

The one thing that I've tried to convey throughout this book is that reusable software saves time and money in the long run. It often does require more time and budget up front, but once everything is in place, the speed at which a team can move and the money that can be saved pays for itself multiple times over.

Regression Testing

Developers who are creating reusable software absolutely need to make sure that they can perform regression tests in a timely and automated manner. According to Wikipedia, regression testing is "a type of software testing which verifies that software which was previously developed and tested still performs the same way after it was changed."[10] In summary, regression testing helps a developer ensure that when they modify their software by fixing bugs, adding new features, or porting it to a new target microcontroller, they can verify that the software behaves as expected without any new bugs being created. If bugs have been created, the regression tests would catch them and developers could deal with them.

The idea behind regression testing is that there is a test set that exists that can be rerun on the system periodically to ensure that all the tests are still able to pass. If regression testing is run often, any tests that fail should be easily traceable to the code that changed and is causing the issue.

---

[10]https://en.wikipedia.org/wiki/Regression_testing

Automating Tests

Any team or developer that is creating reusable software should be creating automated tests. Even the simplest embedded system could require a hundred or more test cases to ensure that the software behaves as expected. Attempting to manually run through these tests will consume a lot of time and could be prone to errors. Therefore, automating test cases is really the best solution for developers.

There are several different methods that teams can use to create automated test cases. The most popular that I have encountered include

- using a C/C++ test harness; and
- creating a Python-based test harness.

There are several example C/C++ test harnesses that developers can leverage, such as Unity or Cpputest. Both C/C++ test harnesses are open source and can be found by searching for them in your favorite web browser. The advantages to using a C/C++ test harness is that

- they are open source;
- developers already know C/C++; and
- they can be used to create automated tests.

There are several disadvantages as well, including the following:

- Being open source, there is limited support to get them up and running.
- I have found that they are difficult to set up initially.

Python test harnesses can be very interesting to developers as an alternative to a C/C++ harness. I have found them to be more flexible for system-level testing, similar to what we discussed in the section on in-line hardware testing. Python is an easy-to-learn scripting language that is very powerful. It also includes libraries specifically designed to perform testing.

The direction that any team chooses to go will be highly dependent on their skillsets and their end requirements. It may also depend on when their products are due and how much time and budget they have allocated for testing. One thing is certain though; if you are planning to create reusable firmware, you need to have automated tests to ensure the software continues to behave as you expect it to.

Using Trace to Verify Application Software

A new testing tool that is now available to embedded-software developers that wasn't available just a few years ago but can be very powerful is application tracing. Application tracing allows a developer to record events that are occurring in their system and offload the event and the timing through the debugger onto a host machine. Event data can be logged by streaming continuously or as a one-shot. An example setup for how a developer can trace their application can be found in Figure 11-3.

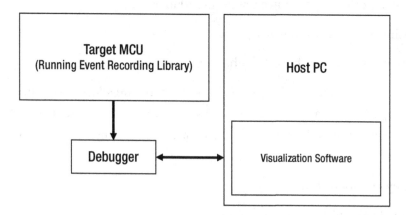

Figure 11-3. *Tracing application data block diagram*

In the setup, a developer runs a small and efficient event-recording library that can communicate with the debugging probe to store the event data on a host PC. The sample rate for the event data will depend on the throughput to the PC along with the buffer size given to the event-recording library. The larger the buffer, the more event data that can be stored locally before it needs to be transmitted upstream. Even on resource-constrained microcontrollers, the event-tracing library uses no more than 1 percent of the CPU and usually has a few kilobytes of RAM allocated to it.

Once a developer has set up tracing and recorded a trace to their PC, they can use their capture software to get statistical information about the system. This information can be viewed in many ways, from simple tables and graphs to task-tracing diagrams. An example trace that monitored a system that had three tasks to control LEDs can be seen in Figure 11-4. This table shows useful information, such as CPU usage and minimum, maximum, and average execution times, along with the task periodicity. A developer can easily use this information to monitor and track not only changes to their application but also whether their code is behaving as expected after porting it to a new microcontroller or product.

Actor	Priority		Count	CPU Usage	Execution Time			Response Time			Periodicity		
	Min	Max		%	Min	Avg	Max	Min	Avg	Max	Min	Avg	Max
Task IDLE	0	0	1	98.948	-	-	-	-	-	-	-	-	-
Task led_blue	1	1	101	0.016	80	81	82	220	221	222	499.998	500.000	500.001
Task led_green	1	1	202	0.033	80	81	83	158	213	270	249.965	250.000	250.034
Task led_red	1	1	504	0.081	80	81	83	156	189	318	99.933	100.000	100.067
Task TzCtrl	1	1	5047	0.923	0	92	111	43	148	378	7.810	10.000	10.100

Figure 11-4. *Trace data demonstrating task statistics*

Another interesting feature that developers can use to test and verify their software is a visual inspection of the trace data. Figure 11-5 shows an example visualization where a developer has discovered that there is a deadlock in their application code. The active task is shown as a solid lifeline, while the task waiting to execute is shown as a hashed line. The highest-priority task is on the right-hand side. Examining the trace reveals when different events occur, such as:

- Task delays

- Context switches

- Giving and taking objects such as semaphores

- Current status of all tasks

This information can be used to dramatically improve the verification process involved with reusable firmware.

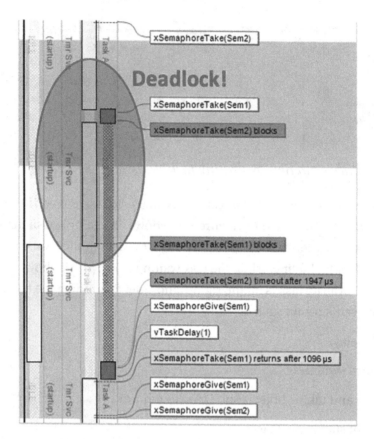

Figure 11-5. *Manually inspecting event data that reveals a deadlock*

A Modern Example: The Renesas Synergy™ Platform

So far in this chapter we have examined quite a few different topics associated with testing portable firmware. Before we conclude, I want to walk you through a real-world example of how a microcontroller supplier is taking their software to the next level by providing not just example code, but also certified, portable firmware that works on their entire series of microcontrollers. This is a real-world example of how Renesas tests the software that it provides with its Synergy microcontrollers.

The Renesas Synergy Platform provides a wide range of microcontrollers, from low-power microcontrollers with an ARM Cortex-M0+ cores all the way through to high-performance ARM Cortex-M4 cores. Rather than expecting its customers to write their own drivers, middleware, and application code, Renesas has built into its platform an entire software framework that provides these components in a configurable and portable manner across the entire microcontroller family! What is so surprising is that Renesas doesn't just supply example code but has also gone through a rigorous software-development cycle that has strict quality-assurance requirements that include many of the testing methodologies that we have been discussing in this chapter.

For example, Figure 11-6 shows the general process that Renesas uses every single night to test that its framework works as expected!

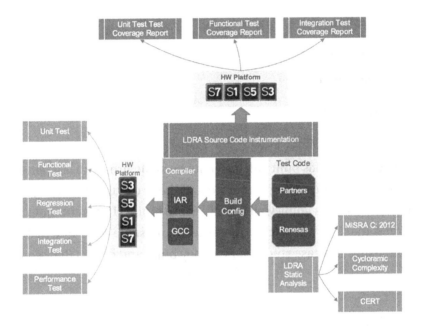

Figure 11-6. *Renesas Synergy™ Platform continuous integration test server[11]*

The reader can easily see that the test setup is a combination of running tests both on the software alone and on the hardware. By quickly surveying the diagram, a developer can see that their software framework is the following:

- Statically analyzed

- Verified against best practices and coding standards

- Compiled under multiple toolchains

---

[11]Renesas Synergy Software Quality Handbook, page 17.

- Tested on target hardware through the following:

  - Unit tests

  - Functional tests

  - Regression tests

- Tested in a software harness that performs the following:

  - Unit tests

  - Functional tests

  - Regression tests

  - Integration tests

  - Performance tests

The way that Renesas has built and tested its reusable firmware is a perfect example of how to apply many of the concepts that we have been discussing throughout this book and in some circumstances going well beyond those topics. The techniques that it is applying are ones that every developer interested in reusable code should be leveraging, examining, and using as a case study for how they build and design their own embedded systems.

Going Further

Testing is critical in any embedded system but especially for developers who are planning to reuse their software. This chapter has covered some basic fundamentals, but once again, an entire book could be spent on the topic. The following are some ideas on how you can put this chapter to use, along with where you can go to learn more:

- Review McCabe's[12] white paper on using cyclomatic complexity for testing, located at http://www.mccabe.com/pdf/mccabe-nist235r. pdf.

- Identify a cyclomatic complexity calculator and run it on your own code base.

---

[12]http://www.mccabe.com/pdf/mccabe-nist235r.pdf

- Reduce the complexity of functions with a value greater than 10 as it makes sense.

- Review each function and identify the test cases that need to be run in order to cover all paths, inputs, and outputs.

- Select a test harness and implement the tests for each function.

- Record how long it takes to implement the tests initially. The next time you port your code, record and compare the development times.

- Invest in a copy of James Grenning's book *Test-Driven Development for Embedded C*. The book has great content, but be warned the examples are a bit strenuous to set up and complete.

- Review your development kit or product under development and list out what would be necessary to perform hardware in-loop testing.

- Download and set up Segger's SystemView trace tool along with Percepio's Tracealyzer. Become familiar with how to set up, automate, and use these trace tools.

- Review the Renesas Synergy™ Platform along with the Renesas Synergy™ Quality Handbook.

CHAPTER 12

A Practical Approach to Code Reuse

"Make everything as simple as possible but not simpler."

—Albert Einstein

Being Practical in an Unpractical Environment

Every software developer knows that there are right and wrong ways to develop software as well as best practices that should be followed. The problem that many teams and individual developers face is that they find themselves in an environment where doing things the right way, whether it is through code reuse, automated tests, or any other technique that we have been discussing, is just not possible. Developers could find themselves in an environment where

- management doesn't understand software development and has unrealistic expectations;

- development timelines are short or impossible and the only option is to crank out code;

- budgets and resources are scarce but the end results still need to be delivered;

- upper management doesn't care about quality, reuse, or even accuracy as long as sales remain strong; and

- any situation where developers are pressured in such a way that they don't develop software the way they know they should.

© Jacob Beningo 2017
J. Beningo, *Reusable Firmware Development*, https://doi.org/10.1007/978-1-4842-3297-2_12

It is important to remember that even if the environment that is being worked in is unpractical, developers can still work in a practical manner that gets the job done the right way. Attempting to cut corners by skipping design or documentation or being stingy on testing will only increase the costs and delay the project.

Early in my career. I worked for several start-ups where chaos ruled the day. Management was always jumping from one fire to the next, and getting anything consistent accomplished was impossible. The development team was pulled from one direction to the next at least daily and sometimes more often. Despite this rough environment, I was able to adapt and create quality, reusable firmware by taking a practical approach that implemented reuse in phases and through carefully planned baby steps.

Phases and Baby Steps

Embedded-software developers start their careers with very little knowledge of how to properly develop software. They start out learning language semantics and how to create a basic program. A developer can spend a few years learning the intricacies of how to properly interact with low-level hardware and developing the skills necessary to properly debug an embedded system. Embedded-software developers learn new skills and gain new insights and understanding over time and in phases. They don't just start with all the knowledge they need to be successful.

Adapting a developer's or a team's software-development practices and processes to improve robustness, be more reusable and portable, and achieve many other positive attributes that we have been discussing will also not happen overnight. A team could decide that going forward everything will be reusable by developing a HAL, APIs, and so on up front, but there are several reasons this may not be possible, such as the following:

- Limited budget

- Limited development resources

- Delivery timelines

- Lack of approval from management

- Chaotic business wildfires

So, what can a developer do?

First, it is important to recognize that reusability and portability in the long run will help decrease the total cost of ownership. Second, given how chaotic firmware development can be when developers don't follow a strict process or best practices or continually jump through management hoops, the chances are that building some reuse into the code up front will still be cheaper and faster in the short term. The trick is to not go overboard and overdesign the reuse, but rather to identify where the maximum benefit will be and aim to achieve it.

When time is short or the pressure is on, take a first pass at creating reusable firmware. Design a HAL with the expectation that it will need to be updated in future releases. Create configuration tables so that drivers and application modules are easily configurable rather than hard coded. Add enough flexibility so that at a later time the software can be improved without bringing down a house of cards.

We have discussed many times in this book that a HAL design, for example, will require multiple iterations to get right. Implementing code reuse will also require several iterations and phases before it is completely in place and being utilized successfully. In general, developers can follow a very simple process that over time will allow them to implement the practices that we have been discussing throughout this book. This process contains five steps:

1) Identify the highest-impact result.

2) Evaluate what is currently being done and what needs to be done.

3) Define a roadmap to get from where you currently are to the desired result.

4) Execute the roadmap and improve the software, process, or practice.

5) Assess the results.

The entire process flow can be seen in Figure 12-1.

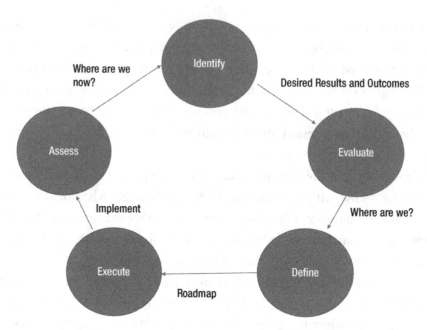

Figure 12-1. Software practice omprovement

This process can follow a very formalized and strict implementation, or it can be done by a single programmer who simply realizes that things need to change. The best results are achieved by focusing on one to three improvements until the desired outcome has been achieved. Let's discuss in more detail how the reader should go about following this simple process and how they can get the most from it.

Identifying Desired Results and Outcomes

There are many possible results and outcomes that a development team may be looking for when they start engaging in improvements in order to develop reusable firmware. Embedded-systems developers may be looking to

- improve code readability;
- decrease number of bugs; and
- improve reuse and portability.

From a business perspective, management and shareholders are going to be looking at

- decreasing time to market;

- decreasing development costs; and

- increasing product quality (at least I hope so).

On the surface, these desired results might not look like they overlap at all, but in many cases the things that a developer wants to improve will have an impact on the business results. In some situations, though, getting management to see and understand the benefits can be difficult, and sometimes vice versa. I've worked with clients where management saw the benefits and were failing to get the developers to buy in on how important reuse and portability are.

The trick is to identify desired engineering results that also mesh with the results management is looking for. If developers want to decrease bugs and rewrite modules, while management is looking to decrease costs, the two are going to clash. Developers need to understand a business need or result first and then translate what can be done at the engineering level to get that result while simultaneously achieving their own desired goals. Sometimes this requires that the individual developer get a read on their management team and forge forward on their own without support in the hope that the end results justify the means.

When all is said and done, there are three primary outcomes or results that a business is looking to get out of reusable firmware. In many cases, a developer should justify their activities to see if their reusable code will improve the odds of achieving their goals. Always choose the low-hanging fruit that will make the biggest impact with the smallest amount of effort. Let's examine these outcomes and a few engineering activities that go with them.

Desired Results: Decreasing Time to Market

A major result that many managers and business owners would love to get from their development teams is decreased time to market. Getting a product to market before the competition can be a major advantage for a business, especially if a product is new. Launching a product sooner can

- provide a revenue stream to fund the company;

- provide a success for the team to celebrate;

- beat competitors to market; and

- result in decrease costs.

Projects that run their full course—or worse, go over schedule—can cost dramatically more, sometimes even to the point that the project is canceled or the business goes bust. This is a primary reason why there is such a big push to decrease development times. We live in a society that is in a hurry, and unless we work for Apple we want to be to market first.

There are several reuse options that developers can employ and suggest in order to decrease their time to market. Several ideas that we have discussed throughout this book are as follows:

- Use a hardware abstraction layer (HALs)

- Develop application programming interfaces (APIs)

- Leverage existing components and frameworks

- Follow best practices for portable firmware

Implementing all or some of these activities can decrease time to market. Sometimes, the results can be obvious, especially if they are tracked through metrics. Other times, the results may be subtle.

Desired Results: Decreasing Development Costs

Decreasing development costs may seem like something that a developer wouldn't necessarily care about. They are paid to design a successful product, not minimize costs. However, the way I always view development costs is that the lower the costs are, the more profitable the company is. The more profitable the company is, the more willing they will be to provide their hard-working employees with bonuses, pay raises, and better benefits. Perhaps that is just my optimistic personality showing through, but there are other benefits that developers may not think about as well.

Decreasing development costs could be the difference between failing and being able to successfully launch a new product, company, or widget that could benefit millions or even billions of people. Many start-ups are strapped for cash, and if they can't find a way to decrease their development costs or keep them in check, there is no hope for their survival.

There are several options available to developers that can help them decrease their development costs. Several ideas that we have discussed throughout this book are as follows:

- Use a hardware abstraction layer (HALs)

- Develop application programming interfaces (APIs)

- Leverage existing components and frameworks

- Use an automated testing framework

- Follow best practices for analyzing software for bugs

- License commercial off-the shelf software

There are many different things that can be done to decrease costs, such as buying a professional debugger and good development tools. Spending money on the right tools for the job can make a huge impact on total cost.

Desired Results: Increased Quality

Developing a quality product is a great way for a business and a development team to set themselves apart from the competition. There is such a push to get to market fast that in many circumstances quality suffers. A product gets to market and is buggy or has terrible performance, which then turns off users and requires marketing to perform damage control. Quality is one of the elements that is critical to every embedded system and sadly can be a major product differentiator.

There are several different strategies that developers can follow to increase their firmware quality, all of which would take an entire book to discuss. However, from what we have discussed in this book, several activities that developers can engage in to ensure their portable and reusable firmware is of high quality are follows:

- Adopt coding standards

- Utilize automated tests

- Perform static and dynamic code analysis

- Perform code reviews

- Follow industry best practices

- Implement a robust software development lifecycle plan

Implementing these will help to ensure that, over time, your firmware becomes high quality.

Evaluating Where You Are

Once a developer has determined the results or the low-hanging fruit that they want to go after first, they need to figure out how they are going to achieve that outcome. Before going too far, it's a good idea to quickly determine the status of the code. For example, if a developer decides that the code base needs to have a HAL, they should survey the software to determine whether it currently contains a HAL, how evolved it is if so, and whether it could be adapted or improved upon.

There are many ways a developer can go about evaluating the current status. A developer may even want to create a spider diagram similar to that in Figure 1-14 from Chapter 1 or simply rank the current status on a scale from one to ten, one being that the feature is not evolved and ten being it is fully evolved. With some numeric value assigned, a developer can then decide what value the ranking *should* be and what it will take to get there.

Getting a stake in the ground for where you currently are and where you need to get to will help determine the roadmap, or the plan, that will be put into place to make the firmware more reusable.

Defining How to Get There

Being practical about reusable firmware really means that a developer doesn't over-design and that they build in enough reuse for the job at hand. A formal process might be the practical way to go, but in many instances just adapting on the fly might be the more practical approach. Whether a formal roadmap and plan are defined or not, developers should still at least identify a few metrics to monitor as part of their plan so that they can measure the improvements and the progress being made toward the goal.

I've worked with companies that are so bogged down in process and metric gathering that a snail is moving at a faster pace than they are. In many cases, developers need to balance the spectrum of no process to too much process. There is a safe balance somewhere in the middle that allows developers to work very rapidly. That said, as you move toward practical code reuse, you should still identify at least a few metrics by which to track your progress.

Getting the Most from Metrics

Metrics shouldn't be something that are tracked just for the sake of tracking metrics. A good metric will have several characteristics, including the following:

- Easily measurable
- Automatically trackable
- Meaningful

Let's be honest—some of these are obvious. The key is to find metrics that adhere to all three of these characteristics. If a developer has to occasionally stop development when they are under pressure to document and record a metric, they aren't going to do it. If they must stop at the end of the day to record a metric when they want to get home and have a beer, they aren't going to record it.

In order to get anything from a metric, it has to be easy to measure, automatically trackable, and meaningful. If it doesn't meet these criteria, then the data will end up with holes that will cloud the result and make the metric meaningless. Let's examine a few metrics that developers should be interested in tracking and for which it is possible to do so automatically.

Metrics Worth Tracking

Everybody loves metrics! Right? In general, while I believe engineers do like to have data that they can use to track progress, most engineers find metric tracking to be a pain. The development cycle is busy with engineers being pulled in every direction, yet they are expected to be disciplined and stop occasionally to take measurements about the development cycle. This can be a tough thing to do but is a necessary evil.

I strongly believe in tracking metrics, but I believe development teams need to take a minimalistic approach to metrics. Any metric that is used needs to have meaning and value if it is to serve any purpose to a team. Having a metric just to have it is not a good use of engineers' or managers' time. So, what metrics should developers be tracking if they want to understand how reusable firmware is affecting their development cycle?

The primary thesis behind reusable firmware is that it will decrease costs and time to market. The metrics that are selected should allow a team to check whether they are decreasing development efforts. There are a million different metrics that could be tracked, but there are just a handful that I find to be the most useful. These metrics all come back to tracking the development for each component in the software.

285

Each component should track several different metrics, which include the following:

- Maximum stack size

- Real-time function execution

- Code size

- RAM usage

- Cyclomatic complexity

- Development time

That's it! One might want to track the time spent debugging because so much time is spent debugging. Identifying and using proper debug techniques could dramatically improve development times and costs. That is beyond this book's goal, however, so let's examine a few of these metrics and understand why we should be tracking them.

First, development time for a component is obvious. We need to understand how long it takes us to develop the component and then how long it takes during each port to get the component up and running. Tracking the time spent on a component from one project to the next can also give a developer a sense of how much time is saved through reuse. For example, the first time I created an SPI peripheral HAL and implementation design pattern it took 40 development hours. The next time I used the SPI HAL and design pattern, it took only eight hours to port and fully test the driver. Before creating a reusable module, it was taking on average 32 hours to implement and test the drivers.

For an extra eight hours of work, I could then save 24 hours of work on every project that followed! That was just for that one component. When you consider that there are at least a dozen components in most projects, it's easy to not just see but to show management and clients the time savings resulting from reusing software. The data is there to justify further improvement efforts, but also can be used as a baseline for estimating future project timelines.

Second, developers should be tracking each component's code and RAM usage. As we discussed earlier in this book, reusable components can potentially use more RAM and code space. That means that when we start looking at the microcontrollers we are using, there may be a trade-off where we need to use a more expensive microcontroller to fit all the code. While we may be saving money and time through reuse, we might be paying back the money portion in more expensive hardware. This doesn't have to be the case, but it's a good metric to track to ensure that the code base doesn't get out of control and to allow developers to easily select the microcontroller they need for a given project.

Tracking these metrics doesn't have to be a big deal. A script can easily be written that parses the map-file output from the compiler to calculate the code and RAM usage and log it to a database or print it in a report. For tracking development time, developers could use online tools such as Trac, but they could also just as easily use a spreadsheet. Figure 12-2 shows an example of how a developer can create a simple activity list for a project containing all the different common software components and then record the development time for each. The data is fake, but it does provide the reader with a general idea of how, if they record this data, they can easily start to get minimum, maximum, and average development hours for different activities.

Figure 12-2 shows just a handful of low-level microcontroller activities, but the list can be fully expanded to include BSP and application components as well. A complete list can be found with the download materials for this book. As a team builds more products, they will very quickly be able to not only improve their estimation skills but also calculate how taking the time up front to do things right can impact their project.

Activity	BE16-10001	BE16-10002	BE16-10003	BE16-10004	BE16-10005	Total	Minimum	Maximum	Average
Project Setup	8	4	2	2	2		2	8	3.6
Start-up Code	4	4	4	4	4		4	4	4
MCU Driver (Clocks)	40	8	8	8	8		8	40	14.4
MCU Configuration	20	4	4	4	4		4	20	7.2
Timer Driver	40	8	8	8	8		8	40	14.4
Timer Configuration	16	2	2	2	2		2	16	4.8
Scheduler / RTOS	80	8	8	8	8		8	80	22.4
Dio Configuration	20	4	4	4	4		4	20	7.2
Dio Driver	40	8	8	8	8		8	40	14.4
ISR Control	20	4	4	4	4		4	20	7.2
Spi Configuration	20	4	4	4	4		4	20	7.2
Spi Driver (blocking)	40	8	8	8	8		8	40	14.4
Spi Driver (non-blocking)	40	8	8	8	8		8	40	14.4
Uart Configuration	20	4	4	4	4		4	20	7.2
Uart Driver (blocking)	40	8	8	8	8		8	40	14.4
Uart Driver (non-blocking)	40	8	8	8	8		8	40	14.4
I2C Configuration	20	4	4	4	4		4	20	7.2
I2C Master Driver (blocking)	40	8	8	8	8		8	40	14.4
I2C Master Driver(non-blocking)	40	8	8	8	8		8	40	14.4
I2C Slave Driver	40	8	8	8	8		8	40	14.4

Figure 12-2. *Component-development metric tracking*

Assess the Results

Once the implementation is under way, developers can continually monitor their progress and assess where they are at in relation to getting the desired results. Having good metrics is key to being able to assess the results appropriately. Once the results have been achieved, developers can move back to the Identify step to determine what their next focus point will be to improve the reusability of their firmware.

Before we conclude this chapter and the book, I would like to point out several additional best practices that developers should keep their eyes out for in order to ensure that they can develop reusable firmware.

Recognizing Design Patterns

A core point in this book that we have been tip-toeing around is that embedded-software developers should not be reinventing the wheel. When it comes to interacting with hardware or software components, pretty much everything has been done before. The C programming language is almost 50 years old! Microcontrollers have been around since 1970. Someone has already figured out the best way to interact with an SPI bus, a GPIO, a UART. Successful embedded-software developers don't reinvent the wheel. They recognize design patterns in the problems that they are trying to solve and then use and adapt those design patterns to the problem at hand.

My biggest complaint when I was an undergraduate taking computer science classes was that our professors wouldn't teach us about design patterns, not even how to recognize them, but instead would force us to reinvent and create from scratch libraries and solutions that already existed. We spent painstaking time inventing and debugging algorithms for which we could have adapted an existing solution. The biggest lesson I took away from these encounters was that for a Phd, it's all about the journey, and there is no real hurry to get to the solution. For an engineer, it's about finding the simplest and quickest solution.

The key to being a successful embedded-software engineer is to recognize design patterns and implement them where appropriate. For example, when using a UART to receive messages from an external source, a developer is going to need a circular buffer. Don't take three days to design a new circular buffer (I see engineers do this all the time); use one of the thousands of solutions that have already been implemented and move on to other design problems that truly deserve your attention.

There are several factors that developers should watch for in order to identify a design pattern. They can all be summed up in just a single point:

- If I've seen this before or think I may need it again, then a design
pattern either already exists or I should create a new one for future use.

It's that simple. It's not rocket science, and believe me, I know!

There are several common design patterns that the reader can find in almost every embedded system. These patterns include:

- Memory-mapping drivers

- Calculating checksums

- Command parsers and interpreters

- Error handling

- Program updating (bootloaders)

- Calibration

- Circular buffers

- and more

The list could go on and on. As you develop your software, ask yourself if this is a problem that someone else may have encountered in the past, or that you have, and, if so, do a quick search or browse your own code for the solution. It can save considerable time and effort. Once a developer starts to recognize these design patterns, they can start creating their own design-pattern templates and checklists.

Creating Templates and Checklists

Over the years, as I have recognized different design patterns in the software that I've written, I have created a template that could be used in the future to implement that pattern faster. The template could be nothing more than a high-level software diagram showing how to implement a solution, or it could be an abstracted low-level implementation. For example, one of the first design patterns I ever implemented was for interacting with external memory devices. We discussed a few chapters back that every memory device follows JEDEC standards, which makes writing, reading, and interacting with those devices the same no matter who the manufacturer is. Interacting with those devices becomes a design pattern, and once a developer creates that pattern once, they can use it every time that problem presents itself.

Another template example is the Doxygen templates that are used to document code. Having a consistent method for documenting code is crucial. It needs to be done over and over again for every project. Rather than creating a new way to document software in every project, I created a template that I could easily use on each and every project. Over time, I do update and adjust those templates, but the base pattern is there, and it decreases the effort tremendously.

Templates are a great way to speed up software development and prevent developers from repeating work that has already done.

Another tool that I have found to be indispensable is using checklists. Checklists can be used to manage everything from creating a new project and checking in a project to revision control and final reviews for releasing software. A checklist is a great way to take a complex procedure, or even one that is not done very often, and ensure that it is repeatable.

For example, I have a project-setup checklist that I use at the start of every project. The checklist doesn't go into low-level details but has the high-level points to remind me what I should set up and configure in order to get the project up and running the fastest. For example, my project-setup checklist is set up to follow several different phases, as shown in Figure 12-3.

Phase 1 – Project Setup

- ☐ Setup revision control
- ☐ Create the project
- ☐ Create the project directory structure
- ☐ Set the white and tab spacing for the project

Phase 2 – Configuration

- ☐ Add Doxygen code templates
- ☐ Configure Doxy wizard
- ☐ Import skeleton HAL's and API's
- ☐ Create a version log
- ☐ Create a hardware configuration module

Phase 3 – Code Analysis

- ☐ Setup static code analysis tool
- ☐ Setup software metrics analyzer
- ☐ Setup dynamic code analysis

Phase 4 – Setup scheduler

- ☐ Setup RTOS or bare-metal scheduler
- ☐ Setup a single task to blink an LED

Phase 5 – Debug Setup

- ☐ Setup RTT and trace tools if applicable
- ☐ Setup printf
  - o Uart driver
  - o Uart mapped to printf
- ☐ Configure assert macro

Phase 6 – Begin Development

- ☐ Write quality, robust, secure, reusable and portable software

Figure 12-3. *Project-startup checklist[1]*

---

[1]https://www.beningo.com/tools-embedded-software-start-up-checklist/

As the reader can tell from the checklist, there is a lot that is done before a single line of code is ever written for the project. Many of these items would be easily overlooked if there were pressure on to start banging out code as quickly as possible. The checklist ensures that proper procedures are followed that will maximize the project's chances for success.

Every firmware project that I work on starts with this checklist. If you examine the checklist carefully, you'll also notice that there are entries that remind me to bring templates into the project. For example, there is mention of the Doxygen templates, along with HALs and APIs. At that bullet point, if the project that is being developed requires a communication protocol, circular buffer, command parser, and so forth, those template components would be added to the code base. By the time the checklist is completed, there is a nearly completed skeleton for the software along with the implementation for any common design patterns.

In many instances, in just a day or so a base system can be brought online that if developed from scratch would easily take a month or more. This is the power that reusability and portability bring to the table.

Version Control Is Your Best Friend

Version-control systems are a great way to share source code between developers. They provide the ability for multiple people to simultaneously work on the same code base without the danger of sending files back and forth constantly. Make a mistake while developing and rest assured that the simple press of a button can roll back the code to a fresh square one. History has shown that working without a version-control system is a disaster waiting to happen! Version-control systems are an essential development tool, and there are several tips developers should follow in order to get the most from them.

Tip #1: Commit Frequently

Embedded software at times takes on a life of its own and tends to have a temperamental attitude. A developer makes a few minor changes and the entire system destabilizes into frenzy. The developer has no fear and reverses the few changes he made and voila! The system is still broken. Without a version-control system, the developer scratches their head in panic and tries to understand what change they made that they don't remember from five minutes ago! The engineer using version control, on the other hand, performs a right click and simply reverts to the previous working version of the code and now cautiously moves forward. But what if the developer had gone days without committing his code? Days' worth of effort could be lost, which is why developers using version control should commit frequently! Complete a feature and commit. Get a partial feature working, commit. This will not only save the engineer time when things go wrong but will also leave a nice trail in the version-control system of the changes that were made.

Tip #2: Fill in the commit log

It is great if an engineer commits their code changes frequently; however, it can prove to be a futile effort if sufficient information is not provided in the change log. Most version-control tools will allow comments to be made at the time the code is committed. Fill in the log with helpful and useful information! Don't leave it blank or put cryptic information here. In the future, a bug may get introduced into the code, and as the developer backtracks the versions, it will be essential that the log contain useful information on what changed. It takes only a few moments and will save many hours of frustration and headaches! Try to come up with a common log format that needs to be filled in before each commit.

Tip #3: Don't forget to add files to the VCS

Version-control systems have been known to play a trick or two on a developer. The biggest is when a developer thinks that he is committing code when he actually isn't! How can this happen? Most systems require that when you create a file you add it to revision control. If this isn't done, then the system will happily commit and ignore those files that haven't been added. So, don't forget to add files to the VCS!

Tip #4: Define a commit process

It is really easy to forget to add files to revision control, properly log changes, and a variety of other tasks associated with version control systems. The best thing that can be done is to create a process for each of the different tasks that need to be performed. For example, create a commit process. It would look something like the following:

1) Update version log within the code base.

2) Copy the changes.

3) Add files to the VCS.

4) Begin the commit process.

5) Paste the change log into the commit comments and add any additional relevant comments.

6) Complete the commit.

Tip #5: Lock modules that are in process

There are times when multiple developers are working on a project and might need to modify the same module. Version-control systems often have a feature that allows the programmer to lock a particular module for editing. This prevents another programmer from modifying the file at the same time and thus helps to prevent conflicts within the code base.

Tip #6: Utilize the code-comparison tools

There will inevitably come a time when a bug creeps into the code unnoticed. At some point it will be discovered, and then the question will be asked, "What changed?" The only way to know for sure is to compare different revision levels of the code. This could be a painful process if it weren't for the fact that most version-control systems include a difference tool. This tool allows a side-by-side comparison of files within the code across different versions of the code. These alterations are highlighted and can then be examined as the potential source of the bug.

Tip #7: Don't fear merging code branches

The concept of branching the code into a separate version, making changes, and then later merging it back into the main version trunk can be scary! What happens if something goes wrong? What if it isn't merged properly and the main branch becomes corrupted? Beginners will often fear merging branches, but do not be concerned! This is a common occurrence, especially when multiple developers are involved in the project. If a mistake is made it is easy to go back a version and restart! The best way to get over this fear is to practice.

What Is the Cost to Do Nothing?

An important question that every developer and every team should ask themselves before beginning any improvement to their embedded-software processes or code base is:

What is the cost to do nothing?

I come across so many developers, teams, and clients who will look at the $2,000 price tag on a compiler, computer, or development tool and instantly say it costs too much. They never stop for a moment to ask what the cost is if they *don't* purchase the tool. Purchasing a $2,000 tool might save the company $10,000 or even $20,000 over the lifetime of that tool. The problem is that most managers and development teams are short-sighted in their thinking, looking only at what is right in front of them and not what is in the best interest of the company in the long-term.

When I first started my business, I had worked at several large and small companies and was absolutely set on making sure that:

1)   I would use the right tools for the job no matter the cost.

2)   I would always evaluate what is in the long-term best interest for my clients.

In several instances, I purchased tools that cost more than $10,000 to the mutual benefit of both myself and my clients. Each client that I served saved the $10,000 on the tools, which they were then able to put back into their own development cycles. In the grand scheme of things, the $10,000 was nothing to those companies, but to those clients it was a huge gesture.

When developers are evaluating whether to start using reusable firmware in their own development cycles, they need to ask themselves what the short-term and long-term costs will be if they do nothing. It may cost the company $10,000, $20,000, or maybe even $50,000 up front to create firmware that is reusable, or those amounts over several years as reuse is increased in iterations. But what is the return on investment over one, two, five, and ten years? It might be that with an upfront investment of $10,000 a company can save $100,000 in the next two years. Perhaps future products can beat the competition to market or improve quality to a point that customers prefer their product.

I see so many teams that make short-term decisions without considering the long-term perspective. Unfortunately, I see many of these teams choke, stumble, and, in some cases, even go out of business. Others are able to just barely survive and end up in a mad dash to implement reusability and best practices that they should have been using all along.

Don't get caught up in short-term thinking. Keep this question on your mind and ask it at every crossroads. The costliest mistakes that I've seen in the industry and in life happen not when people jump into a situation, but rather when they do nothing and hope for the best.

Final Thoughts

When looking back over my short career so far and examining what has made the greatest impact on my clients' products and software, I can sum it up in one word: reuse. It's a simple idea to reuse embedded software. Reuse has been going on for decades in the PC world. Yet, firmware developers have always opted for writing software in a one-off fashion, ignoring reuse and opting to just get it done and deal with the fires that are burning today.

As we progress through the coming decades, it is absolutely clear in my mind that the teams that will be the most successful are the teams that utilize reuse to the furthest extent. Teams that leverage HALs, APIs, microcontroller platforms, and even automatically generated code will develop software far faster than today's standards. Teams that reuse code can focus on their product's key features, the differentiators that set it apart from the competition.

Embedded-software developers have always been experts in the microcontroller, the low-level bits and bytes. That is going to change over the coming decades. More and more developers are going to be experts in HALs and APIs and have little to no knowledge about the hardware. As we move to 32-bit microcontrollers, the complexity will become so high that the only way we can possibly expect to get a product to market in a year or less will be to reuse what we have already created and leverage existing code.

Microcontroller manufacturers, as experts in their own hardware, are starting to provide frameworks and HALs for developers to use. We will see the hardware abstracted, but even when that does happen, teams that utilize reusable concepts will still have an edge over teams that are just getting things done for today with no thought about tomorrow.

I've had the pleasure of working with teams in more than a dozen different countries to improve software-development processes and help teams get their products to market. As you contemplate the material and concepts in this book, I encourage you to start with the low-hanging fruit that will have the most dramatic impact on your software and business in the shortest amount of time. Reinvesting the time saved to further implement and improve your software will have a powerful effect on your products and end users.

Going Further

We have covered many topics in this book, and we are only at the beginning. Don't forget that this will be an iterative process that very well might take you years. These are exciting times, and the following are a few more thoughts on where you can go from here:

- Consider purchasing my *API Standard*[2] book, which provides a Doxygen-documented starting point for many microcontroller peripheral features and provides the Doxygen template source code with it.

- Determine whether this will be a personal development effort to start developing more reusable firmware or whether this is a team effort that will have management support. Get the key players and decision makers on board.

- Identify three potential areas to immediately improve in. What is your company's low-hanging fruit? Could it be:

  - Implementing Doxygen templates for readability?

  - Leveraging the APIs and HALs in this book?

  - Identifying design patterns used in your products?

- Once you have your top three priorities, rank each priority and review how well you are currently doing in this area.

- Create a roadmap of how these three priorities will be implemented in the next several months and what needs to happen in order to be successful. Don't forget that this doesn't need to be a detailed, formal plan.

- Identify metrics that need to be tracked in order to monitor the improvements and also the results that they are getting for the company.

---

[2]https://www.beningo.com/store/an-api-standard-for-mcus/

- Schedule reviews to monitor progress; adjust the roadmap and plan if necessary.

- Review your products and identify common design elements and procedures that could be turned into templates and checklists. Schedule time to convert these design patterns and procedures.

- Calculate the cost in opportunity, project delays, troubleshooting, and development costs that doing nothing could incur.

- Enjoy developing reusable firmware and improving the products that you work on.

Index

A

Abstract Data Types (ADTs)
 abstractions, 80
 definition, 81
 implementation data structure, 82
 initialization function, 83
 interface specification, 81
 operations, 81
 pop method, 84
 stack method initialization, 83
 Stack_Push, 85
Abstractions, *see* Abstract Data
  Types (ADTs)
Application Programming Interfaces
  (APIs), 23
 architecture, 24
 characteristics, 49
  consistent look and feel, 53
  const keyword, 49
  documentation, 53
  flexible and configuration, 53
  Micrium uc/OS-III, 54
  naming conventions, 50
  uOS III, 52
 comparison (API and HAL), 58
 designing process, 53
 embedded-software developers, 49
 FreeRTOS TaskCreate, 54
 HAL design, 57
 scope, 48

ThreadX tx_thread_create, 55
 wrappers, 55
Assertion fundamentals
 assert.h header file, 68
 definition, 68
 input and pre-condition, 69
 macro implementation, 69
Automating tests, 269

B

Boogeyman
 integration issues, 35
 issues, 33
 microcontroller vendors, 34
 peripheral technique, 35
 ramifications, 34
 readability issues, 35
Bootloaders framework, 252

C

Callback functions
 ArrayInit function, 88
 definition, 86
 elements to random numbers, 89
 implementation, 87
 initialization code, 87
 instances, 86
 lower-level code, 87
 signal handler, 87

© Jacob Beningo 2017
J. Beningo, *Reusable Firmware Development*, https://doi.org/10.1007/978-1-4842-3297-2

I, J, K, L

M, N

V, W, X, Y, Z

Get the eBook for only $5!

Why limit yourself?

With most of our titles available in both PDF and ePUB format, you can access your content wherever and however you wish—on your PC, phone, tablet, or reader.

Since you've purchased this print book, we are happy to offer you the eBook for just $5.

To learn more, go to http://www.apress.com/companion or contact support@apress.com.

Apress®